ACCESS 2007 PURE SQL:

Real, power-packed solutions for business users, developers, and the rest of us.

Pindar E. Demertzoglou, Ph.D.

Alpha Press – Albany, New York 2009

About the Author

Pindar's exciting relationship with databases started with DBase III back in 1991, continuing with all versions of Access since early 1993, and working with MS SQL Server, MySQL, Oracle, and IBM DB2 for a number of years. From then on, he is still in love with all of them. After almost twenty years, he still works with data, information processing, integration, and dissemination.

Pindar is currently a Clinical Assistant Professor of Information Systems at the business school of Rensselaer Polytechnic Institute in Troy, New York where he is teaching databases for the last ten years. Pindar also completed and collaborated on a myriad of database projects for organizations or in collaborative efforts between the University and various corporations.

Pindar's interests in information science, transactional systems, and analytics focus on creating more efficient and flexible organizations. The idea is to accomplish more with fewer resources and in less time leaving a small footprint on the environment. Pindar's education includes a BS from the American College in Thessaloniki Greece, an MS, MBA, and a PhD in the United States. He received national and international distinctions for his work in the field and faculty awards for his teaching methods.

Nevertheless, the majority of the authror's experience came from participating in a multitude of industry projects. There, everything has to work efficiently, reliably and above all be acceptable by the people of the corporation. Theoretical knowledge, though useful, takes a second place in these cases. A solid application and strong promotion within the organization are the primary success factors. This is the main reason for which theory takes a secondary part in this book and when it does it is only to support a business task.

No matter what the restrictions of time, Pindar will find the time to grow his tomatoes, eggplants, peppers, squash, onions, and in general anything he can find for his vegetable garden.

BRIEF TABLE OF CONTENTS

DETAILED TABLE OF CONTENTS

BUSINESS TABLE OF CONTENTS

Introduction

The goal of this book is to provide the database professional and power user with working solutions for everyday actual business tasks. The continuous thought has been to reduce needless writing and concentrate on the daily needs of database usage and development. As a new database developer back in 1993, I needed a book like this one but never had it. Instead, I used to buy books with hundreds of pages, which seemed to be a repetition of what one could find in the help file.

An efficient database developer, in my humble point of view, does not need a book to tell him or her how to execute a query or how many types of queries Access 2007 supports; the answers are a click away in the help file or online. What power users and database developers actually need is thought-out code to show them the way to achieve their difficult tasks without having to look around for hours, days, or sometimes weeks. In addition, they need a book to show them when something is possible, when it is not, how many ways exist to achieve a task, and which one is the most efficient.

Furthermore, the table of contents is not arranged by topic (tables, queries, reports, etc) but by solution. Not only the content of the book should be practical but the book itself and its layout should help the professional find what he or she needs in seconds.

CHAPTER 1
CREATE, EDIT, AND DELETE
TABLES USING SQL

In Access 2007, you can use design interfaces to create tables, queries, forms, and reports. However, you can use pure SQL code, practically text, to create highly complex tables, indexes, constraints, and relationships. When we use SQL to create database objects, we call the SQL code Data Definition Language (DDL). When we use SQL to retrieve and manipulate data, we call the SQL code Data Manipulation Language (DML).

The ability to use SQL to create database objects does not represent just one additional way to work with Access. Through SQL statements, you can understand in detail the inner structure of the objects you are creating, you can use your knowledge of SQL to enter the realm of other databases like MSSQL Server or MySQL to create objects independent of any design interface, and you can create and delete temporary objects on the fly.

To make an analogy, let us assume that you want to learn how to create web pages. You can buy or download an HTML editor, as there are plenty to choose from. However, what is your strategic goal? Learn how to work with an editor, or understand how to develop web code? The function of HTML editors is always the same: They convert your clicks to HTML code.

The same is true with SQL. There are many design interfaces that you can use either integrated to the program like the ones in Access 2007 or others that you can download and use to work with a relational database. The result here is always the same; they convert your clicks to SQL code.

Consequently, if you understand how to work with SQL, you will, in essence, be able to work with any relational database, commercial or open source, because all of them use SQL. That is why I have included three chapters in this book for DDL. In all subsequent chapters and all the way to the end of the book, you will use SQL code as DML for data manipulation. For all chapters, however, you can paste the code provided in a query and magically see the design interface adapt to your code. Enough with words, however, let's delve right into work.

For all of the examples in this chapter, you can download the sample database from http://www.databasechannel.com/sampledata/Access2007.

In this chapter, we will work with three DDL statements: CREATE TABLE, ALTER TABLE, and DROP TABLE. We use the CREATE statement to create new tables, the ALTER statement to modify existing ones, and the DROP statement to delete existing tables. The basic structures of the three statements appear below:

CREATE TABLE "tablename" (
fieldname1 datatype (size),
fieldname2 datatype (size),
fieldname3 datatype (size)
)

ALTER TABLE "tablename"
[ADD] [ALTER] [DROP] COLUMN fieldname datatype(size)

DROP TABLE "tablename"

1.   Create a table using SQL

Create a customer table using pure SQL
Discussion:
This is a simple example of creating a table using SQL in Access 2007. The Access 2007 help file says that we need to use data definition queries to create objects. Actually, we can enter this code in any SQL view of any query, and it will work. The table in this example contains only six text fields. The table is bare without any primary keys defined, NULLs handling, or indexes.

Code:

```
CREATE TABLE Customer1 (
[LastName] text(50),
[MiddleName] text(50),
[FirstName] text(50),
[Address] text(100),
[State] text(2),
[Zip] text(5));
```

Result:

2.   Create a table using SQL, and populate it with data on the fly

Create a customer table, and populate it with data from an existing table

Discussion:

In most of our work tasks, we do not just need to create a table. We also need to put some data in it on the fly. Creating a table and populating it on the fly is possible using the SELECT INTO statement in Access 2007. In this example, we create the table customer1, and we populate it with data from the customers table.

Code:

```
SELECT * INTO Customer1
FROM customers
```

Result:

The table customer1 will be created and populated with all of the records from the customers table. Of course, you can modify the SQL statement above to move specific fields and records.

3. Create a table using SQL, and populate it with data in one step

Create a customer table, and populate it with specific columns and rows from an existing table

Discussion:

In this example, we create the table customer1 that we populate with only three fields and 14 records from the customers table.

Code:

```
SELECT lastname, firstname, address INTO Customer1
FROM customers
WHERE city = "Boston"
```

Result:

4. Create a table defining its primary key

Create a customer table, and assign CustomerID as the primary key

Discussion:

In this scenario, we create a table with a primary key of data type "Number" and two simple text fields. Notice the primary key picture on the left of the CustomerID field in the table design view in the picture below:

Code:

```
CREATE TABLE Customer1 (
[CustomerID] number Primary key not null,
[LastName] text(50),
[FirstName] text(50));
```

Result:

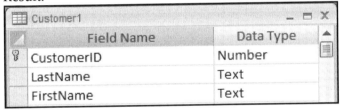

5. Create a table defining the primary key as autonumber

Create a customer table, and assign the PK CustomerID as an autonumber

Discussion:

In this scenario, we create a table with the primary key of data type "AutoNumber" and two simple text fields.

Code:

```
CREATE TABLE Customer1 (
[CustomerID] Counter Primary key not null,
[LastName] text(50),
[FirstName] text(50));
```

Result:

Field Name	Data Type
CustomerID	AutoNumber
LastName	Text
FirstName	Text

6.   Create table with a field that does not accept nulls

Create a customer table, and assign the lastname field as required

Discussion:

On some occasions, we might want to create a table with a field that will not accept null values. Null values are different from zero-length strings or zeros. (Check chapter 23 for a full discussion of null values). To avoid nulls for a field, we simply make the field required. In other words, we force users to enter a value, or they will not be able to save the record in the database. We can do this with the following code, which makes the lastname field required.

Code:

```
CREATE TABLE Customer1 (
[CustomerID] Counter PRIMARY KEY NOT NULL,
[LastName] text(50) NOT NULL,
[FirstName] text(50),
[Address] text(50));
```

Result:

7. ALTER table: add a column

Add a city field in the customer table

Discussion:

On most occasions, we need to modify the design of existing tables instead of creating new ones. We can alter table designs almost at will using pure SQL. In this example, we add the city field to the customer1 table.

Code:

```
ALTER TABLE Customer1
ADD COLUMN City TEXT(25)
```

or if you would like to make it a required field:

```
ALTER TABLE Customer1
ADD COLUMN City TEXT(25) NOT NULL
```

Result:

8. ALTER table: delete a column

Delete the city field from the customer table

Discussion:

We can easily delete a field from a table using the ALTER and DROP statements in combination. For instance, in this case, we delete the "city" field from the customer1 table.

Code:
ALTER TABLE Customer1
DROP COLUMN City

9.   ALTER table: modify a an existing column

Change the size of the lastname field from 50 to 80 characters
Discussion:
Let us say that we want to modify the size of the lastname field from 50 characters to 80.
Notice that the data type of the lastname field is already text. We can also change the
data type or the name of the field, if we wish, using the ALTER COLUMN statement.

Code:
ALTER TABLE Customer1
ALTER COLUMN LastName TEXT(80)

Result:

10.   Delete Table

Delete the table customer1 from the database
Discussion:
We can use SQL to delete tables using the DROP statement. In this example, we delete
the customer1 table. We must pay attention, however, when we delete tables using the
DROP statement because there is no warning or undo action for it. The table will be
deleted permanently from the database.

Code:
DROP TABLE Customer1

Result:
The table customer1 has been deleted from the database.

CHAPTER 2
CREATE, EDIT, AND DELETE
INDEXES USING SQL

The use of indexes is another low-lighted topic in the world of databases. It is common knowledge that indexes are useful, but the guidelines to use them are obscure at best. First, indexes will speed up searching operations. They work great with WHERE and ORDER BY clauses. However, they will slow down INSERT and UPDATE statements since every insert or update needs to be saved in both the table and the index. Third, they should be avoided in small tables with few records. They work better in large tables with thousands of records. Fourth, it is a good idea to create indexes for fields that we use a lot in searching operations. If we have a form in Access or a web form that we use as the front-end in which we provide the users with the option to search customers by first and last name fields, then we need to index those two fields.

In addition, indexes can be set up as unique or non-unique. In this case, the indexes accept unique or non-unique values so that they can function as constraints disallowing duplicate values for the indexed field or fields. For example, if we set up a unique index on a last name field, all of the last names in the table will have to have unique values. Furthermore, primary key columns in Access 2007 tables are automatically indexed when created, and these indexes are set up as unique.

We can also use indexes as constraints to disallow null values for fields in Access 2007 tables. If we want to make the last name field a required field, we can use an index to assign a field as required. In this case, we force the users to make an entry for this field.

Additionally, we can set up indexes to take into consideration or ignore existing null values for the entries of a field. For instance, let us assume that we would like to index a last name field, which contains null values for 15 records while it has entries for the rest of the 500 records. We can create indexes that will either take those null values into consideration or simply ignore them.

Finally, we can create multi-field indexes that will index the combination of values of multiple fields instead of just indexing the values of each individual field. For example, if we create a unique index on last name and a unique index on first name, what we practically told the database is not to accept duplicate values for last names and not to accept duplicate values for first names. In other words, we cannot have two Smiths or two Johns in the database, which is, of course, impractical. However, we can create a multi-field unique index on both the last and first name fields that will accept any number of duplicate values for the individual last and first name fields but will not accept duplicate values for the combinations.

Let's go through some examples to demonstrate the points we mentioned above in practice. For all of the examples in this chapter, you can download the sample database from http://www.databasechannel.com/sampledata/Access2007.

11.   Create a table and set a unique index for one of its fields

Optimize customer searches on the last name field
Discussion:
Since we expect heavy searching activity on the LastName field, we need to create an index to accelerate these searches. In this scenario, we create a new table and an index on the LastName field.

Code:
```
CREATE TABLE tblCustomer1 (
[CustomerID] Counter Primary key not null,
[LastName] text(50),
[FirstName] text(50),
[Address] text(50),
CONSTRAINT indLastName UNIQUE (LastName));
```

Result:

In the figure above, the LastName field is indexed and, at the same time, does not accept duplicates. This is because we created a unique index on this field with the SQL code in this example.

Now, if we click on the "Indexes" button in the "Show/Hide" group in the "Table Design" tab, we see that there are two indexes for the table we just created. One is the default index that Access 2007 creates every time we define a primary key. The second is the index named "indLastName" exactly as we defined it in our SQL code.

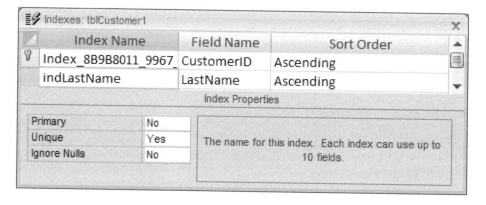

12. Create a non-unique index for an existing table

Add a non-unique index for the first name field in the customer table

Discussion:

Let us assume that we have created a table and we have data in it. After some time, we decide we would like to add an additional index using SQL. We can easily do this by using the following code:

Code:

```
CREATE INDEX indFirstName ON tblCustomer1 (FirstName);
```

Result:

Notice in the figure below that the indFirstName is non-unique. This means that we allow duplicate values for the FirstName field. In other words, we can have two "Johns" or two "Marys" in the table, but they definitely have to have different last names as defined by the indLastName, which is a unique index.

13. Create a unique index for an existing table

Add a unique index for the last name field in the existing customer table

Discussion:

As we can see from the figure in the previous example, the indFirstName index is non-unique, and it does not ignore nulls. What is the exact meaning of a unique index? What is the meaning of an index ignoring or not ignoring nulls?

First, by a unique index, we mean that no duplicate values are allowed for that field. We know very well that unique values are not allowed for fields that have been designated as primary keys. However, by defining a unique index, we can disallow duplicate values for a field that is not the primary key of the table. For example, if we are working with the LastName field, and we create a unique index on it, we cannot have two customers in our table with the same last name. If we try to enter two customers with the same last name, the database will not allow their entry. The SQL code below will create a unique index on a field other than the primary key for an existing table.

Code:

CREATE UNIQUE INDEX indLastName ON tblCustomer1 (LastName);

Result:

As we can see from the figure below, the indLastName is a unique index now. However, this is not always a desirable scenario since there might be multiple customers with the same last name. How can we set up index constraints so that we allow multiple customers to have the same last name and allow multiple customers to have the same first name, but disallow multiple customers to have the same last and first names at the same time? Let us see the next example with multiple-field indexes.

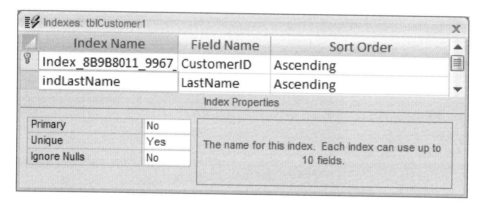

14.   Create multiple-field indexes to avoid duplicates

Add a unique multi-field index for the last and first name fields
Discussion:

When working with customers, we would like to make sure that no duplicate customer records exist in our database. At the same time, it is logical that many customers might have the same last name, and many of them will have the same first name.

What we actually need to do is to allow multiple customers to have the same last name. In addition, we need to allow multiple customers to have the same first name. Finally, we need to disallow multiple customers to have the same combination of last and first names. We can easily solve this problem with a multi-field index.

With a multi-field unique index, our database will accept values such as Smith John and Smith Tracy. However, if we try to enter another Smith John in the database, then we will get a message that such an entry violates existing index rules and will not be accepted. Multi-field indexes are extremely useful to keep our data in a good state.

Code:
CREATE UNIQUE INDEX indLastFirst ON tblCustomer1 (LastName, FirstName);

Result:

Index Name	Field Name	Sort Order
Index_8B9B8011_9967_	CustomerID	Ascending
indFirstName	FirstName	Ascending
indLastFirst	LastName	Ascending
	FirstName	Ascending

Index Properties

Primary	No	
Unique	Yes	The name for this index. Each index can use up to 10 fields.
Ignore Nulls	No	

15. Create an index that ignores nulls

Create an index on lastname that ignores null last name values

Discussion:
By default when we create an index for a field, this index will include the field's null values in the indexed entries. We might, however, want nulls to be excluded from our index and only entries with data in the field to be included. Note that this is not the same as setting a field to not accept nulls. Our index will simply not include any null values from this field.

Code:

CREATE UNIQUE INDEX indLastName ON tblCustomer1 (LastName) WITH
IGNORE NULL;

Result:

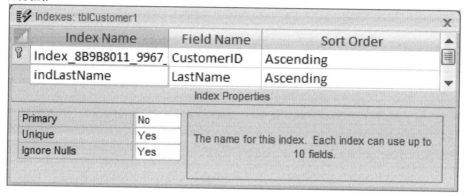

16.   Create an index on a field that will not accept nulls.

Add a unique index for the last name field that will not allow null values
Discussion:

In this scenario, we would like a field to be indexed, not accept duplicate values, accept
zero-length strings, and not accept null values at the same time. This piece of code
becomes even stronger when we want to apply it with multi-field indexes. For example,
we might have a situation in which we would like to have the combination of two fields
indexed, disallow duplicates, and not accept nulls at the same time. With indexes, we
can apply data validation rules on the combined values of fields. In this scenario, we
work with one field to keep it simple.

Code:

CREATE UNIQUE INDEX indLastName ON tblCustomer1 (LastName) WITH
DISALLOW NULL;

Result:

As we can see, the LastName field is indexed, accepts no duplicates (UNIQUE), and it
will require an entry (DISALLOW NULL). Pay close attention because Access 2007 does
not indicate a field as required in the table design view when we use an index constraint.
In the picture of the table design view below, we see that the field last name looks like it
is not required when it is actually required. Try to go to data view to add an entry for

first name, while leaving the last name field empty. We will get a constraint violation error.

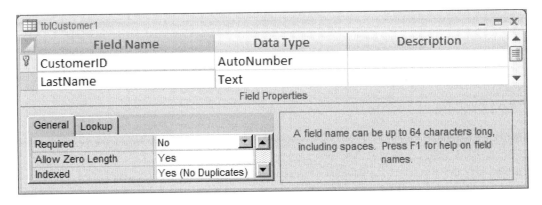

17. Delete Index

Delete the "indLastName" index from the customer table using SQL

Discussion:

In our previous examples, we have created an index on the LastName field for the tblCustomer1 table and we named it indLastName. In this case, we can write a DROP statement to delete the index from our tbl1Customer1 table.

Code:

DROP INDEX indLastName ON tblCustomer1

Result:

The index "indLastName" will be deleted from the tblCustomer1 table.

CHAPTER 3
CREATE, EDIT, DELETE
RELATIONSHIPS USING SQL

Our manager asked us to create a customer database to store information about our customers and their orders. One of our tasks will be to create relationships among tables. After almost 20 years of working with databases, I can attest that this process is much more art than science. There are neither rigid rules to follow nor guidelines to cover all of the situational scenarios we might encounter.

However, we have two great tools at our disposal: First, we have a total and complete understanding of the meaning of relationships and their related topics like primary keys, foreign keys, referential integrity, cascade updates, cascade deletes, and join types. Second, we can use our logic to achieve a well-built relationship resulting in a solid database. The purpose of this chapter is to completely demystify the obscure area of relationships not only with respect to building them but, most importantly, with respect to their interpretation and usage.

18. Why and how to create a one-to-many relationship
Create a one-to-many relationship between customers and orders

Our first task is to create a relationship between the customers and orders tables. The logic here is that each customer can have multiple orders while one order definitely belongs to one customer only. This is the case for a one-to-many relationship. This one-to-many relationship is depicted graphically in the figure below. I have included data values on purpose to actually show how records from one table relate to records in the other table. This is because when we talk about relationships among tables, we are actually talking about record relations.

CUSTOMERS		ORDERS		
CustID	Name	OrderID	CustID	OrderDate
1	John	1	2	9/10/2009
2	Mary	2	2	10/10/2010
3	George	3	1	11/10/2010
4	Stacy	4	3	11/11/2010

Primary Key   Primary Key   Foreign Key

The steps for creating a one-to-many relationship between two database tables (customers and orders in this case) are the following:

1. Assign a primary key to both tables if they do not already have one. In this example, the primary key for the Customers table is "CustID", and the primary key for the Orders table is "OrderID".

2. Make sure your primary key is not a "natural" key like a social security number, or driver's license number. The data types for the primary keys in both tables should be of the "Auto Number" data type.

3. Create a field in the Orders table, which we will name "CustID." The "CustID" field in the Orders table is the "Foreign key" of the table. The data type of the "CustID" field in the Orders table should be of the number data type so that it can be joined with the CustID in the Customers table.

4. In Access 2007, click on the "Database Tools" tab on the ribbon. In the "Show/Hide" group, click on the relationships button. The "Show Table" dialog box opens. Add the tables we would like to join.

5. The relationships window in Access 2007 shows the entity relationship diagram (ERD) of the database. In the ERD, all related tables appear along with the field names and the primary and foreign keys. The ERD allows us to understand the structure and design of the database, and it constitutes the place in which we can create, edit, and delete relationships. In this case, we will create a new relationship between customers and orders.

6. Click on the CustomerID field in the Customer table, and drag it on the CustomerID field on the Orders table. The "Edit Relationships" window will come up.

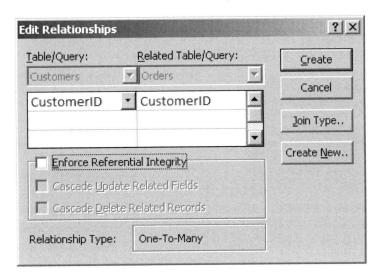

7. We can just click "Create", and our relationship is ready. However, in this case, we will also click on "Enforce Referential Integrity" so that our database remains sound when inserting new records and deleting existing ones. For example, with referential integrity on, we will not be able to add an order in the orders table without an existing customer in the customers table. In addition, we will not be able to delete a customer from the customers table for whom there are orders in the orders table. We will have to first delete the orders for that customer and then delete the customer. For a full and detailed understanding of referential integrity and its important implications, read the corresponding section in this chapter.

8. Finally, our Entity Relationship Diagram (ERD) will look like this:

19.   How to read, understand, and use a one-to-many relationship

The meaning of one-to-many relationship between customers and orders

Learning how to create a one-to-many relationship is really a minimal goal in itself. The essential objective is to actually understand its meaning, be able to apply it, use it, and take advantage of its many powers and possibilities. In this respect, let us try to read what is happening in our two related tables of customers and orders.

First, when looking at the foreign key values in the orders table (the values of the CustID field in the Orders table), we notice that only John, Mary, and George have orders. Second, we see that John and George have one order each, while Mary has two orders. Third, we see that Stacy does not have any orders at all, so we might want to initiate a marketing effort for her. Fourth, when we look at the orders table and examine order number 3 (with OrderID = 3), we immediately understand that this order belongs to John because the corresponding foreign key value is 1. If we look up this value in the customer table, we find that the corresponding customer name is John. This is the way relational databases work and are able to retrieve related records from two or more tables.

CUSTOMERS		ORDERS		
CustID	Name	OrderID	CustID	OrderDate
1	John	1	2	9/10/2009
2	Mary	2	2	10/10/2010
3	George	3	1	11/10/2010
4	Stacy	4	3	11/11/2010

Primary Key	Primary Key	Foreign Key

20.   Why and how to create a many-to-many-relationship

Create a many-to-many relationship between orders and products

Our task this time is to create a database to keep track of customers, orders, and products.   We already know how to create a one-to-many relationship between customers and orders.   Now, we need to create a relationship between orders and products. Whenever we design a database, the setup of relationships is the cornerstone of the design process. We do have an ally in this process, which is our logic.

In this respect, we examine and make conclusions on the relation of each table to the other or of relations among entities because this is how we refer to tables in database parlance. From the orders point of view, we conclude that each order in the orders table can contain more than one product. It is only logical that a customer can order multiple products in one order. From the products point of view, we conclude that each product can participate in more than one order. It is logical that we can sell the same product to multiple customers through their orders. When this is the case, we need to establish a many-to-many relationship between Orders and Products.

CUSTOMER	
CustID	Name
1	John
2	Mary
3	George
4	Stacy

ORDERS		
OrderID	CustID	OrderDate
1	2	9/10/2009
2	2	10/10/2010
3	1	11/10/2010
4	3	11/11/2010

Products_Orders		
OrderID	ProductID	Quantity
1	2	2
2	2	5
3	1	3
4	2	4

Products	
ProductID	ProductName
1	A
2	B
3	C
4	D

To create a many-to-many relationship between the Orders and Products tables, we need to create a join table between them like the Products_Orders table in this example. The primary key of the join table is the combination of the primary keys of the tables that we would like to join in a many-to-many relationship. In other words, the primary key of any join table in a many-to-many relationship is a composite key consisting of two fields. As we know already, the values of a primary key in a relational table must always be unique, and this uniqueness is expressed in this case by the combination of the values of OrderID and ProductID. For example, the value (1,2) of the first record in the Products_Orders table is different from the value (2,2) in the second record. This is how we obtain uniqueness of primary key values of join tables in many-to-many relationships.

To create a many-to-many relationship in Access 2007, we follow these steps:
1. Make sure that the two tables that you are about to join in a many-to-many relationship already have primary keys. These primary keys should be of the autonumber data type.
2. Create a new table whose name is the combination of the names of the two tables that you would like to join—in this case "Products_Orders." You can follow any

other naming convention you prefer as long as you can remember in the future that this is a join table between Orders and Products.

3. In the join table "Products_Orders", create two fields whose names are: ProductID and OrderID. The data types of both OrderID and ProductID should be "Number". This is because we need to join these fields with the corresponding keys in the Orders and Products tables, and we cannot join two fields with dissimilar data types. Your table should look like this:

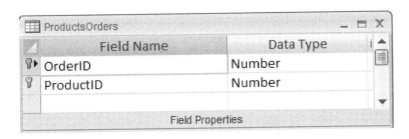

4. We are not finished yet, however. Let us assume that a customer orders two units of product (A) and three units of product (B). This customer is ordering multiple quantities of the same product in the same order. In addition, we might want to give discounts on particular products in the same order while extending no discounts for other products. How do we accomplish this? The answer is to include additional fields in the Products_Orders table so that we can enter this information. Our final table will look like this:

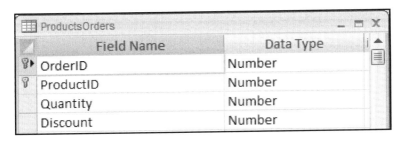

5. The next step is to join the Orders table to the ProductsOrders table by dragging the OrderID field from the Orders table on the OrderID field in the ProductsOrders

table. We do the same by dragging the ProductID field from the Products table on the ProductID field in the ProductsOrders table. Our relationships window will now look like the figure below:

21. How to "read", understand, and use a many-to-many relationship

The meaning of many-to-many relationship between orders and products

The important goal in any database work is to understand what we are doing and not so much the process of doing it. If we do not remember the series of clicks to achieve a task, we can always resort to a handy reference. However, if we do not understand how many-to-many relationships work, we are reluctant to use them or, at the very least, cannot take full advantage of them.

Let us examine the meaning of a many-to-many relationship from A to Z. The figure below depicts a many-to-many relationship between the Orders and Products tables. Let us try to answer a couple of questions:

CUSTOMER		ORDERS		
CustID	Name	OrderID	CustID	OrderDate
1	John	1	2	9/10/2009
2	Mary	2	2	10/10/2010
3	George	3	1	11/10/2010
4	Stacy	4	3	11/11/2010

Products_Orders			Products	
OrderID	ProductID	Quantity	ProductID	ProductName
1	2	2	1	A
2	2	5	2	B
3	1	3	3	C
4	2	4	4	D

What specific products were included in John's order?

To answer this question, we should go to John's record in the customer table. There, we see that John's primary key value is 1 (PK=1). Then, we proceed to the Orders table, which is joined with the customer table through a one-to-many relationship. There, we see that John appears in the third record of the table where CustID = 1. In database parlance, this translates to foreign key value = 1 or FK=1. Next, we see that the corresponding OrderID value for FK=1 is 3 (OrderID =3). From there, we are looking for OrderID = 3 in the ProductsOrders table. We see that we have one OrderID with the value of 3 in the ProductsOrders table. The corresponding ProductID value is 1. Next, we go to the Products table and see that ProductID = 1 corresponds to product A. Since the quantity for the pair (3,1) in the Products_Orders table is 3, we can finally answer that John ordered three units of product (A). This is exactly how relational databases use associations (relationships) to store and retrieve information.

What specific products were included in Mary's orders?

Mary's PK is 2. For FK=2 in the orders table, the corresponding PK values are 1 and 2. We now know that Mary placed two orders. For OrderID 1 and 2 in the ProductsOrders table, the corresponding ProductIDs are 2 and 2. The quantities are 2 and 5. Therefore, we know right away that Mary ordered seven product Bs in two separate orders. We also note that Mary has a pattern of ordering only product Bs, which allows us to direct our marketing efforts.

22.   Create a one-to-many relationship using pure SQL

Use SQL to create a one-to-many relationship between customers and orders
Discussion:
In this scenario, we create a one-to-many relationship between the tblCustomer1 and tblOrders1tables using CustomerID as the joining field.

Code:

```
ALTER TABLE tblOrders1
ADD CONSTRAINT C_OrdersRelationship
FOREIGN KEY (CustomerID)
REFERENCES tblCustomer1 (CustomerID);
```

Result:

Go to "Database Tools", and click on "Relationships" in the "Show/Hide" group. Right click on the pane, and make the two tables show in the relationships pane. The two tables will appear with a one-to-many relationship established already. In addition, you will notice that referential integrity is already set as well. This is really cool, isn't it?

23.   What is referential integrity, how to apply it, and what it means

The meaning and implications of referential integrity in table relationships

Referential Integrity is a concept misunderstood and underused in the database professional world. Some developers will turn this option on in Access because it is a good "thing" to do even though they do not fully understand its implications. Let us take it one step at a time and explain the ins and outs of referential integrity.

Referential integrity in relational databases means that relationships among joined tables remain consistent. Of course, as is the case with all definitions, we do not understand much. Let us try to approach it from a more practical perspective. First, we set referential integrity on table relationships (not tables themselves), and we have the choice to apply it when we create those relationships.

Let's first see how we do it before we discuss what it means. Let's say that we would like to create a one-to-many relationship between customers and orders. To achieve this, we drag the CustomerID field (PK in the Customer table) on the CustomerID field in the Orders table (FK in the orders table). The relationships window then opens up as we can see below:

The only thing we need to do is to click on the Referential Integrity check box. In some cases, you might find that the database does not allow you to apply referential integrity. If this is the case, then you should immediately look for orphaned records in the table at the many part of the relationship. In this particular example, it means that we have orders with CustomerID (FK) values without corresponding CustomerID values (PKs) in the customers table. In short, we have orders without corresponding customers. Check chapter 22 for a full explanation of orphaned records. I have devoted a whole chapter on orphaned and unrelated records because this topic is crucial in any database work.

Once referential integrity is on, we have several consequences. First, the database will not allow us to enter an order in the orders table without a corresponding customer. If we have an order from a new customer, we have to enter that customer's data in the Customers table first and then, the orders in the Orders table. Actually, this is what you will see if you try to enter an order without an existing customer:

Second, the database will not allow us to delete a customer who has orders in the database. First, we need to delete all of the orders for that customer and try to delete the customer. If we try to delete a customer with existing orders, the following message will appear.

If we want to delete a customer with existing orders in one step, we can also click on "Cascade Deletes". This option helps the professional delete all related information about a customer in the database, but it is very dangerous to leave on because end users might delete customers and their related information by mistake. Check chapters 27 and 28 on "Cascade Updates" and "Cascade Deletes" for full details on their use since they are an important productivity tool for developers and power users.

CHAPTER 4
THE SELECT STATEMENT

The SELECT statement is the most widely used keyword in any relational database, and it constitutes the basis for a multitude of Structured Query Language (SQL) code statements. In this chapter, we will go through examples of how to use the SELECT statement alone or in combination with its various clauses like WHERE, GROUP BY, HAVING, and ORDER BY. However, we will devote whole chapters to some of its clauses since there are many ways and tricks in using them to achieve the intricate results we need in our daily business tasks.

In this chapter, we will focus on the SELECT statement in detail, and you will be surprised to see that SELECT can be used in many more ways than simply selecting records. The general structure of the SELECT statement in Access 2007 appears below:

```
SELECT field1, field2, field3
FROM table
[WHERE]
[GROUP BY]
[HAVING]
[ORDER BY]
```

24.   SELECT with * to retrieve all columns and rows from a table

Create a quick report selecting all columns and rows from the customer table

Discussion:

We can use the * wildcard character to quickly retrieve all of the columns and records from a table. Note that a SELECT statement used this way will retrieve records in the order they are stored in the table.

Code:

SELECT *
FROM Customers

Result:

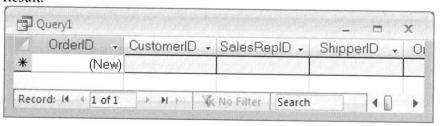

25.   SELECT to retrieve only field names

Provide documentation for the Orders table by retrieving a list of its fields

Discussion:

There are occasions when we would like to retrieve only the field names and not any records. This is usually for documentation purposes or for just having a look at the field names before we write a query. We can easily do this by using the following code, which will result in no records because there is no way for 0 to equal 1.

Code:

SELECT *
FROM Orders
WHERE 0=1;

Result:

26.   SELECT to retrieve specific columns from a table

Create a quick customer list for mailing labels

Discussion:

Experience indicates that in the vast majority of cases, we need to retrieve only a subset of columns from a table. We can define exactly what columns to get using the SELECT statement. In this particular example, we need to send out letters to our customers, and we only need to retrieve address related fields.

Code:

SELECT lastname, firstname, address, city, state, zip
FROM Customers

Result:

lastname	firstname	address	city	state	zip
Demarco	John	11 Lark Street	New York	NY	12189
Demania	Mary	12 Madison Ave	New York	NY	12189

Record: 10 of 201   No Filter   Search

27.   SELECT to retrieve columns in the order you prefer

Retrieve a customer list arranging the columns in a specific order

Discussion:

We can specify the order in which we would like to see columns in the query output. In this case, we would like to see the state field first, followed by the last and first names of our customers. When rearranging columns in SQL statements, pay attention to your commas. It is prohibited to have a comma after the last field before the FROM clause.

Code:

SELECT state, city, lastname, firstname
FROM Customers

Result:

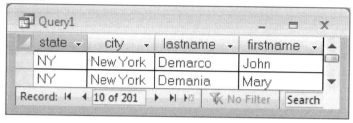

28. SELECT to retrieve specific records from a table

Create a report of customers in Boston

Discussion:

SQL statements provide great flexibility for retrieving records. For instance, we can retrieve all columns from a table, all rows, some columns and all rows, some rows and all columns, or some rows and some columns. In this example, we are retrieving all of the columns from the customer table but limiting the rows by selecting customers who reside in Boston. Notice from the result set that the database returned only 14 customers.

Code:

```
SELECT *
FROM Customers
WHERE city = "Boston"
```

Result:

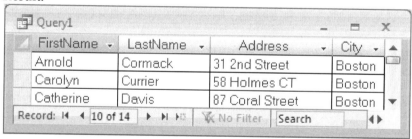

29. SELECT to retrieve specific columns and specific rows

Create a list of suppliers from NY but do not display the state

Discussion:

Sometimes, we need to retrieve specific columns and specific rows from a table. When in this situation, always work with the process of getting the columns first and then, apply

34

the appropriate clauses (WHERE) and criteria ("Houston", "Texas") to get the rows that you need. In this example, we are retrieving only the company name and the contact name of suppliers who operate in New York. In addition, notice that although we use the state as a criterion field, the state itself will not appear in the result set.

Code:
SELECT companyname, contactname
FROM suppliers
WHERE (state = "NY")

Result:

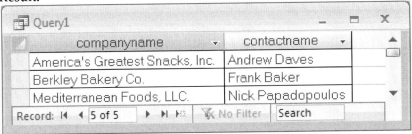

30. SELECT AS: column aliases

Retrieve data from the suppliers table but change the column titles
Discussion:
In many cases, table fields have names that make sense to the database developer but not the end user. For example, Cust_LN and Cust_FN might make sense to the database developer because they represent naming conventions for the customer last name and customer first name fields. However, if we use them as titles for queries or reports, no one will be able to discern their meaning.

In these cases, we use the SELECT AS statement to assign field aliases or column titles that make sense for all of us. We can do this on the fly in a SELECT statement. In the example below, we change the titles of the fields for two columns in the suppliers table. Notice we enclose the second alias [Supplier Contact] in brackets because we have a space between the two words. If we forget the brackets, the SQL statement will not run.

Code:

SELECT companyname AS Company, contactname AS [Supplier Contact]
FROM suppliers

Result:

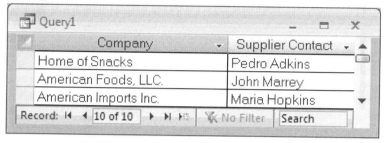

31.   SELECT combined with plain text

Create a quick letter to customers

Discussion:

SQL allows us to mingle field data with plain text, which results in the creation of some interesting results. In this example, we are writing a quick letter to customers. Notice that we enclose plain text in double quotes (" "). In addition, note that the characters (+ ' ' +) add spaces between fields and plain text. Finally, the whole statement in the code below is just one concatenated field named "CustomerLetter." For a full understanding of concatenated fields, refer to chapter 15 where you will find many tips and tricks working with them.

Code:

SELECT "Dear" + ' ' + [firstname] + ' ' + "We would like you to know that our full product catalog is on sale in the city of" + ' ' +[city] + ' ' + "Please visit our website at: http://www.company.com" As CustomerLetter
FROM customers

Result:

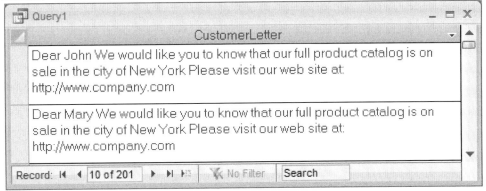

32.   SELECT with ORDER BY

Sort a customer list by last name

Discussion:

In this example, we use the * wildcard character to retrieve all of the columns and rows in the customers table and then, sort the data on last name. To sort data in SQL, we use the ORDER BY clause. Specifically, to sort in ascending order, we use ORDER BY ASC, and to sort in descending order, we use ORDER BY DESC. In this example, the ORDER BY clause is not followed by the ASC or DESC keywords. This is fine since when we use the ORDER BY clause alone, it will sort in ascending order by default.

Code:

```
SELECT *
FROM Customers
ORDER BY lastname
```

Result:

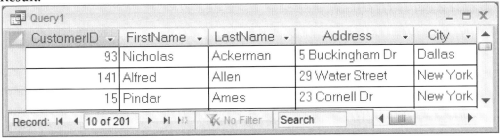

37

33.   SELECT with WHERE and ORDER BY

Retrieve all customers except those in Boston and sort by last name

Discussion:

In this example, we use the * wildcard character to retrieve all columns in the customers table. For rows, we filter the result set by using the WHERE clause with the inequality predicate "<>" to select all customers except those in the city of Boston. Then, we sort ascending on lastname. Note that there are 187 customer records returned out of 201.

Code:

```
SELECT *
FROM Customers
WHERE city <> "Boston"
ORDER BY lastname
```

Result:

CustomerID	FirstName	LastName	Address	City
93	Nicholas	Ackerman	5 Buckingham Dr	Dallas
141	Alfred	Allen	29 Water Street	New York
15	Pindar	Ames	23 Cornell Dr	New York

Record: 10 of 187 No Filter Search

34.   SELECT with WHERE, GROUP BY, HAVING and ORDER BY

Calculate the number of customers in all states except NY and show states with more than ten customers

Discussion:

Our business manager asked us to calculate the number of customers in each state. In addition, she asked us to exclude New York State from the results. From the remaining states, she also asked us to exclude states with less than ten customers. Finally, states with bigger numbers of customers should appear first in the result set.

To comply with the above requirements, we need to use SELECT, WHERE, GROUP BY, HAVING, and ORDER BY in combination. Let us examine the purpose of each statement: First, we use the SELECT statement to select two fields from the customers table. Specifically, we select the state field as it is and the CustomerID field on which we apply the Count() function to calculate the number of occurrences of CustomerID in the table. Since CustomerID is the primary key of the table, we know that Count() will produce reliable results because there is no way to have null values in a primary key field.

Then, we use the WHERE clause with the inequality operator "<>" to exclude from the calculations customers in New York State. Practically, "<>" means retrieve everything else except 'NY'. Next, we use the GROUP BY clause to aggregate calculations by state. The database will calculate the number of customers and produce results by state since we group on that field.

The next point is a bit tricky if not understood well. The WHERE and HAVING clauses are both filtering statements. We use them both to obtain a subset of records. They do, however, have their specific roles in SQL statements, and they can be used individually or in combination. In this specific example, we use the WHERE clause to exclude customers from the state of New York from the result set. The WHERE clause will run before any groupings and calculations by the GROUP BY clause. In this particular example, the WHERE clause will exclude customers from NY, and the GROUP BY clause will produce groups and count customers for the remaining records. After the groups of customers by state are generated from the GROUP BY clause, and the customer numbers are calculated by the count() function, the HAVING clause takes effect. It will exclude from the final result any states with less than ten customers. Therefore, the HAVING clause will wait until the groupings and calculations are complete before it takes effect. This is logical since the numbers produced by the count() function are not known in advance.

Finally, the ORDER BY clause takes effect, and it will sort results by the highest number of customers. What you need to remember in one sentence is that when using the WHERE and HAVING clauses in combination, the WHERE clause always takes effect first, while the HAVING clause takes effect after the groups by the GROUP BY clause have been established. The ORDER BY clause will take effect last.

Code:

```
SELECT State, Count(CustomerID) As NumberOfCustomers
FROM Customers
WHERE State <> "NY"
GROUP BY State
HAVING Count(CustomerID) >10
ORDER BY Count(CustomerID) DESC
```

Result:

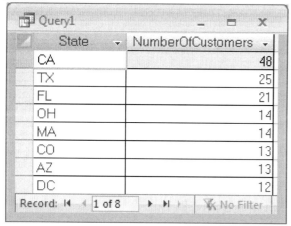

35.   SELECT with INSERT INTO to append records in an existing table

Append records from the customer table to a historical customer table

Discussion:

Our goal in this example is to copy (append) a number of records from our customer table to another table in which we keep historical customer data. This scenario applies in situations where we no longer do business with some customers, but we do not want to delete them from the database. At the same time, we do not want these old customers to clutter our operational customer table, slow it down, or interfere with our calculations. We can easily copy them to a historical table by using the INSERT INTO statement. The general structure of the INSERT INTO statement appears below:

```
INSERT INTO TargetTable (field1, field2, field3...)
SELECT (field1, field2, field3...)
FROM SourceTable
```

In this particular example, we copy records from the customers table to the customer2 table. Since customer2 does not exist, we create it with the CREATE statement below. Then, we use the INSERT INTO statement to append three fields with 201 records (all records in the customer table) in the customer2 table.

Code:
```
CREATE TABLE Customer2 (
[CustomerID] Counter Primary key not null,
[LastName] text(50),
[FirstName] text(50),
[Address] text(100),
[City] text(50));

INSERT INTO Customer2 (firstname, lastname, address, city)
SELECT firstname, lastname, address, city
FROM customers
```

Result:

36.   SELECT with INSERT INTO to append specific records in a table

Append selected customer records to a historical table

Discussion:

In some occasions, we might want to copy only a subset of records in one table into another table. We can easily achieve this by using the INSERT TO statement and the WHERE clause in combination. In this specific example, we append customer records from NY only.

Code:

INSERT INTO Customer2 (firstname, lastname, address, city)
SELECT firstname, lastname, address, city
FROM customers
WHERE State = 'NY'

Result:

37.   SELECT INTO to create a backup or temp table

Create a quick backup copy of the products table
Discussion:

The SELECT INTO statement accomplishes two tasks simultaneously. First, it can create a new table, and second, it can populate this table with records from another table. We do not need to use the CREATE statement to create a new table. In addition, we do not need the INSERT INTO statement to copy records from one table to another. The SELECT INTO statement can accomplish both tasks at once.

We can use the SELECT INTO statement to create quick backup copies of tables, or we can create temporary tables and work on their data leaving the original tables untouched. For instance, we might want to manipulate data in the products table, but we would like to see the results of the edits first before we apply them in the operational products table. In this particular example, we create a backup copy of the products table, and we name it Products_Backup.

Code:

SELECT *
INTO Products_Backup
FROM Products

Result:

38.   SELECT INTO to create a backup table with a subset of data from the original table

Create a temporary table that contains a subset of data from the products table

Discussion:

We can use the SELECT INTO statement and the WHERE clause in combination to create a new table that will contain a subset of data from the original table. The choice of the word "data" is not accidental. In fact, using the SELECT INTO statement in combination with the WHERE clause, we can transfer any fields and records we wish. In this particular example, we create a new table named "Products_Subset" which will contain only three fields and product records from suppliers with supplier ID 1, 2, 3, and 4 only.

Code:

```
SELECT ProductName, UnitsInStock, UnitsOnOrder
INTO Products_Subset
FROM Products
WHERE SupplierID IN (1,2,3,4)
```

Result:

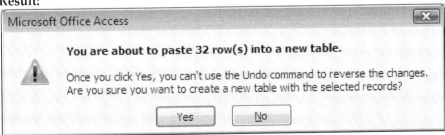

39.   SELECT INTO to create a new table with a subset of data from three joined tables

Create a new table that contains data from the three joined tables

Discussion:

The SELECT INTO statement can create a new table that contains data from multiple joined tables. In this example, we create a new table that contains fields from the customers, orders, and productsorders tables. In addition, we restrict the number of records it will contain by using the WHERE clause for customers in NY only. Why do we need to create a new table since we can easily retrieve the same records using a query? Actually, a move like this one serves multiple purposes. First, we might want to give access to this data to other people and not worry if they edit or change it any way they want. If we provide them with a query, they could affect the data in the underlying tables. Another scenario might be that we would like to hide the complexities of the joins to the people working with this data. It is much easier to work with one table than with two inner joins from three tables. Finally, we might be in a business scenario in which this table is the data source for XML or PHP or ASP.Net or other server side pages on our website, and we generate this table every week. Those pages will return results much faster working out of a table data source instead of multiple joins and WHERE clauses.

Code:

```
SELECT customers.lastname, customers.firstName, Orders.OrderDate,
ProductsOrders.UnitPrice, ProductsOrders.Quantity
INTO TempCustomersOrders
FROM (customers INNER JOIN Orders ON customers.CustomerID =
Orders.CustomerID) INNER JOIN ProductsOrders ON Orders.OrderID =
ProductsOrders.OrderID
WHERE (((customers.State)="NY"));
```

Result:

CHAPTER 5
THE OR AND AND OPERATORS

The OR and AND operators are widely used in relational databases. There are four points you need to remember about them: First, their task is to produce a subset of records from the total records in a table or query. Second, they have no effect on what columns we retrieve from that table or query. Third, they are always used with other operators such as LIKE, with equality and inequality predicates, or with wildcard characters. They cannot be used by themselves in SQL statements. Fourth, the OR and AND operators can be used individually or in combination with varying results as we shall see in the following examples.

The OR operator is inclusive so that records will be returned for every OR condition satisfied in our query. For example, if we want to retrieve invoice information from suppliers in three different cities (New York, Texas, and Houston), we will use the OR operator twice. The AND operator is exclusive, and it will produce results only when all of the multicolumn conditions are met.

40.   Using OR on the same column
Create a quick report with customers in New York or Houston
Discussion:
Let us suppose we have a request to create a list of all customers who reside in New York or Houston. In this case, we need to use the OR operator on the city field with two equality predicates. Note that since we used the SELECT statement with *, the database will return all columns in the table. However, when it comes to records, only 43 out of 201 will be returned. This is because we filtered the recordset to include customers in the cities of New York or Houston only.

Code:

SELECT *

FROM customers

WHERE (city = "New York") OR (city = "Houston")

Result:

CustomerID ▾	FirstName ▾	LastName ▾	Address ▾
1	John	Demarco	11 Lark Street
2	Mary	Demania	12 Madison Ave
3	George	Demers	23 New Scotlan Ave
4	Phillip	Demetriou	22 Academy Road

Record: I◄ ◄ 10 of 39 ► ►I ►⊞   ✖ No Filter   Search

41.   Use the IN operator to replace multiple OR operators

Produce a report of customers from four cities

Discussion:

The OR operator works fine with two cities as we have seen in the previous example. What if we need to use OR on the city field but use five or six cities as criteria? We have two problems in this case: First, we need to write a long SQL statement using multiple OR operators. Second, if we have a big number of records in the table, the query will be slow to return results. In cases like this one, we can use the IN operator that produces much cleaner code. It is easy to modify and maintain as you can see below:

Code:

SELECT lastname, firstname, city, state

FROM customers

WHERE city IN ("Albany", "Denver", "Houston", "Phoenix")

ORDER BY lastname ASC

Result:

lastname	firstname	city	state
Bink	Jim	Huston	TX
Bittel	David	Huston	TX
Clark	Allen	Huston	TX

Record: ◄ ◄ 10 of 42 ► ►► No Filter | Search

42. Using OR on multiple columns

Create an inventory report listing product quantities for units in stock and units on order

Discussion:

A very efficient way to use the OR operator is to apply it on multiple columns. For instance, we might have a business request to create an inventory report that lists products for which we have more than 10 units in stock or products for which we have more than 10 units on order. As you can see from the result set, we obtained a total number of 70 products. This means that 70 records satisfied at least one condition. This is because any record that satisfies at least one of the conditions will appear in the result set.

In addition, this is why the second record in the result set with 32 units in stock and 0 on order appears as well. We asked for units in stock >10 or units on order >10. This particular record satisfies only the first condition, and this is enough to appear in the result set. The outcome will be very different when we use the AND operator as we will see later on.

Code:
```
SELECT productname, unitsinstock, unitsonorder
FROM products
WHERE (UnitsInStock > 10)
OR (UnitsOnOrder > 10)
```

47

Result:

productname	unitsinstock	unitsonorder
Almonds, Hickory Smoked - 12 oz. B	40	5
Almonds, Roasted and Salted - 18 o	32	0
Banana Chips - 20 oz. Bag	25	0
Berry Cherry in 8 oz. Bag	50	0

Record: 10 of 70 No Filter Search

43.   Use UNION instead of OR to speed up results

Create an inventory report using UNION instead of OR operators

Discussion:

We can use the UNION statement instead of multiple OR operators to speed up the response time of the database engine. This is a trick used in databases, and the difference in response time is enormous. The SQL statement below with the UNION operation achieves the exact same results as the SQL code in the previous example. However, the response is instant using UNION, while it takes quite a few seconds using the OR operators.

Response times deteriorate as the number of records or the number of OR operators increase. Consequently, if you have statements with multiple OR operators that you use often, you might consider replacing them with UNION statements. The only difference is the order in which the retrieved records appear since in this case, the results of the first SELECT statement in the UNION operation will appear first. The results of the second SELECT will follow. You can easily reorder the recordset using the ORDER BY clause with a UNION statement. For a full understanding of UNION operations, plus related tips and tricks refer to chapter 21.

Code:

SELECT productname, unitsinstock, unitsonorder
FROM products
WHERE (UnitsInStock > 10)
UNION

SELECT productname, unitsinstock, unitsonorder
FROM products
WHERE (UnitsOnOrder > 10)

Result:

productname	unitsinstock	unitsonorder
All-Purpose Marinade I	27	15
All-Purpose Marinade II	26	15
Almonds, Hickory Smoked - 12 oz. E	40	5
Almonds, Roasted and Salted - 18 c	32	0

Record: 10 of 70   No Filter   Search

44.   Using AND on multiple columns

Produce a report of customers from a specific state and a specific city

Discussion:

This time, we have a business request to produce a report of customers who reside in the state of NY and, in particular, the city of Albany. In this case, we need to use the AND operator to isolate records which satisfy both criteria at the same time. Note that if we use the OR operator, we will get all of the customers in the state of NY irrespective of city and all the customers from all of the cities named "Albany" around the country. This is a problem because there are 28 cities in the U.S. named Albany! If we do business worldwide, there are six additional cities named Albany. An experienced database user will always use AND to isolate the customers only for Albany, New York. As you can see from the result set, we have only four customers that satisfy both criteria.

Code:

SELECT lastname, firstname, city, state
FROM customers
WHERE (state = "NY")
AND (city = "Albany")

Result:

lastname	firstname	city	state
Vanton	Kenneth	Albany	NY
Trindan	Luis	Albany	NY
Riegert	Joanne	Albany	NY
Miller	Anthony	Albany	NY

Record: 1 of 4 — No Filter — Search

45. Using OR and AND in combination

Produce a report of customers from one state and two cities

Discussion:

Our objective in this scenario is to produce a report that will list customers from the cities of Albany and New York in NY State. In this case, we need to use the AND operator twice and the OR operator once as it appears in the code below:

Code:

```
SELECT lastname, firstname, city, state
FROM customers
WHERE
state = "NY" AND city = "Albany"
OR
state = "NY" AND city = "New York"
ORDER BY lastname
```

Result:

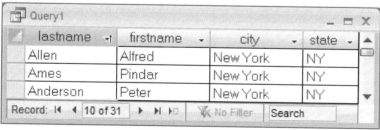

lastname	firstname	city	state
Allen	Alfred	New York	NY
Ames	Pindar	New York	NY
Anderson	Peter	New York	NY

Record: 10 of 31 — No Filter — Search

46. Using multiple OR and multiple AND operators in combination

Produce a report of customers from three states and three cities

Discussion:

This time, we have a request to create a customer report that will list customers in the cities of Houston, Albany, and Phoenix from the states of Texas, New York, and Arizona respectively. In this case, we need to use the AND operator three times and the OR operator twice as it appears in the code below. The database returned 29 records.

Code:

```
SELECT lastname, firstname, city, state
FROM customers
WHERE
state = "NY" AND city = "Albany"
OR
state = "TX" AND city = "Houston"
OR
state = "AZ" AND city = "Phoenix"
ORDER BY lastname
```

Result:

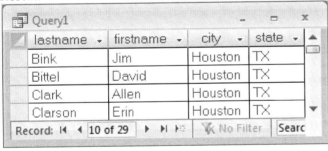

CHAPTER 6
SORTING RECORDS: THE ORDER BY CLAUSE

The ORDER BY clause, with the ASC or DESC keywords, allows the sorting of records in ascending or descending order respectively. The ORDER BY clause is much stronger than what is generally assumed, and it allows for some cool tricks with our data.

47.   Sorting ascending on one column
Create a list of customers sorting by last name in ascending order
Discussion:
This is a basic example of how to sort our customers by last name and in ascending order. Customers whose last names start with an "A" will appear first. The keyword "ASC" is not required to sort records in ascending order. If we leave the keyword "ASC" out, the ORDER BY clause will sort ascending by default.

Code:
```
SELECT *
FROM Customers
ORDER BY lastname ASC
```

Result:

48. Sorting descending on one column

Create a list of customers sorting by last name in descending order

Discussion:

Sometimes, we want to see names in reverse alphabetical order—names that start with Z, Y, or X first. In this case, we add the DESC keyword to our SQL statement. Note that if we want to sort descending, the DESC keyword is required.

Code:
```
SELECT *
FROM Customers
ORDER BY lastname DESC
```

Result:

CustomerID	FirstName	LastName	Address
48	Stephen	Zinter	110 Johnson Ave
21	Lauren	Zentons	23 Crescent Dr
18	Charles	Zensons	23 Tampa Ave
20	Lisa	Zartons	34 Home Ave

Record: 10 of 201 No Filter Search

49. Use the ORDER BY clause to sort multiple columns

Create a customer list sorting by city and last name simultaneously

Discussion:

We can sort records on the values of multiple columns. For example, we might want to obtain a report which will include a list of customers sorted first by city and then, by last name.

Let's say we have some customers in Albany and some customers in Boston. Sorting ascending on both city and last name fields will create the following result: The records with the city of Albany will appear first in the result set, followed by the records with the city of Boston. Now, within the Albany records, customers will be sorted alphabetically and in ascending order. Within the city of Boston records, customers will again be sorted alphabetically and in ascending order. We should not be surprised to see a customer

53

from Boston whose last name starts with an "A" being listed after a customer in Albany whose last name starts with a "Z".

Code:

```
SELECT city, lastname, firstname
FROM Customers
ORDER BY city, lastname ASC
```

Result:

50. Use ORDER BY clause with null values

Find customers who do not have a first name registered in the database

Discussion:

Let us suppose that we have a suspicion that some first name values are missing from our records. How can we quickly find out which ones they are? We can simply create a query that includes the fields we would like to check and sort ascending on the field we suspect includes blank entries. In this instance, we sort ascending on the first name field from our customers table. As you can see from the result set, we immediately found one customer without a first name.

Code:

```
SELECT lastname, firstname
FROM Customers
ORDER BY firstname ASC
```

Result:

51.   Use the ORDER BY clause with numbers

Create an inventory report sorting products by quantity on hand

Discussion:

In this scenario, we would like to list products from our inventory with the biggest quantities on hand. We can easily achieve this task using the DESC keyword with numbers. When sorting numbers, the DESC keyword will cause the biggest ones to show first, while the ASC keyword will cause the smallest numbers to show first.

Code:

```
SELECT productname, unitsinstock
FROM products
ORDER BY unitsinstock DESC
```

Result:

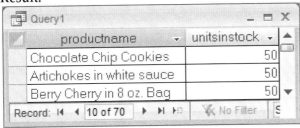

52.   The ORDER BY clause with dates

Create a list with the latest orders on top

Discussion:

The ORDER BY clause works with dates the same way it works with numbers. So, to list the latest dates first, we use the DESC keyword. If we would like to show the oldest dates first, we use the ASC keyword.

Code:

```
SELECT orderid, orderdate, shippeddate
FROM ORDERS
ORDER BY orderdate DESC
```

Result:

orderid	orderdate	shippeddate
4	12/14/2010	12/19/2010
874	12/11/2010	12/16/2010
165	12/9/2010	12/14/2010

Record: 10 of 1001   No Filter   Sea

53.   TIP: Combine the ORDER BY and TOP clauses to control the result set

List the top five products in the inventory with the biggest quantities on hand

Discussion:

The ORDER BY clause produces very meaningful results when used in combination with the TOP clause. For instance, what if we want to list the top five products in our inventory with the biggest quantities on hand? We can achieve this task by combining the ORDER BY and TOP clauses. Notice the number of records in the result set. Only five products appear, and these five products have the largest unit quantities in stock in our inventory.

Code:

```
SELECT TOP 5 unitsinstock, productname
FROM products
ORDER BY unitsinstock DESC
```

Result:

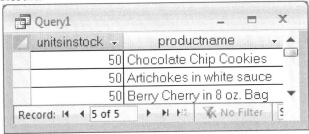

CHAPTER 7
WORKING WITH WILDCARD CHARACTERS

Wildcard characters like (*, ?, !, [], -) provide essential functionality and power in databases. They are used in combination with operators such as (LIKE, OR, AND, BETWEEN, IN, etc.) and predicates like (<, >, <>, =, >=). They also allow for the formulation of very sophisticated search criteria.

54. The * wildcard character

Create a list of customers whose last name starts with D

Discussion:

The * is the wildest of the wildcard characters, and it will match any number and type (letters or numbers) of characters whether we put it in the beginning, middle, or end of a search condition. For example, we can search for all of the customer last names that start with the letter D. As we can see, every customer whose last name starts with a D will appear in the result set. Notice in the code of this example that the * is positioned after the letter D. This means that entries such as Dem, D1a, d123, or Dzo will appear in the result set.

Code:
```
SELECT *
FROM customers
WHERE ((lastname) Like "D*")
```

Result:

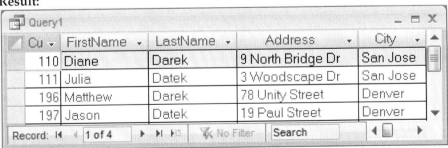

55. The ? wildcard character in combination with *

Create a customer list using ? and * to create intricate search patterns

Discussion:

The ? character matches any single character. Though not used as much as the *, it can still make the difference and enable us to get exactly the results we want in certain cases. Usually, we use it in combination with other wildcard characters. For instance, let's say we want to find names starting with "Da", have any character after the "Da" pattern, and the next letter is "e" followed by any number of characters—"Da?e*". This will give us results such as Darec, Datek, Dale, and Daleney.

Code:
```
SELECT *
FROM customers
WHERE ((lastname) Like "Da?e*")
```

Result:

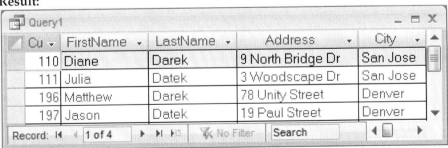

56.　Create multi-character search strings with [ ]

Create a customer list using multi-character search patterns

Discussion:

Let us assume we would like to search for a number of specific characters within a character string such as a name field. We can do this by using the brackets [ ]. Any character or characters that we include within the brackets will be included in our search. For example, C[ru]* will find Croney, Culey, but not Colonie. Note that we use the * in this example to allow any characters to be included after the brackets.

Code:

```
SELECT *
FROM customers
WHERE ((lastname) Like "C[ru]*")
```

Result:

Cu	FirstName	LastName	Address	City
99	Kenneth	Crondos	158 West Lawrence	Huston
100	Pindar	Crooney	16 Warren Street	Huston
101	Joseph	Crandil	192 Tampa Ave	Huston
107	Mary	Crawford	21 Aegean Dr	Huston

Record: 8 of 8　　No Filter　Search

57.　Use the ! and [ ] wildcard characters to create exclusion patterns

Create a customer list using specific characters as exclusion search patterns

Discussion:

Sometimes, we need to exclude a set of characters to obtain the results we need. For example, we might want to retrieve all of our customers from the customers table except those whose names start with an A, B, C, D, or E. How about using the [!] wildcard to get the results we want? Note that the returned recordset is sorted by last name, and the first customer record to appear has a last name value starting with "F". All of the customers whose names start with a letter before that have been excluded from the recordset.

Code:
SELECT *
FROM customers
WHERE ((lastname) Like "[!abcde]*")
ORDER BY lastname

Result:

Cu ▾	FirstName ▾	LastName ▾	Address ▾	City ▾
115	Sonya	Ford	5 Beach Ave	San Jose
166	Cristopher	Geisler	93 Kate Street	Boston
116	William	Gibson	17 Grove Street	San Jose
117	Kathy	Giordano	21 Garden Ave	San Diego

Record: ◄ ◄ 10 of 130 ► ►I ►⬚ ⬚ No Filter | Search | ◄ ⬚ ►

58.   Use the ! and [ ] and - wildcards to create exclusion ranges

Create a customer list using sets of characters as exclusion ranges

Discussion:

What if we continue from the previous example using ! and [], but instead of typing in all of the characters, we use ranges? For example, we might want to obtain a recordset of customers whose names do not start with a letter in the range A-P. We can do this by using the "[!a-p]*" exclusion pattern. As you can see from the figure below, the customers who appear in the list have names starting with an "R", which is the one immediately following "P" that was included in our exclusion range.

Code:
SELECT *
FROM customers
WHERE ((lastname) Like "[!a-p]*")
ORDER BY lastname

Result:

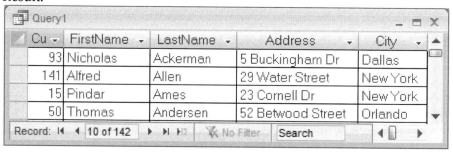

59. Use the - and [ ] wildcards to create inclusion ranges

Create a customer list using sets of characters as inclusion ranges

Discussion:

We can continue from the previous example and use [] and - to obtain a recordset of customers whose names do start with a letter between A and P. Simply put, we need to take out the exclamation mark.

Code:

```
SELECT *
FROM customers
WHERE ((lastname) Like "[a-p]*")
ORDER BY lastname
```

Result:

CHAPTER 8
THE LIKE OPERATOR

The major aspect of the LIKE operator is its flexibility in creating search expressions. In other words, it has the flexibility to work on text, number, and date data types using intricate expressions to produce results. In addition, its usefulness is greatly enhanced when used in combination with wildcard characters like (*, ?, !, [], -) for the creation of elaborate search expressions.

However, we need to remember two points when using the LIKE operator. First, to supply this flexibility and functionality, it consumes resources, so it should not be the first operator that we resort to for all of our search expressions. Second, we should really know how to use it to get the results we need since it might not always return the expected results.

In this chapter, we approach the usage of the LIKE operator from all perspectives, and we point out tips for using it optimally. To demonstrate the cool functionality of the LIKE operator, all of the examples in this chapter use the table called tbls_CustomerOrders. The records of this table are edited with special values to show how LIKE applies to various circumstances in our working environment.

60.   The LIKE operator with the * wildcard character
Create a list of customers whose last name starts with M
Discussion:
This simple example uses the LIKE operator to find customers whose last names start with an "M". The LIKE operator is used within the WHERE clause, and we enclose the search expression in double quotes. In addition, we use the * wildcard to obtain the result we need.

Code:

```
SELECT *
FROM tbls_CustomerOrders
WHERE (lastname like "M*")
```

Result:

Ord	lastname	firstname	city	state
3	Moore	Gerald	Phoenix	AZ
32	Madsen	Patricia	Boston	MA
37	Millman	Arnold	Los Angeles	CA

Record: 10 of 79 — No Filter — Search

61. The LIKE operator with [ ] and * to search for ranges

Find customers whose zip code starts with a number between 1 and 4

Discussion:

This time, we have a request to prepare a customer report showing customers whose zip codes start with numbers between 1 and 4, such as 12189, 26890, 34123, or 41289 (as opposed to 58659, which would not be eligible). To obtain the report, we use the LIKE operator with the [ ] and * wildcard characters—LIKE with two wildcard characters simultaneously. The [ ] wildcard will identify all zip codes starting with 1, 2, 3, and 4. The * will then allow for the retrieval of any number of characters after 1, 2, 3, and 4. So, even if we had to work with zip codes comprising of ten characters like 23546-1295, the SQL code in this example would work the same. Of course, we could modify the search condition as "[1-4]????" to only look for five digit zip codes.

Code:

```
SELECT lastname, firstname, city, zip
FROM tbls_CustomerOrders
WHERE (zip like "[1-4]*")
```

Result:

lastname	firstname	city	zip
Riegert	Joanne	New York	12189
Read	Lisa	Washington	11882
Moore	Gerald	Phoenix	44895

Record: I◄ ◄ 10 of 492 ► ►I ►✱ | 🍸 No Filter | Search

62. The LIKE operator with date fields

Create a report of orders for the month of April for all years

Discussion:

The LIKE operator can produce very useful pieces of information when used with date fields. In this particular example, we look for orders in the month of April irrespective of the day or year they were placed. To achieve what we need, we use the LIKE operator with the * wildcard character. Notice how we use the * twice for days and years, while we fix the month at 4 (April). I know from experience that in your own working environment, dates might not be in the format of "Month number/Day number/Year" (1/1/2010), but perhaps like January 12 2010, for example. This is not a problem at all since we can manipulate dates and change their format on the fly any way we want. I have devoted a whole chapter (chapter 26) on date manipulation for your reference. In addition, using LIKE, we can fix the day, the year, or any combination of month, day, and year and retrieve the corresponding results.

Code:

```
SELECT lastname, firstname, orderdate
FROM tbls_CustomerOrders
WHERE (OrderDate Like "4/*/*")
```

Result:

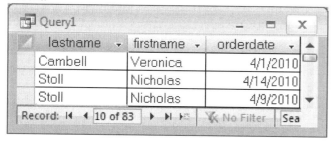

63.   The LIKE operator with number fields

Create a report of customer orders with order totals of $200
Discussion:
The LIKE operator can as easily be used with number fields as it can with text and date data. In this example, we have a request to find all customer orders with a total of $200. When we use LIKE with numbers, we do not enclose the numbers in quotes.

Code:
SELECT lastname, firstname, orderdate, OrderTotal
FROM tbls_CustomerOrders
WHERE (OrderTotal Like 200)

Result:

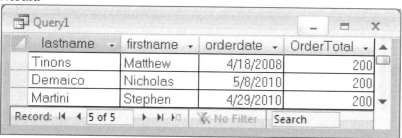

Although we can use LIKE to search for numbers, it is a better practice to use equality and inequality predicates such as (<, >, <>, =, >=). The above example could be written with the equality predicate "=", and it will produce the same results.

Code:

SELECT lastname, firstname, orderdate, OrderTotal
FROM tbls_CustomerOrders
WHERE (OrderTotal = 200)

Result:

lastname	firstname	orderdate	OrderTotal
Tinons	Matthew	4/18/2008	200
Demaico	Nicholas	5/8/2010	200
Martini	Stephen	4/29/2010	200

Record: ◄ ◄ 5 of 5 ► ►► No Filter Search

64. Compare LIKE, BETWEEN, and "<=" "=>" for number ranges

Create a report of customer orders with order totals between $200 and $400

Discussion:

In this scenario, we have a request from management to prepare a report showing customer orders with order totals between $200 and $400. To achieve this goal, we have three alternatives: We can use the LIKE operator, the BETWEEN operator, and the "<=" "=>" predicates. Which one is the best solution? Let us explore the three cases before we make a decision. In the first case, we use the LIKE operator with the [ ] wildcard for ranges and the "?" to establish the number of characters to be returned at 3. In other words, we are looking for numbers such as 234, 345, or 385. If we have used * after the [ ], we will also get numbers such as 26, 30, and 35, which is not what we want. The result set includes 230 records starting with order totals at $200 and going all the way up to the order total of $393.

Code:

SELECT lastname, firstname, orderdate, OrderTotal
FROM tbls_CustomerOrders
WHERE (OrderTotal LIKE "[2-3]??")
ORDER BY OrderTotal ASC

Result:

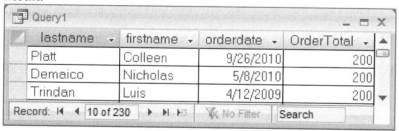

Discussion:

We use the BETWEEN operator to achieve the same task. What we must know about the BETWEEN operator is that it is inclusive. For ranges of order totals between $200 and $400, it will include order totals of exactly $200 and exactly $400 if they are available. As you can see from the result set in the following image, the results are the same as those with the LIKE operator!

Code:

SELECT lastname, firstname, orderdate, OrderTotal
FROM tbls_CustomerOrders
WHERE (OrderTotal BETWEEN 200 AND 400)
ORDER BY OrderTotal ASC

Result:

lastname	firstname	orderdate	OrderTotal
Platt	Colleen	9/26/2010	200
Demaico	Nicholas	5/8/2010	200
Trindan	Luis	4/12/2009	200

Record: 10 of 230 No Filter Search

Discussion:

In this case, we are using the "<=" "=>" predicates to achieve the same goal of finding orders between $200 and $400. You can see from the result set that the "<=" "=>" predicates produced the exact same result as the LIKE and BETWEEN operators. When it comes to numbers, however, the "<=" "=>" predicates are the most flexible and trusted to work with. For example, we can use the "<" ">" to exclude lower and upper limits. In addition, predicates will produce consistent results, while operators have issues with result accuracy and performance.

Code:

SELECT lastname, firstname, orderdate, OrderTotal
FROM tbls_CustomerOrders
WHERE (OrderTotal >= 200 AND OrderTotal <= 400)
ORDER BY OrderTotal ASC

Result:

lastname	firstname	orderdate	OrderTotal
Platt	Colleen	9/26/2010	200
Demaico	Nicholas	5/8/2010	200
Trindan	Luis	4/12/2009	200

Record: 10 of 230   No Filter   Search

65.   The NOT LIKE operator

Find customer orders with order totals different than $200

Discussion:

We can use the negation keyword "NOT" to completely change the result set of an operation using LIKE. In this particular example, we are looking for order totals different from $200. Though we can use LIKE to achieve this, we will be better off using the inequality predicate "<>" for which I include the code below as well. Both pieces of code will produce the same result but prefer to use the predicate instead of the operator.

Code1:

SELECT lastname, firstname, orderdate, OrderTotal
FROM tbls_CustomerOrders
WHERE (OrderTotal NOT Like 200)

Code2:

SELECT lastname, firstname, orderdate, OrderTotal
FROM tbls_CustomerOrders
WHERE (OrderTotal <> 200)

Result:

lastname	firstname	orderdate	OrderTotal
Riegert	Joanne	11/6/2009	30
Read	Lisa	7/25/2009	210
Moore	Gerald	6/29/2009	231

Record: ◄ ◄ 10 of 914 ► ►I ►* No Filter Search

66.   TIP: Use LIKE with the trim() function to get the right results

Filter customer names effectively by eliminating blank spaces

Discussion:

We have a request from our manager to find all orders for which the first name is Mary so that she can have a look and send them a card for their name day. We know how to use the LIKE operator, so we write a statement like the one below and get 20 records. We provide the report to our manager, and two weeks later, she comes back and says we missed three customers. What happened? Well, for three Marys, there were spaces in front of their first names and the LIKE operator did not pick them up. When it comes to LIKE, the statement (LIKE " Mary") is different from (LIKE "Mary"). Consequently, if there are any spaces, the two LIKE statements above will produce different results. What can we do about it? Let us look at the trim() function in the SQL statement after the one shown below:

Code:

SELECT lastname, firstname, orderdate, OrderTotal
FROM tbls_CustomerOrders
WHERE (firstname LIKE "Mary")

Result:

lastname	firstname	orderdate	OrderTotal
Simmons	Mary	9/16/2010	115
Stewart	Mary	7/29/2008	84
Simmons	Mary	3/7/2010	57

Record: 10 of 20   No Filter   Search

Discussion:

The trim() function will eliminate any spaces before or after a string in a field, and this will allow the LIKE operator to function properly or give us the results we want since LIKE will always function as it should. We can use it in the WHERE clause together with the LIKE operator as you can see in the code below. Notice that this time, the database returned 23 records instead of 20. For a full understanding of string functions and their cool functionality, please refer to chapter 25 where I list multiple examples.

Code:

```
SELECT lastname, firstname, orderdate, OrderTotal
FROM tbls_CustomerOrders
WHERE (trim(firstname) LIKE "Mary")
```

Result:

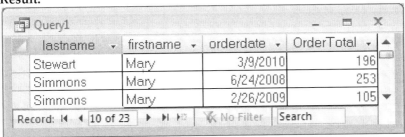

lastname	firstname	orderdate	OrderTotal
Stewart	Mary	3/9/2010	196
Simmons	Mary	6/24/2008	253
Simmons	Mary	2/26/2009	105

Record: 10 of 23   No Filter   Search

67.   TIP: Use LIKE to test a field for the presence of spaces

Check for the presence of blank spaces in a city field

Discussion:

The same supervisor comes back and says she needs a report of customers from certain cities. This time, we are wise enough to know that to get the right results, we need to check for spaces first. Then, however, we reason that some city names should contain spaces. For example, New York contains a space, and Los Angeles contains a space. In addition, we realize that the trim() function is good enough for leading and trailing spaces. What if we have a space right in the middle of the word, however? We can actually look for spaces using the LIKE operator with the * wildcard character. In this example, we are looking for two spaces in any part of the field value. To achieve this, we use the * three times. We can test for one space using two asterisks ("* *"). The cool thing is that we have found two city names with two blank spaces as you can see in the figure below:

Code:
SELECT lastname, firstname, city, orderdate
FROM tbls_CustomerOrders
WHERE (city LIKE "* * *")

Result:

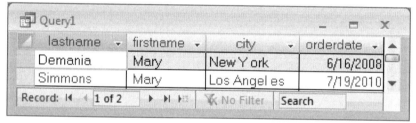

68.   TIP: Use LIKE to test a field for the presence of numbers

Check for the presence of numbers in a city field
Discussion:
Now, what if someone entered some city names and did not pay attention, and as he was typing, he mingled some numbers with the name of the city? For example, he might have entered "New 9York". How can we check a field for the presence of numbers within text strings? The answer is by using the LIKE operator, the [ ] wildcard character for ranges, and the * wildcard character as in the code below. Notice that we use the [ ] to check for any number between 0 and 9. In addition, we use the * twice to look for the presence of a number at any part of the field, including the end and the beginning of its value. We actually caught two records with numbers mistyped in them.

Code:

SELECT lastname, firstname, city, orderdate
FROM tbls_CustomerOrders
WHERE (city LIKE "*[0-9]*")

Result:

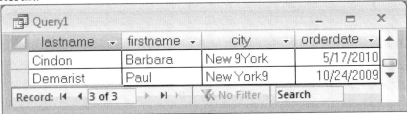

69. TIP: Create an index on a field used often with LIKE

Create an index on the city field

Discussion:

In chapter two, we discussed indexing in detail. Specifically, we mentioned that if a field is often used in searches, we need to create an index on it. We can easily create an index on the city field using the code below. This SQL statement will create a non-unique index because we want to be able to store two cities with the same name in the field "city".

Code:

CREATE INDEX indCity ON tbls_CustomerOrders (city)

Result:

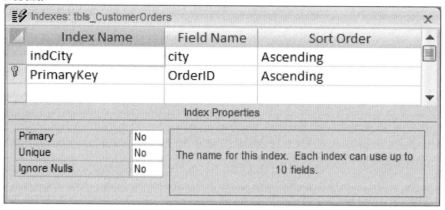

CHAPTER 9
EQUALITY AND INEQUALITY
PREDICATES

The primary goal of equality and inequality predicates in search expressions is to find absolute matches. They are more flexible than using the LIKE operator, and their results are solid and unquestionable. They are used in the WHERE clause of a SQL statement, and they can be used by themselves to construct a search condition without the need of any wildcard characters. For instance, the statement (WHERE lastname = "Smith") is valid. They should be given preference over operators such as LIKE, BETWEEN, and TOP.

70. Access 2007 equality and inequality predicates reference

Meaning	Predicate
Equal to	=
Not equal to	<>
Less than	<
Less than or equal to	<=
Greater than	>
Greater than or equal to	=>

71. The equality predicate "=" for absolute searches in text data

Find a specific customer record searching on last name

Discussion:

In this example, we use the equality predicate to retrieve the record of a particular customer. What we need to know about the equality predicate is that we search for a known value. In other words, we know the last name of the customer we are looking for in advance. Then, we use the equality predicate to find that customer. This is very different when we conduct approximate searches using the LIKE operator where we might know that the customer last name starts with "Ma", but we are not certain about the rest of it. That is why we use the expression (LIKE "Ma*") to find all of the customers whose last names start with "Ma" and then, select the one we need to work with. The point to remember is that whenever we can, we should give preference to the equality predicate over the LIKE operator because it will retrieve exactly what we need, faster, with less overhead for the database, and less clutter in the results.

Code:
SELECT *
FROM Customers
WHERE (lastname = "Delaney")

Result:

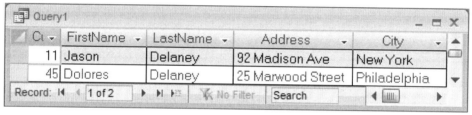

72. The equality predicate "=" for absolute searches in number data

Find a specific customer record searching on CustomerID

Discussion:

The equality predicate is very efficient with numbers as well. Actually, it should be preferred and used in multiple working scenarios involving numbers and especially primary keys. For example, let us assume we need to use an UPDATE statement to change the record of a customer. We should unequivocally identify the customer using the equality predicate on the primary key of the table so that we are certain we are updating the right customer. The same logic is valid with DELETE statements where we should use the equality predicate to identify the correct customer for deletion. Another scenario is for those who work with server side pages like ASP.Net, PHP, ASP, JSP, etc. and who need to connect back to the database server to get customer records. Obviously, they would want to transfer as little data as possible between the database server and web server, so the equality predicate is the one of choice. In this example, we retrieve all of the information on a particular order searching on the OrderID, which is the primary key of the Orders table.

Code:

SELECT *
FROM Orders
WHERE OrderID = 972

Result:

OrderID ▾	CustomerID ▾	SalesRepID ▾	ShipperID ▾	OrderDate ▾
972	199	10	3	8/19/2008
(New)				

Record: I◄ ◄ 1 of 1 ► ►I ►⁑ ﹀ No Filter | Search

73. The ">" inequality predicate with date data

Retrieve orders placed after a certain date

Discussion:

The ">" inequality predicate means "greater than", and we can freely use it with numbers and dates. For instance, we might want to find orders placed after June 2010. We can easily achieve this using the code below. The last day of June will not be included in the result set because we are using a "greater than" argument. In the next example, we will see how we can include the last day of June as well. In addition, we sort by orderdate ascending so that older orders appear first. We can sort descending (DESC) to get the latest orders. When sorting ascending, the ASC keyword is not needed in Access 2007. The ORDER BY clause defaults to ascending order when no ordering keyword is used (ASC, DESC).

Code:

SELECT OrderID, OrderDate, ShippedDate, ShippingCost
FROM Orders
WHERE OrderDate > #6/30/2010#
ORDER BY OrderDate

Result:

OrderID	OrderDate	ShippedDate	ShippingCost
601	7/1/2010	7/6/2010	36
620	7/1/2010	7/6/2010	36
484	7/3/2010	7/8/2010	41

Record: 10 of 172 — No Filter — Search

74. The "=>" inequality predicate with date data

Retrieve orders placed after a certain date including the date specified

Discussion:

The ">=" inequality predicate means "greater than or equal to", and we can use it with numbers and dates as well. In this example, we want to find orders placed after June 2010 including the last day of June. In addition, we sort by orderdate ascending so that older orders appear first.

Code:

```
SELECT OrderID, OrderDate, ShippedDate, ShippingCost
FROM Orders
WHERE OrderDate => #6/30/2010#
ORDER BY OrderDate
```

Result:

OrderID	OrderDate	ShippedDate	ShippingCost
474	6/30/2010	7/5/2010	41
517	6/30/2010	7/5/2010	45
620	7/1/2010	7/6/2010	36

Record: 10 of 174 — No Filter — Search

75. The "<" inequality predicate with number data

Find orders for which the shipping cost was less than $35

Discussion:

The "<" inequality predicate means "less than", and, in this example, we use it to find shipping costs lower than $35 per order regardless of the date placed. Notice that we do not use quotes or other symbols to enclose numerical data in criteria expressions. We simply type the number. In addition, the first number appearing in the result set is 34 because we specifically asked for "less than 35".

Code:

SELECT OrderID, OrderDate, ShippedDate, ShippingCost
FROM Orders
WHERE ShippingCost < 35
ORDER BY ShippingCost DESC

Result:

OrderID	OrderDate	ShippedDate	ShippingCost
833	6/2/2010	6/7/2010	34
305	2/14/2008	2/19/2008	34
816	7/13/2008	7/18/2008	34

Record: 10 of 181   No Filter   Search

76.   The "<=" inequality predicate with number data

Find orders for which the shipping cost was less than or equal to $35

Discussion:

The "<=" inequality predicate means "less than or equal to", and we can use it with numbers and dates. In this example, we want to find shipping costs of less than 35 per order, including those orders with a shipping cost of exactly 35.

Code:

SELECT OrderID, OrderDate, ShippedDate, ShippingCost
FROM Orders
WHERE ShippingCost <= 35
ORDER BY ShippingCost DESC

Result:

77.   The "<>" inequality predicate with number data

Find orders for which the shipping cost is not equal to $35
Discussion:

The "<>" inequality predicate means "not equal to". This time, we want to find shipping costs different from the amount of $35 per order. Notice that we do not use quotes or other symbols to enclose numerical data as criteria. In addition, we can use the inequality predicate efficiently with date and text data.

Code:

```
SELECT OrderID,  OrderDate, ShippedDate, ShippingCost
FROM Orders
WHERE ShippingCost <> 35
ORDER BY ShippingCost DESC
```

Result:

OrderID	OrderDate	ShippedDate	ShippingCost
914	7/31/2009	8/5/2009	52
435	7/16/2008	7/21/2008	52
442	2/2/2010	2/7/2010	52

Record: 10 of 961   No Filter   Search

78.   The ">" predicate with number and date data concurrently

Find orders placed after a certain date and with shipping cost less than $35
Discussion:

In this example, we are looking for orders placed after June 2010, which also have shipping costs of less than $35.

Code:

SELECT OrderID, OrderDate, ShippedDate, ShippingCost
FROM Orders
WHERE OrderDate > #6/30/2010#
AND ShippingCost < 35
ORDER BY ShippingCost DESC

Result:

CHAPTER 10
THE BETWEEN OPERATOR

The BETWEEN ... AND operator is designed to retrieve subsets or ranges from a data set. It works primarily with number and date data. In this sense, it can be used to retrieve records that lie between two values acting as boundaries. Those two boundary values can be numbers or dates. In addition, while we cannot use BETWEEN with wildcard characters or predicates, we can still use functions to augment its range of applicability. It is important to stay aware that BETWEEN is inclusive such that the values acting as boundaries will be included in the recordset. For example, if we use BETWEEN with two date values, the records containing those date values will be included in the result set.

79.   The BETWEEN operator with numbers

Find products with prices between $15 and $18
Discussion:

In this example, we are looking for product prices between the $15 and $18 values. The BETWEEN operator is inclusive, so the products with unit prices of 15 and 18 are included in the result set.

Code:
SELECT productname, productunitprice
FROM products
WHERE productunitprice BETWEEN 15 AND 18
ORDER BY productunitprice

Result:

80. The BETWEEN operator with the left function()

Find suppliers with zip codes starting between 12 and 22

Discussion:

In this example, we are looking for a range of zip codes between 12 + any number and 22 + any number. We can use the left() function to extract the two leftmost characters of the zip code and get the result we need.

Of course, one might raise an objection and say: Why do we need to use the left function and not put the lower and upper boundaries in directly as 12189 and 22459? The answer is that in working with the supplier table, we deal with only 10 records. If we have hundreds of records to work with, we need to run two SQL statements with the min() and max() functions first to identify the boundaries and then, use BETWEEN. Even if we do that, however, Access 2007 will give us a type mismatch error since the zip code is a text field (and it should be). If we use the left() function, we will not have to run three SQL statements, and we will also not receive any errors.

Code:

SELECT companyname, address, city, zip
FROM suppliers
WHERE left(zip, 2) BETWEEN 12 AND 22
ORDER BY zip

Result:

Companyname	address	city	zip
Nature's Food, Inc.	12 Boston Street	New York	12189
BayLine Farms Co.	89 Sterner Ave	New York	12189
Mediterranean Foods, LLC.	28 Parkwood Ave	New York	12189
Berkley Bakery Co.	35 Kensington Ave	New York	12189
America's Greatest Snacks, Inc.	12 Avon Ln	New York	12189
American Imports Inc.	10 Silver Street	Boston	22459
American Foods, LLC.	30 Maplewood Ave	Boston	22459
Home of Snacks	22 Taft Street	Boston	22459

Record: 1 of 8   No Filter   Search

81.   The BETWEEN operator with dates

Find orders placed within a date range

Discussion:

In this example, we would like to retrieve order dates that fall between 6/15/2009 and 8/15/2009. The BETWEEN operator is inclusive, and it will include orders placed on 6/15/2009 and 8/15/2009 as it is shown in the result set. In addition, notice the # symbol we use to enclose date values in Access 2007.

Code:

```
SELECT OrderID, orderdate, shippeddate
FROM orders
WHERE orderdate BETWEEN #6/15/2009# AND #8/15/2009#
ORDER BY orderdate DESC
```

Result:

OrderID	orderdate	shippeddate
787	8/15/2009	8/20/2009
433	8/14/2009	8/19/2009
761	8/14/2009	8/19/2009

Record: 10 of 69   No Filter   Search

82.   The BETWEEN operator with the year() function

Find orders placed within a year range

Discussion:

In this example, we use the year() function to extract the year out of the orderdate field so that we can use year values as the lower and upper boundaries. All orders from 2009 and 2010 will be included in the result set due to the inclusivity characteristic of the BETWEEN operator.

Code:

SELECT OrderID, orderdate, shippeddate

FROM orders

WHERE year(orderdate) BETWEEN 2009 AND 2010

ORDER BY orderdate DESC

Result:

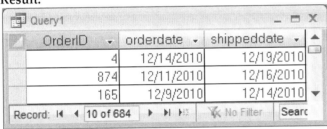

83.   The NOT BETWEEN operator with numbers

Find products with prices outside a price range

Discussion:

In this instance, we are looking for products with prices outside the $10 to $40 range, so we are asking the database to give us all products whose prices do not fall between $10 and $40. In practical terms, when we use the BETWEEN operator with NOT, we are usually looking for extreme values or outliers. The products with prices of exactly $10 or $40 will not be included in the result set.

Code:

SELECT productname, productunitprice
FROM products
WHERE productunitprice NOT BETWEEN 10 AND 40
ORDER BY productunitprice ASC

Result:

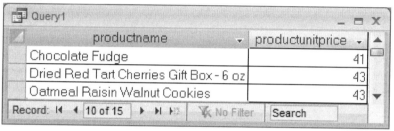

84.   Comparison of BETWEEN with "<=" or "=>"

Find products with prices within a price range

Discussion:

In this paradigm, we show that using the BETWEEN operator is the same as using the two inequality predicates "<=" and "=>". Both SQL statements below will produce the same results.

Code:

SELECT productname, productunitprice
FROM products
WHERE productunitprice BETWEEN 15 AND 18
ORDER BY productunitprice ASC

Or

SELECT productname, productunitprice
FROM products
WHERE productunitprice >=15 AND productunitprice <=18
ORDER BY productunitprice ASC

Result:

CHAPTER 11
THE IN OPERATOR

The major role of the IN operator is to participate in search conditions for filtering records. It is always used within the WHERE clause of a SQL statement and usually takes the place of multiple OR operators. It is an extremely useful search operator, and it will check the existence of a value against a list of values provided or constructed dynamically. Moreover, the IN operator can be used with text, number, and date data, making it suitable for a wide range of applications. Finally, it is really indispensable when used with subqueries as it will be shown in this chapter and in chapter 30. Using IN with subqueries allows the database professional to obtain results that would have been very difficult or impossible to obtain otherwise. The IN operator should be well understood and at the top of the toolbox of a database user or developer.

85.   The IN operator with text data
Create a report of customers from multiple cities
Discussion:
Our supervisor is requesting a report that lists all customers from the cities of New York, Boston, Chicago, Los Angeles, and Dallas. Of course, we could use the OR operator to produce this report:

```
SELECT LastName, FirstName, city
FROM customers
WHERE (city="New York")
OR (city="Boston")
OR (city="Chicago")
OR (city="Los Angeles")
OR (city="Dallas")
```

Using multiple OR operators to obtain a solution is rather tedious in both time and effort. Then, as soon as we provide the report to the supervisor, she comes back and says: "This is excellent; can I please have another report with our customers in the rest of the cities in the country?" To produce the second report, we will need to create an additional multitude of OR statements with the remaining cities.

The IN operator solves these problems quickly and efficiently. Note that enclosing the names in single or double quotes will produce the same results in Access 2007. In addition, since the ORDER BY clause is not used, the records will appear in the order they are stored in the table.

Code:

SELECT lastname, firstname, city

FROM customers

WHERE city in ('New York', 'Boston', 'Chicago', 'Los Angeles', 'Dallas')

Result:

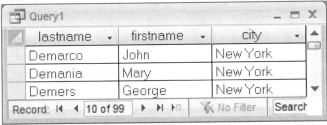

86. The NOT IN operator with text data

Create a report of customers excluding several cities

Discussion:

This time, our supervisor reverses the request and asks for a report of customers from all cities not included in our previous report—every city except New York, Boston, Chicago, Los Angeles, and Dallas. Since we have the code using the IN operator from the previous example, the only thing we need to do is put the keyword "NOT" in front of the IN operator!

Code:

SELECT lastname, firstname, city

FROM customers

WHERE city NOT IN ('New York', 'Boston', 'Chicago', 'Los Angeles', 'Dallas')

Result:

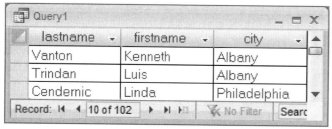

87.   The IN operator with numeric data

Create a report of products based on prices

Discussion:

In this scenario, we need to produce a business report that lists products from our product catalog with the following prices: 15, 19, 22, 23, and 42. Since the numbers are not sequential, we cannot use the BETWEEN operator to get our results. We can, however, use the IN operator to produce the report almost as fast. In addition, when we employ IN with numbers, we do not use quotes.

Code:

```
SELECT productname, quantityperunit, productunitprice
FROM products
WHERE productunitprice in (15, 19, 22, 23, 42)
```

Result:

88.   The IN operator with date data

Create a report of products based on prices
Discussion:

We have a request from the sales department to have a look at the orders in the first day of the three summer months because they are missing an order. They want to know what happened so that they can communicate it to the customer. We can absolutely use IN with date fields as can be seen in the code below. Notice the special character (#) in which we enclose date criteria in Access 2007.

Code:

```
SELECT OrderID, OrderDate, ShippedDate, ShippingCost
FROM Orders
WHERE
OrderDate IN (#6/1/2009#, #7/1/2009#, #8/1/2009#)
```

Result:

OrderID	OrderDate	ShippedDate	ShippingCost
762	6/1/2009	6/6/2009	41
942	7/1/2009	7/6/2009	48

Record: 1 of 2   No Filter   Search

89.   Create dynamic lists for the IN operator using subqueries

Generate a report of orders in which there is at least one non-discounted product
Discussion

The IN operator shows its real power when used with lists generated dynamically through SQL code. Instead of typing the values we would like to use with IN in the parenthesis, we can actually use SQL to create value lists automatically. This leads to the concept of subqueries, which we will discuss in detail in chapter 30, but we will go through a few examples here to understand the ultimate use of the IN operator.

In this specific example, management wants to have a report of orders in which no discount was extended for at least one of the products included in the order. Each order might contain multiple products, and for each product, we might or might not have extended a discount. In other words, the database is set up so that discounts are given on a per product basis and not per order. This way, we have the flexibility to extend discounts on a product-by-product basis, which is a much more flexible way of doing business.

To answer this request, we need information from two different tables: the Orders table and the ProductsOrders table. The subquery in this case will generate a list of OrderIDs from the ProductsOrders table for which the discount = 0. Then, this list of OrderIDs will be used as filtering criteria by the IN operator in the main query. Therefore, we have dynamically created a list of values for the IN operator. There are 136 orders with at least one non-discounted product.

Code:

```
SELECT orderid, orderdate, shippeddate
FROM orders
WHERE orderid
IN (SELECT orderid FROM ProductsOrders WHERE (Discount) =0)
```

Result:

orderid	orderdate	shippeddate
2	7/25/2009	7/30/2009
5	11/14/2008	11/19/2008
7	11/26/2009	12/1/2009
24	3/7/2008	3/12/2008

Record: 10 of 136   No Filter

90.   The IN operator with GROUP BY and HAVING in subqueries

Generate a report of orders for which the total extended discount was 0

Discussion

Continuing from the previous example, we now have a request to produce a report that will list orders in which all of the included products have a discount of zero. So, if four products are included in an order, the discount rate for all four of them will be zero. To reply to this request, we will again use the IN operator to look in the ProductsOrders table for OrderIDs of orders with zero total discounts. The problem here is that we cannot use the WHERE clause since it always runs first and excludes records before the

SQL statement is executed. However, our goal is to sum up the discounts for each product in each order first. Our second concern is to somehow make calculations in the ProductsOrders table and find the sum of discount for every order. Third, we need to keep in the result set only the orders with a total discount of zero, and we need to filter out everything else. The final issue is that the filtering needs to happen after the results of the sum() function.

All of the above issues can be solved by using the IN operator, a subquery, the GROUP BY and HAVING clauses, and the sum() function as per the example below. In the example, the GROUP BY clause with the sum() function will run first and produce a list of unique orders and their total discounts. From this list, the HAVING clause will keep only the ones with a zero total discount. Then, the SELECT statement in the subquery will generate a list of OrderIDs as filtered out by the HAVING clause. Finally, the WHERE clause from the main query will use the OrderIDs generated from the subquery to filter orders from the Orders table and produce a result set of orders whose orderID matches the OrderID produced by the subquery.

At this point, we could easily answer the following question as well: Generate a report of orders for which the total extended discount was not 0. We can answer this in no time by replacing the IN operator with NOT IN!

Code:
```
SELECT orderid, orderdate, shippeddate
FROM orders
WHERE orderid
IN (SELECT orderid FROM ProductsOrders GROUP BY orderid HAVING sum(Discount) =0)
```

Result:

orderid	orderdate	shippeddate
30	5/28/2008	6/2/2008
124	1/25/2009	1/30/2009
273	3/21/2009	3/26/2009
356	2/26/2009	3/3/2009

Record: 10 of 10   No Filter   Sea

91. The IN operator with subqueries and dates

Find customers who have not placed any orders in the second half of 2009

Discussion

Our task in this scenario is to find customers who have not placed any orders in the second half of the year 2009. Management needs this information for initiating promotions to inactive customers. To achieve this task, we will use the NOT IN and BETWEEN operators and a subquery. Remember that the purpose of the subquery is always the same—to generate a list of values to be used by the IN operator. Here, the subquery will generate a list of CustomerIDs from the Orders table, which will be used by the main query to filter records from the Customers table. In total, 70 customers have not ordered anything during this six-month period.

Code:
```
SELECT *
FROM Customers
WHERE CustomerID NOT IN
(Select CustomerID FROM Orders WHERE
OrderDate BETWEEN #6/1/2009# AND #12/1/2009#)
```

Result:

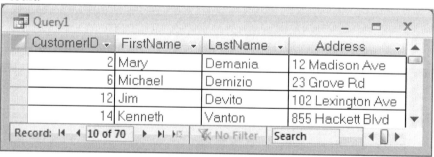

92. The IN operator with subqueries, dates, and date functions

Find customers who have not placed any orders in the year 2009

Discussion

The request in this case is to find customers who have not placed any orders for the year 2009. Of course, we do not track years separately in the orders table, but we can easily

94

extract the year out of the OrderDate filed using the year() function. Then, we can use it in the subquery as shown below. Only 36 customers have not placed any orders in the year 2009. This type of query is excellent to keep track of customer retention rates in a business.

Code:
SELECT *
FROM Customers
WHERE CustomerID NOT IN
(Select CustomerID FROM Orders WHERE
year(orderdate) = 2009)

Result:

CHAPTER 12
THE DISTINCT PREDICATE

The DISTINCT predicate is used to eliminate duplicate rows from the results of a SELECT statement. It belongs to a set of four predicates (ALL, TOP, DISTINCT, DISTINCTROW) which we can use to manipulate the number of records returned from a SQL statement. All four of them are used right after the SELECT keyword, and all of them are optional. If we do not use a predicate with the SELECT statement, [ALL] is assumed by Access 2007.

SELECT [ALL] [TOP] [DISTINCT] [DISTINCTROW] field1, field2, ... fieldn
FROM table

From the four predicates above, we will focus on DISTINCT in this chapter and TOP in the next one, since they are the two most useful ones. [ALL] is assumed as the default when no predicate is used and the DISTINCTROW has very specific applications. We will look at an example in this chapter. However, we should understand the DISTINCT and TOP predicates well because they are essential to retrieving the results we need in various scenarios.

The column on which we use the DISTINCT predicate will return only its unique values. Also, note that if we apply the DISTINCT keyword on a combination of columns—lastname and firstname, for example—the database will return the unique combinations of their values. Let us see how this works through examples in our familiar customers and orders database.

93.   Run a SELECT statement without the DISTINCT predicate

Find cities in which we have customers

Discussion:

Using a classic SQL statement to retrieve the column "city" from the customers table will return multiple instances of the same city since it is logical to have multiple customers in the same city. For example, as we can see from the result set, New York appears as many times as the number of customers we have in this city. There are 201 records returned with multiple instances of various cities.

Code:

SELECT city
FROM customers

Result:

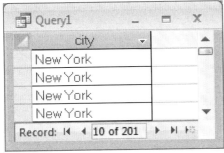

94.   Run a SELECT statement with the DISTINCT predicate

Find unique cities in which we have customers

Discussion:

There are cases, however, in which we just want to obtain a report that shows only the unique or distinct names of the cities where we have customers. The business goal is to create a list of cities to know where we do business. Maybe we want to set up shipping centers in several regions. In this scenario, we would like New York to appear only once, Boston only once, and Los Angeles only once. This is a case where we use the DISTINCT predicate. This time, only 15 records returned, and the value for each city is unique. From this recordset, we know that the number of cities where we have customers is 15.

Code:

SELECT DISTINCT city
FROM customers

Result:

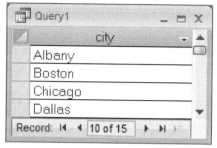

95. Use DISTINCT on one column

Finding unique job titles

Discussion:

Suppose our next business goal is to retrieve the unique job titles of people who replenish our inventory and manage our orders from various corporate suppliers. It is a good thing to know if we deal mostly with managers, directors, or other positions. Maybe we can get better discounts if we talk to people in higher positions with more decision-making flexibility. We can easily achieve this goal using the DISTINCT keyword. The unique corporate titles of people with whom we do business are seven.

Code:

SELECT DISTINCT ContactTitle
FROM suppliers

Result:

96. Use DISTINCT on multiple columns

Finding unique customer names in various states

Discussion:

Experience indicates that DISTINCT works at its best when applied on a single column. However, if we want to apply DISTINCT on multiple columns, we need to know exactly what to expect. Let's work with our customers table and go through some examples to fully understand this concept.

Code Case 1:

If we run a simple SELECT statement such as:

SELECT firstname, state
FROM customers
WHERE (firstname="John")

We will get four customers with a first name John. Actually, these are all the Johns we have in our customers table.

Result:

Code Case 1:

If we include the DISTINCT clause such as:

SELECT DISTINCT firstname, state
FROM customers
WHERE (firstname="John")

We will get only three customers with a first name John. This is because we told the database to return unique combinations of first names and states. In the previous result set, we have two Johns in Texas. When we use DISTINCT on both firstname and state, only one of the two appear. This is a problem with DISTINCT on multiple columns. We cannot exactly control which ones will appear in the result set, and we might get results that we haven't intended. So, be very careful when using DISTINCT on multiple columns.

Result:

97.   Getting more information beyond DISTINCT

Find unique job titles and their Corresponding Numbers
Discussion:
Although it does not thematically belong here, your logical next thought is probably: Okay, I know how to retrieve unique values for names, states, job titles, and other fields. However, what is the total number I have from each? To answer this question, we need to use the GROUP BY clause, which we explore in detail in chapter 16. Here, we will use the job titles as an example to find the number of people holding each title.

As we can see from the result set, we know that we have four sales managers and one of each of the other titles. We simply use one aggregate function count() and the GROUP BY clause to get the result we need. The "CountNumber" is the title we give ourselves to the counting column.

Code:
SELECT ContactTitle, Count(ContactTitle) AS CountNumber
FROM suppliers
GROUP BY ContactTitle

Result:

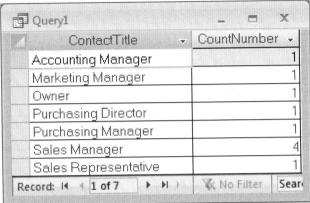

98.   Use DISTINCT with the max() function

Find the latest order from every customer

Discussion:

Now, our supervisor is emboldened by our expertise and asks for another report. This time, she wants a report that will show her the latest orders from each customer. No matter how many total orders any customer made, she wants to see only the latest one from each customer. We reply that this task needs many aggregations, and it will take a couple of hours. Then, we spend about 20 seconds to write the following statement and 1 hour, 59 minutes, and 40 seconds to download favorite music.

Code:

```
SELECT customerID, max(orderdate) as LatestOrder
FROM Orders
GROUP BY CustomerID
```

Result:

customerID	LatestOrder
1	1/9/2010
2	6/2/2010
3	6/2/2009
4	9/23/2010

Record: 1 of 191

99.   The DISTINCTROW predicate

Find customers with at least one order

Discussion:

In this scenario, we are looking for customers who have at least one order in the Orders table. There are three ways to achieve this goal. We can use a subquery (see chapter 30), a join (chapter 29), or DISTINCTROW. I would suggest using a subquery to obtain this result because it is the cleanest way and will provide guaranteed results. We can do it by using joins, but we will create a lot of code, while DISTINCTROW has its own peculiarities. From the result set below, we see that we have 190 unique customers with at least one order. However, we used fields only from the customers table. If we include at least one field from the Orders table, the DISTINCTROW will not work. DISTINCTROW will work with any number of joined tables as soon as we select fields from some of the joined tables but not all of them. Finally, I have included the code using a subquery which will produce the exact same result.

Code:

```
SELECT DISTINCTROW lastname, firstname, city, zip
FROM Customers
INNER JOIN Orders ON Customers.CustomerID = Orders.CustomerID
```

Code:

```
SELECT lastname, firstname, city, zip
FROM Customers
WHERE CustomerID
IN (SELECT CustomerID from tbls_Orders)
```

Result:

CHAPTER 13
THE TOP PREDICATE

The TOP predicate is useful for selecting a specified number or a certain percentage of records from a data source like a table or query. It belongs to a set of four predicates (ALL, TOP, DISTINCT, DISTINCTROW) used to manipulate the number of records returned from a SQL statement. All four of them are used right after the SELECT keyword, and all of them are optional. If we do not use a predicate with the SELECT statement, [ALL] is assumed by Access 2007.

SELECT [ALL] [TOP] [DISTINCT] [DISTINCTROW] field1, field2, ... fieldn
FROM table

The TOP predicate used alone is not useful at all since it does not return records in any special order; it simply returns the first n or n% of the records as they are stored in the table. However, when the TOP predicate is used with the ORDER BY, GROUP BY, and WHERE clauses, it shows its real potential and practicality. For instance, by using TOP with ORDER BY, we can control exactly which and how many records will appear in the result set.

100.   The TOP predicate alone with numbers
Retrieve 5 records from the products table
Discussion:
The TOP predicate in this example will return the first five records from the products table in the order these records are stored in the table. This process is practically useless for our corporate needs since it does not provide any special information at all. This example is given to demonstrate that TOP by itself will not produce any useful results.

Code:

SELECT TOP 5 productname, unitsinstock, unitsonorder

FROM Products

Result:

productname	unitsinstock	unitsonorder
Almonds, Hickory Smoked	40	5
Almonds, Roasted and Sa	32	0
Banana Chips - 20 oz. Bag	25	0
Berry Cherry in 8 oz. Bag	50	0
California Original Pistachio	35	0

Record: 5 of 5   No Filter   Search

101.   The TOP predicate with ORDER BY and numbers

Find the five products with the most units in stock

Discussion:

In this example, the business goal is to find the five products with the highest levels of inventory. The use of the TOP predicate in combination with the ORDER BY clause can show its usefulness and practical application. As you can see from the result set, the five products with the highest inventory levels appear first. We use the DESC keyword with the ORDER BY clause so that highest quantities appear first (chapter 6).

Code:

SELECT TOP 5 productname, unitsinstock, unitsonorder

FROM Products

ORDER BY unitsinstock DESC

Result:

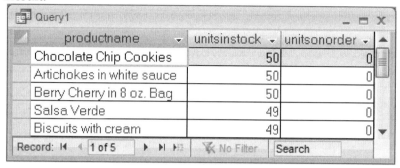

102. The TOP predicate with ORDER BY and percentages

Retrieve 20% of the products with the highest prices

Discussion:

This time, management asked for the top 20% of the most expensive products in the inventory. We can easily reply to this request by using the TOP predicate with the ORDER BY clause as shown below. In Access 2007, we actually used the word "20 PERCENT" and not "20%" with the TOP predicate. The database returned 14 products because the total number of products in the products table was 70.

Code:

```
SELECT TOP 10 PERCENT productname, productunitprice
FROM Products
ORDER BY productunitprice DESC
```

Result:

103. The TOP predicate with ORDER BY and text data

Select exactly 5 employees sorted by name

Discussion:

In this example, we use TOP in conjunction with ORDER BY to get the first five employees ordered by last name. Of course, the obvious question is: What is the difference with a simple SELECT and ORDER BY without the use of the TOP predicate? The answer is that we can define the exact number of employees to appear in the result set when using the TOP clause. The ASC keyword is not used with the ORDER BY clause because it is assumed by default in Access 2007 (chapter 6).

Code:

```
SELECT TOP 5 lastname, firstname, title
FROM SalesReps
ORDER BY lastname
```

Result:

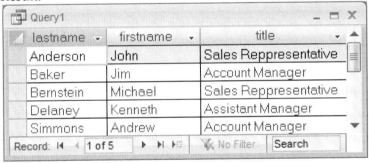

104. The TOP predicate with ORDER BY and dates

Find the 5 most recently hired employees

Discussion:

The TOP predicate is very useful when used with dates. In this example, we are looking for the five most recently hired employees in the corporation. We use the DESC keyword with ORDER BY to obtain this result. We could use the ASC keyword or the ORDER BY clause by itself to retrieve the 5 most senior employees of the corporation.

Code:

SELECT TOP 5 lastname, firstname, DateofHire
FROM SalesReps
ORDER BY DateofHire DESC

Result:

lastname	firstname	DateofHire
Simmons	Andrew	5/11/2006
Baker	Jim	1/10/2006
Williams	Gerald	1/11/2005
Spicer	George	5/15/2004
Zensons	Phillip	6/10/2001

Record: ◄ ◄ 1 of 5 ► ►► No Filter Sear

105. The TOP predicate with the GROUP BY clause

Find the 10 largest orders from customers

Discussion:

Let us assume that our manager wants to see the 10 largest orders received from our customers. One somewhat crude way to prepare this report would be to calculate order subtotals (multiply the quantity of each product with its price) for all of the products contained in one order and do a GROUP BY on the orderid, followed by SORT DESC to get on top of the recordset of the largest orders. This way, we get what we need, but the whole affair is a mess. In addition, we get all of the orders we have, which might be a very long list for a printout.

Let us start by assuming that we only have two orders to work with (1 and 2 in the table below). We also notice that order number 1 contains three products, and order number 2 contains two products. We also see the product quantities our customers ordered in the "Quantity" field, as well as the corresponding product prices that we extended to the customers. By the way, the product prices that we finally extended to the customers can be different from the prices in our catalog, which we store in the products table.

ProductsOrders			
OrderID	ProductID	UnitPrice	Quantity
1	1	15	2
1	2	12	3
1	3	18	5
2	1	15	2
2	3	18	8

Code:

SELECT orderid, Sum(([unitprice]*[quantity])) AS orderamount
FROM ProductsOrders
GROUP BY orderid
ORDER BY Sum(([unitprice]*[quantity])) DESC

When using the code above, the database will first multiply the UnitPrice with the Quantity for each product. This temporary calculation is shown in the table below so that you know how the database thinks.

ProductsOrders				
OrderID	ProductID	UnitPrice	Quantity	Temp
1	1	15	2	30
1	2	12	3	36
1	3	18	5	90
2	1	15	2	30
2	3	18	8	144

Then, the database calculates the total (SUM) for each order (this is due to the GROUP BY clause on the ORDERID). Since we have two orders, the grouping looks like the table below. The OrderAmount is an alias or a name that we gave to the calculated field.

OrderID	OrderAmount
1	156
2	174

Still however, we gave another command to the database: to ORDER BY the largest order. The database then shows the following result since 174 is larger than 156.

OrderID	OrderAmount
2	174
1	156

At this point, we are able to get a report of the biggest orders, but we still have a problem with the above code. All of the orders will appear. As you can see from the figure below, 919 orders appear even though we only need to see the 10 largest.

Result:

Let us see how we can quickly get the results we need by using the TOP clause.

Code:

```
SELECT TOP 10 orderid, Sum(([unitprice]*[quantity])) AS orderamount
FROM ProductsOrders
GROUP BY orderid
ORDER BY Sum(([unitprice]*[quantity])) DESC;
```

Result:

106. The TOP predicate with calculated fields and WHERE

Get the largest sales for a particular product

Discussion:

As in our previous discussion, we can, of course, use ORDER BY, DESC, and WHERE to create result sets that give us powerful information. However, we need to include TOP if we want to get a manageable number of records returned. In this scenario, we have been asked to prepare a report that contains the 15 largest orders for a particular product—for example "Almonds, Roasted and Salted - 18 oz. Bag" (the product with productid = 2).

Code:

```
SELECT TOP 10 orderid, productid, (unitprice*quantity) AS orderamount
FROM ProductsOrders
WHERE (productid=2)
ORDER BY (unitprice*quantity) DESC;
```

Result:

orderid	productid	orderamount
764	2	90
379	2	90
314	2	90
978	2	90

Record: 10 of 14

CHAPTER 14
CALCULATED FIELDS

Calculated fields are temporary columns created using arithmetic operators such as (*, -, /, ^, Mod). In Access 2007, you can use calculated fields in queries, forms, and reports. You should never save the results of a calculated field in a table, however. In addition, you cannot create a calculated field in a table in Access 2007. In other words, you cannot create a field that is the result of an arithmetic operation from two or more fields in the same table.

You can create calculated fields in a variety of ways. For instance, you can multiply a numeric field by a certain number or a certain percentage, and you can multiply two numeric fields themselves. You can multiply two fields and divide the result by another field. You can also create calculated fields conditionally by using the iif() and switch() functions. You can also generate powerful pieces of information by using calculated fields with aggregate functions. Of course, you can use calculated fields in a query with the WHERE clause so that your calculations are applied only to a subset of records. You can also use calculated fields in the HAVING clause in a GROUP BY statement for filtering records after the aggregations from the GROUP BY clause are completed. Finally, you can use calculated fields with UPDATE statements to change hundreds or thousands of records instantly. The applications of calculated fields in databases are essential, and in this chapter, I will present you with multiple examples. However, we will also deal with numeric calculations only. I have devoted two additional chapters on operations with dates and strings so that you can explore each in detail. The arithmetic operators available in Access 2007 appear in the following table:

Operator	Meaning
+	Addition
*	Multiplication
-	Subtraction
/	Division
^	Exponential
mod	Remainder

107. Add a number to a numeric field

Create a product catalog with updated prices on the fly

Discussion:

The business goal here is to create a new product catalog that will appear on the corporate website for a promotional campaign. Management does not want the product prices in the underlying products table to change, however, since this campaign will last only two weeks. We can easily create a query using the SQL code below and use it as the data source for our web catalog. Using these assumptions, management asked to add $2 to the price of each product.

Code:

```
SELECT productname, productunitprice + 2 AS productprice
FROM Products
```

Result:

113

108.   Add a percentage to a numeric field

Update product prices on the fly by a certain percentage

Discussion:

This time, due to increased replenishment costs (receiving goods from suppliers), our manager tells us to add a 2% markup for the product catalog we are sending out this month. We multiply by 1.02 and not by 0.02 since the latter will give us only the percentage increase and not the entire new price.

Code:

SELECT productname, productunitprice * (1.02) as productprice
FROM Products

Result:

productname	productprice
Almonds, Hickory Smoked - 12 oz. Bag	35.7
Almonds, Roasted and Salted - 18 oz. Bag	22.44
Banana Chips - 20 oz. Bag	27.54

Record: 10 of 70   No Filter   Search

109.   Add two numeric columns

Calculate product inventory quantities

Discussion:

Management asks us for a report about product inventory quantities. Specifically, they want to know not only what units we have in the warehouse but how many are on order as well. To answer this request, we create a new column named TotalUnits, which is simply the sum of the units that we have in stock and the ones we have on order that have not arrived yet.

Code:

SELECT productname, unitsinstock, unitsonorder,
(unitsinstock + unitsonorder)
AS TotalUnits
FROM products

Result:

productname	unitsinstock	unitsonorder	TotalUnits
Almonds, Hickory Smok	40	5	45
Almonds, Roasted and	32	0	32
Banana Chips - 20 oz. B	25	0	25
Berry Cherry in 8 oz. Bag	50	0	50

Record: 10 of 70 — No Filter — Search

110. Multiply two columns and group their results

Find order totals by order

Discussion:

The request this time is to find order totals for all of the orders that we have had to this date. Each order might contain multiple products with multiple quantities for each product. We first need to multiply product prices with quantities for every product in each order and sum the results. Then, we need to group by OrderID so that we can obtain the total for every order. A sample data set on which to make these calculations appears below. The order with OrderID = 1, contains three different products with prices of 15, 12, and 18 and quantities of 2, 3, and 5 respectively. We need to first multiply the product unit price times the quantity for each product, get the subtotals, and sum up the results for each order.

ProductsOrders			
OrderID	ProductID	UnitPrice	Quantity
1	1	15	2
1	2	12	3
1	3	18	5
2	1	15	2
2	3	18	8

Code:

```
SELECT OrderID, Sum([UnitPrice]*[quantity]) AS OrderSubtotal
FROM ProductsOrders
GROUP BY OrderID
```

115

Result:

OrderID	OrderSubtotal
1	30
2	210
3	231
4	45

Record: 10 of 919

111.   Subtract a percentage from a numeric column

Provide customers with a 20% discount on every product

Discussion:

Management decided to aggressively sell this month, and they have initiated a promotional campaign with a price discount of 20% for every product in the product catalog. We need to create a new product catalog, which the company wants to send out immediately. We can easily respond to this request using a calculated field as is shown in the code below:

Code:

```
SELECT ProductName, ProductUnitPrice * (1-0.2) as PromotionalPrice
FROM Products
```

Result:

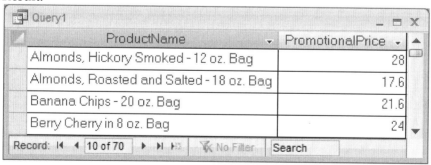

ProductName	PromotionalPrice
Almonds, Hickory Smoked - 12 oz. Bag	28
Almonds, Roasted and Salted - 18 oz. Bag	17.6
Banana Chips - 20 oz. Bag	21.6
Berry Cherry in 8 oz. Bag	24

Record: 10 of 70   No Filter   Search

116

112. Use calculated fields with the WHERE clause

Provide customers with a 20% discount on specific products

Discussion:

Since a 20% discount is too much to provide for every product, management has decided to apply it only on products from suppliers with SupplierID 1 and 4. We can quickly change the product catalog to:

Code:

SELECT ProductName, ProductUnitPrice * (1-0.2) as PromotionalPrice

FROM Products

WHERE supplierid = 1 or supplierid = 4

Result:

ProductName	PromotionalPrice
Almonds, Hickory Smoked - 12 oz. Bag	28
Almonds, Roasted and Salted - 18 oz. Bag	17.6
Banana Chips - 20 oz. Bag	21.6
Berry Cherry in 8 oz. Bag	24

Record: ◄◄ ◄ 10 of 16 ► ►► ►* | No Filter | Search

113. Calculated fields with multiple conditions

Provide customers with different discounts based on their city

Discussion:

The previous scenario of providing product discounts by filtering on supplier ids is fine for some cases, but it also has two major drawbacks. First, the same discount rate is applied to every supplier included in the WHERE clause. Second, discount rates can be applied only to suppliers included in the WHERE clause. In some cases, we might want to provide different discount rates for each supplier and include all products from all suppliers in the result set. Suppose we want to provide a 20% discount for products from SupplierID=1, 15% for those from SupplierID=2, 18% for those from SupplierID=3, and 25% for those from SupplierID=4. In addition, we might want to provide a 10% discount for all of the rest of the products regardless of supplier. The switch function comes to the rescue here, providing the flexibility to give us the results we need.

Code:

```
SELECT productname,
SWITCH(
SupplierID = 1,        ProductUnitPrice*(1-0.2),
SupplierID = 2,        ProductUnitPrice*(1-0.15),
SupplierID = 3,        ProductUnitPrice*(1-0.18),
SupplierID = 4,        ProductUnitPrice*(1-0.25),
TRUE,                  ProductUnitPrice*(1-0.1)
)
AS ProductPrice
FROM Products
```

Result:

114.   How to use calculated fields with the iif() function

Determine employee bonus eligibility

Discussion:

In this example, we are looking for sales representatives who are eligible for a bonus. To be eligible for a bonus, a sales rep needs to have accumulated sales of $5,000 or more for the year. The SQL code in this example is long but easy. First, notice that we use three fields only: LastName, Bonus, and OrderDate. We use the OrderDate field to filter orders for 2009 only. Then, we use the lastname field with a GROUP BY clause to display results by employee name. The last field is that of the Bonus. Here, we use the iif() function with the syntax iif (expression, result if expression is true, result if expression is false) to actually make the calculations and determine bonus eligibility:

IIf(Sum([unitprice]*[quantity])>5000,"Bonus","No Bonus") AS Bonus

The iif() function above reads: If the total amount of orders serviced by the sales rep exceeds $5,000, give the sales rep a bonus. Otherwise, no bonus. The AS part means display this field name as "Bonus". Do not pay attention to the joins in this example since we only use them to get fields from three different tables. For a full overview of joins, see chapter 29.

Code:

```
SELECT SalesReps.LastName, IIf(Sum([unitprice]*[quantity])>5000,"Bonus","No
Bonus") AS Bonus
FROM
(SalesReps INNER JOIN Orders ON SalesReps.SalesRepID = Orders.SalesRepID)
INNER JOIN ProductsOrders ON Orders.OrderID = ProductsOrders.OrderID

WHERE (((Orders.OrderDate) Between #1/1/2009# AND #12/31/2009#))

GROUP BY SalesReps.LastName
```

Result:

115.   Use calculated fields with GROUP BY and aggregate functions

Calculate total discount amounts by order

Discussion:

This time, we have a request to provide a report that will show the total discount amount for each order. Remember that each order might contain multiple products. In addition, for each product in the same order, we might have provided a different discount rate. Our goal is to calculate the discount amount for each product in each order and sum the results. To achieve this task, we will use the ProductsOrders table, which includes the unitprice (the one finally extended to the customer, not the one in the products table used for the product catalog), the quantity of each product, and the discount rate for each product. A sample from the table with two orders appears below:

ProductsOrders				
OrderID	ProductID	UnitPrice	Quantity	Discount
1	1	15	2	20%
1	2	12	3	0
1	3	18	5	15%
2	1	15	2	10%
2	3	18	8	15%

For each product in an order, we need to multiply the unit price by the quantity to get the amount invoiced for that product. Then, we multiply the result by the discount rate to get the total discount for each product in each order. Then, we sum all of the discount amounts in each order. Finally, we group on orderid so that we get the total discount amount by order.

Code:
```
SELECT OrderID, Sum((([UnitPrice]*[Quantity])*[Discount]) AS OrderDiscount
FROM ProductsOrders
GROUP BY OrderID
```

Result:

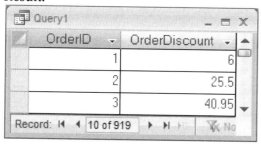

116. Use a calculated field with an aggregate function

Calculate the average discount amount for all orders

Discussion:

Our business goal is to find the average discount amount we have given away for all of our orders. Discounts are excellent, but we need to keep track of them and evaluate them on a continuous basis. Fortunately, we can do this in no time by simply using the AVG (average) function to get the average amount from all the orders.

Code:

SELECT Avg((([UnitPrice]*[Quantity])*[Discount]) AS AverageOrderDiscount
FROM ProductsOrders

Result:

Then, we can compare the above result with the actual average order amount using the code below. Now, we can make the conclusion that an average $9 discount for an average total order of $58 is an acceptable discount rate.

Code:

SELECT Avg([UnitPrice]*[Quantity]) AS AverageOrderAmount
FROM ProductsOrders

Result:

I know you noticed the number of decimals in the results above. We can decrease the number of decimals or eliminate them altogether by using a type conversion function. Actually, calculated fields are extensively used with type conversion functions to format numbers in the most appropriate way. Here, we use the cInt() function to convert the decimal number to an integer. For the full range of type conversion functions, read chapter 24, where they are explained in detail.

Code:

SELECT cInt(Avg([UnitPrice]*[Quantity])) AS AverageOrderAmount
FROM ProductsOrders

Result:

117.   Use a calculated field with an aggregate function and WHERE

Calculate the average discount amount for specific orders
Discussion:

Knowing the average discount amount for all of our orders is excellent, but we might want to go a step further and ask: What is the average discount amount provided for customers in the city of Boston? We can easily isolate discount amounts for any city by using multi-table queries like the one below:

Design Code:

Code:

SELECT Avg((([UnitPrice]*[Quantity])*[Discount]) AS AverageOrderDiscount
FROM Customers

INNER JOIN (Orders INNER JOIN ProductsOrders ON Orders.OrderID =
ProductsOrders.OrderID) ON Customers.CustomerID = Orders.CustomerID

WHERE (((Customers.City)="Boston"));

Result:

118. Storing the results of calculated fields with SELECT INTO

Storing total order amounts in a separate table

Discussion:

Sometimes, we might want to store the results of our calculations in a backup, archive, or temporary table. This is very easy to achieve using SELECT INTO statements that were covered in the SELECT chapter. Storing results of calculated fields in production tables is not a good idea because these fields will interfere with normalization rules. However, for archiving purposes, we can go ahead.

In this example, we take the OrderID and OrderTotal fields from the ProductsOrders table and transfer their records in a new table named ArchivedOrders. Of course, the OrderTotal field is calculated from three different fields in the ProductsOrders table.

Code:

```
SELECT OrderID, SUM((unitprice*Quantity)*(1-Discount)) AS OrderTotal
INTO ArchivedOrders
FROM ProductsOrders
GROUP BY OrderID
```

Result:

The database will first ask you if you want to go ahead.

Then, in the objects pane, we see the new table with a name exactly as we defined it in the SQL code.

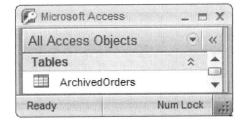

CHAPTER 15
CONCATENATED FIELDS

Concatenating columns means nothing more than displaying the contents of two or more columns in one. The operation of concatenation happens through a query on the fly, and the resulting column and its contents are not saved in the underlying table. There are no special arithmetical or logical calculations involved. Simply put, if we want a query or report to display the contents of the first and last name fields as one, we just concatenate the two fields. Though the concept is simple, its applicability in every day work tasks is indispensable.

Concatenation in databases can achieve much more than simply displaying the contents of two or more columns together, however. We can create mailing labels, write letters with the correct punctuation, combine field data with plain text, perform conditional concatenation based on the values of any field, and use string and other functions for truly powerful results.

To concatenate fields in MS Access 2007, we can use the & character or the + character. Since the + character is the one used with most databases, we will be using this one for our examples.

119. Column concatenation without spaces
Put all customer address information in one field
Discussion:
Suppose we have a job to create mailing labels for letters to our suppliers. My experience indicates that most people will go to Word, connect to Access, and go through multiple steps and a painful process to achieve this task. There is no need to go to this trouble since we can easily achieve this task using Access 2007 alone. There are two steps we need to follow: First, we create a query, namely qry_suppliers_labels, with a field that combines or concatenates values from the address, city, state, and zip fields from the suppliers table. Second, we create a report that formats our data to the label size we

want, and we set the query with the concatenated field as its data source. This is it—we are done forever.

Why? Because let's say in the future, we need to create mailing labels only for a subset of our suppliers in the city of Boston or in the state of California. We can just modify our qry_suppliers_labels, add the city field or the state field, and enter any criteria expressions we need. Then, we can just run our report again. We might also face another scenario in which we need to create labels of different sizes. It will take a few seconds to modify our report and get the label sizes we need. The bottom line is that there is no reason to use two programs (Word and Access) and a painful process to achieve this task.

I will show you how to use punctuation and spaces for formatting your concatenated columns so that you can do everything in Access. In this example, we create a simple concatenation of four fields. Using this code, there will be no spaces between the field values in the result set.

Code:
SELECT (address+city+state+zip) AS FullAddress
FROM Customers

which is the same as

SELECT (address&city&state&zip) AS FullAddress
FROM Customers

Result:
As you can see, the four fields are concatenated into one. However, the data is cramped in a continuous string of characters. We need to add spaces between the fields so that we can easily read them and print the results in a way that will make sense to USPS.

120.   Column concatenation with spaces

Put all customer address information in one field with spaces between values
Discussion:
In this example, we just add spaces between the concatenated columns. We use single quotes with a space between them to achieve this output.

Code:
```
SELECT  (address +' '+ city +' '+ state +' '+ zip)  AS FullAddress
FROM Customers
```

Result:

121.   Concatenation of columns and text

Writing customer letters in Access 2007
Discussion:
What if we would like to write a letter using a database? We can indeed combine plain text with field data with enough flexibility to write automatic letters! There is a sample letter below. Notice how punctuation marks are enclosed in double quotes. In addition, the SELECT statement is practically one field named ""CustomerLetter".

Code:

SELECT "Dear" + ' '+ (lastname + ' ' + firstname) +"." + ' '+ "It is our pleasure to announce that we reviewed your resume, and we have set up an interview time for you. Can you please verify that your address is" + ' ' + (address +' '+ City +' '+ State +' '+ Zip) + ' ' + "to send you corporate policy details and directions?" AS CustomerLetter

FROM Customers

Result:

122. Use the left() string function with concatenated fields

Displaying only the first letter from the customers' first names.

Discussion:

Let's say we want to write a letter, but instead of using the complete first name of the customer, we only want the first letter to appear. We can achieve this result and more by using string (text) functions. In this example, we use the left() function, but we can use anyone that suits your needs. (I have devoted a whole chapter on string functions to which you can refer for details). The left function in this example will extract the first character from the first name field.

Code:

SELECT "Dear" + ' '+ (lastname + ' ' + left(firstname, 1)) +"." + ' '+ "Please complete the enclosed forms so that we can ship your order to your country." AS CustomerLetter

FROM Customers

Result:

123. Use the ucase() string function with concatenated fields

Uppercasing customer last names

Discussion:

This is an additional example of using a string function in conjunction with concatenated columns. Consult chapter 25 regarding text and string operations for a full understanding of the role of string functions, as well as some cool examples. Our goal here is to have the last and first names of our customers capitalized.

Code:

SELECT "Dear" + ' '+ (ucase(lastname)) + ' ' + (ucase(firstname)) +"." + ' ' + "Please complete the enclosed forms so that we can ship your order to your country." AS CustomerLetter
FROM Customers

Result:

124.   Use concatenated fields with criteria

Send letters to a select group of customers

Discussion:

The goal behind this example is to show that we can use additional fields in a query with concatenated fields to sort and filter data. This way, we have total control to retrieve exactly the records we want for concatenation. In this particular example, we restrict the output to customers from the city of Boston.

Code:

```
SELECT "Dear" + ' '+ (ucase(lastname)) + ' ' + (ucase(firstname)) +"." + ' ' + "Please
complete the enclosed forms so that we can ship your order to your state." AS
CustomerLetter, city
FROM customers
WHERE city = "Boston"
```

Result:

125.   Using commas, periods, and other characters

Use correct punctuation with concatenated columns

Discussion:

Commas, periods, question marks, and other punctuation characters can become a pain when constructing concatenated fields. The answer is to enclose them in double quotations. In addition, if they come right after or before the concatenated field, we need to use the + character as well. For example, notice the period, in both statements below at the end of the parenthesis of the first name.

This will work: SELECT (lastname) + ' ' + (firstname) + "." FROM Customers

This will not work: SELECT (lastname) + ' ' + (firstname) "." FROM Customers

Code:

SELECT (lastname) + ' ' + (firstname) + "." AS CustomerName
FROM Customers

Result:

126. Conditional concatenation with the iif() function

Concatenating supplier fields using state as a condition

Discussion:

Sometimes, we might not want to apply the same concatenation rules for all of the records in the query. For example, we might want to create a certain label or letter for suppliers in NY and a different label or letter for everyone else, all in the same query. We can absolutely do this by using conditional statements and the iif() function in particular. However, someone might ask why we need to do this and not use simple criteria to do the same thing. First, in databases, we can achieve the same task in 20 different ways. There is always another less time-consuming and more effective way. Second, in this case, if we use a simple criterion such as (state = 'NY'), we only get the suppliers in NY. What we want is to send two different letters—one formatted for the state of NY and one for everyone else!

Using the iif(condition, true, false) function below, we tell the database to concatenate the companyname, contacttitle, and contactname fields if the state is NY. If it is not, we tell the database to concatenate only the contacttitle and contactname fields. This way, we can create two different sets of labels in the same query. Of course, we can use our imagination and modify the SQL statement below to use it for letters with plain text or any other concatenation task we need.

Code:

```
SELECT IIf((([State]='NY'),[Companyname]+' '+[ContactTitle]+' '+[Contactname],
[ContactTitle]+' '+[Contactname]) AS MailTo
FROM Suppliers
```

Result:

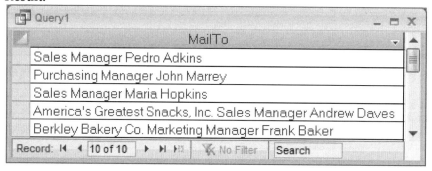

127. More powerful conditional concatenation with the switch() function

Concatenating supplier columns different for each city

Discussion:

Now that we know conditional concatenation is possible, what if we want to create different letters for suppliers based on the city where they reside? Notice in the suppliers table that there are three cities: Boston, New York, and Dallas. Our task is to create a different letter for suppliers in each city using the same query. We cannot use the iif() function to achieve this task since it takes only two parameters, and we need three. We can, however, use the switch() function as shown below:

Code:
```
SELECT
SWITCH(
[city]= 'Boston',      "Dear" +' '+ [contactname]+"," +' '+ "for our current sale we
offer a 25% discount in" +' '+ [city] ,
[city] ='Dallas',      "Dear" +' '+ [contactname]+"," +' '+ "for our current sale we
offer a 10% discount in" +' '+ [city] ,
[city] ='New York',    "Dear" +' '+ [contactname]+"," +' '+ "for our current sale we
offer a 25% discount in" +' '+ [city] ,
)
AS SupplierLetter
FROM suppliers
```

Result:

128. Conditional concatenation with the switch(), left(), and instr() functions

Concatenate supplier fields conditionally for each city

Discussion:

In the previous example, we saw how to use the switch() function to create a different letter for suppliers based on the city where they reside. However, we used the full name of the supplier since the contactname field in the suppliers table contains both the first and last names of the supplier. This time, we would like to send a more personal letter to them by using only the first name. This means that we need to isolate the first name from the contactname field and use it in the query. We can achieve this task by using the instr() function to find the space between the first and last name strings in the contacttitle field. Then, we can use the left function to isolate whatever characters are left from the space we found with instr(). The whole SQL statement is shown below. As you can see in the result set, only the first names of the suppliers appear now.

Code:
```
SELECT
SWITCH(
[city]= 'Boston',        "Dear" +' '+ left(contactname, InStr(1,contactname," ")-1)
 +"," +' '+ "for our current sale we offer a 25% discount in" +' '+ [city] ,
[city] ='Dallas',        "Dear" +' '+ left(contactname, InStr(1,contactname," ")-1) +","
 +' '+ "for our current sale we offer a 10% discount in" +' '+ [city] ,
[city] ='New York',     "Dear" +' '+ left(contactname, InStr(1,contactname," ")-1) +","
 +' '+ "for our current sale we offer a 25% discount in" +' '+ [city] ,
)
AS SupplierLetter
FROM suppliers
```

Result:

CHAPTER 16
THE GROUP BY CLAUSE

The GROUP BY clause is one of the foggiest keywords for both beginners and intermediate database professionals. Because of its intricacies, users and developers do not have a clear understanding of the circumstances when the GROUP BY clause is used. In this chapter, we have two goals: First, to understand in detail how and when the GROUP BY clause should be used, and second, to understand exactly what results to expect from it. The fundamental goal of the GROUP BY clause is to summarize data. The general syntax of the GROUP BY clause appears below but you do not need to memorize it since we will explore the role of each option in detail in the subsequent examples.

SELECT fields, aggregate function (field or calculated field)
FROM table
WHERE criteria
GROUP BY field(s)
HAVING criteria
ORDER BY field

Before we do anything else, let's have a look at the table I prepared especially for this chapter. It is a simple table with only twelve records about customers and their orders. The goal is to run the GROUP BY examples on this table and give you the ability to do the calculations manually so that you know exactly how every result is obtained. The name of the table is tbls_customersgr.

LastName ▾	OrderID ▾	OrderDate ▾	ProductNε ▾	UnitPrice ▾	Quantity ▾	▲
Riegert	1	11/6/2009	Dried Red T	15	2	
Mahoney	57	5/29/2008	Dark Chocol	28	5	
Mahoney	57	5/29/2008	Mushrooms	5	2	
Mahoney	57	5/29/2008	Chocolate Cl	15	1	
Martin	494	9/30/2009	Traditional S	5	5	
Martin	494	9/30/2009	Cream and h	32	3	
Mahoney	502	8/3/2010	Sesame Cra	15	3	
Mahoney	502	8/3/2010	Roasted No-	15	1	
Spicer	509	9/17/2009	Dark Chocol	28	3	
Spicer	509	9/17/2009	Corn Chips B	15	2	
Spicer	509	9/17/2009	Oatmeal Rai	8	3	
Spicer	509	9/17/2009	All-Purpose	15	2	▼

Record: I◄ ◄ 1 of 12 ► ►I ►⊞   ✖ No Filter   Search

First, notice that there are four customers in total. Second, the customer, Mr. Mahoney, ordered twice: orders 57 and 502. Third, the rest of the three customers have one order only. Fourth, Mr. Riegert has one order with one product only, but he ordered two units of it. Fifth, orders 57, 494, 502, and 509 contain multiple products. Sixth, dark chocolate is a product included in two orders (in 57 and 509). At this point, we are ready to go through our first example.

129.   The GROUP BY clause on one column and one aggregated field

Retrieve the total product units ordered by customer

Discussion:

In this scenario, the objective is to calculate the total product units ordered by the customer. There are only two fields used in the SQL code below. LastName is the field on which we apply the GROUP BY clause, and TotalUnits is the aggregated field that results from applying the sum() function on the Quantity column.

Code:

```
SELECT LastName, SUM(quantity) AS TotalUnits
FROM tbls_customersgr
GROUP BY LastName
```

Result:

LastName	TotalUnits
Mahoney	12
Martin	8
Riegert	2
Spicer	10

Record: 1 of 4 — No Filte

130. The GROUP BY clause on one column and one aggregated-calculated field

Retrieve the total order amount by customer

Discussion:

In this scenario, we have a request from management to calculate the total order amounts by customer to create a list with our best customers. There are two fields used in the SQL code. LastName is the field on which we apply the GROUP BY clause. TotalUnits is the aggregated field. However, this time, the aggregation occurs on the result of the multiplication of two columns. It is necessary to multiply the unitprice with the quantity columns to retrieve the total for each product in each order and then, sum the results by customer lastname.

Code:

```
SELECT LastName, SUM(unitprice*quantity) AS OrderTotal
FROM tbls_customersgr
GROUP BY LastName
```

Result:

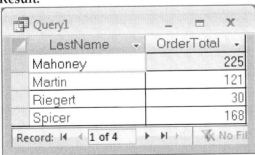

LastName	OrderTotal
Mahoney	225
Martin	121
Riegert	30
Spicer	168

Record: 1 of 4 — No Fil

We see some interesting results here. First, since we grouped by customer last name, the result set produced four records, which is the exact number of unique customers we have in the tbls_customersgr table. We need to check the results to verify the database made the calculations correctly. We use Mahoney as an example.

LastName	Unit Price	Quantity	UnitPrice* Quantity
Mahoney	15	1	15
Mahoney	15	3	45
Mahoney	15	1	15
Mahoney	5	2	10
Mahoney	28	5	140
		SUM()	225

First, the database will do the multiplication of (unitprice * quantity) as we defined it in the calculated field named OrderTotal. This means that the database will multiply the price of each product ordered * its quantity ordered for all products in all orders for the particular customer. Then, it will simply SUM()results since we used the sum() function. Doing the calculations manually, we arrived at 225 for Mr. Mahoney, which is the same number the database produced for this customer.

131.   The GROUP BY clause on one column and two aggregated fields

Find total and average order amounts by customer

Discussion:

In this scenario, the goal is to produce a report that will show the total and average order amounts grouped by customer. There are three fields used in the SQL code: LastName, OrderTotal, and AvgOrder. The lastname is the field used with the GROUP BY clause. The fields OrderTotal and AvgOrder are the two aggregated fields.

Code:

```
SELECT OrderID, SUM(unitprice*quantity) AS OrderTotal,
AVG(unitprice*quantity) AS AvgOrder
FROM tbls_customersgr
GROUP BY lastname
```

Result:

lastname	OrderTotal	AvgOrder
Mahoney	225	45
Martin	121	60.5
Riegert	30	30
Spicer	168	42

Record: 1 of 4   No Filter   Search

132.   The GROUP BY clause on one column, one aggregated field, and WHERE

Find total order amounts for a subset of customers

Discussion:

Sometimes, we want to exclude certain records from our aggregate calculations. In these cases, we can use the WHERE clause to exclude records we are not interested in working with. Using WHERE, we exclude records before the GROUP BY clause takes effect. Therefore, if we have a source dataset with 3,000 records and use WHERE, the GROUP BY clause takes effect on the remaining records only. Later, you will learn the use of HAVING, which is a filtering statement like WHERE that takes effect after the GROUP BY calculates the summarized field values. Consequently, you need to know exactly what you want to do and use the appropriate filtering statement with GROUP BY.

In this example, we look for order totals by customer, but we want to exclude the orders from our customer Spicer. Mr. Spicer has only one order with orderid = 509. We use three fields in this SQL statement: Lastname, OrderTotal, and OrderID. LastName is the GROUP BY field, OrderTotal the aggregated field, and OrderID the filtering field.

Code:
```
SELECT LastName, SUM(unitprice*quantity) AS OrderTotal
FROM tbls_customersgr
WHERE orderid <> 509
GROUP BY LastName
```

Result:

133. The GROUP BY clause on one column, one aggregated field, and HAVING

Find customer orders with total order amount exceeding $100

Discussion:

In this example, we want to exclude from the result set all customers whose order totals are less than $100. However, we do not know beforehand who these customers are. We need to run the GROUP BY clause, find the totals, and exclude those below $100. This is exactly the case in which HAVING is used. Using HAVING with GROUP BY is a powerful and flexible way to filter records. Looking at the result set, we can see that only three customers appear. The customer named Riegert does not appear because his order total is only 30.

Code:

```
SELECT LastName, SUM(unitprice*quantity) AS OrderTotal
FROM tbls_customersgr
GROUP BY LastName
HAVING SUM(unitprice*quantity)>100
```

Result:

134.   The GROUP BY clause on one column, one aggregated field, WHERE and HAVING

Calculate order totals above $100 excluding a subset of products

Discussion:

In this example, pay attention to the combined use of WHERE and HAVING. We want to calculate customer order totals, but we want to exclude from the result set customers whose order totals are less than $100. In addition, we want to exclude the calculation amounts related to the product "Chocolate Chip Brownie". Perhaps management wants to see how customer order amounts differ if this product is excluded from their orders. Maybe they are thinking of discontinuing this particular product.

In general, when it comes to filtering records in GROUP BY statements, we need to make some quick decisions: Do we need to use WHERE, HAVING, or a combination of the two? Your way of thinking should always be the same: Use the WHERE clause to exclude records that you do not want to be included in the aggregate calculations, and use HAVING to exclude values after the aggregations by GROUP BY are made. In this case, we use WHERE to exclude the product "Chocolate Chip Brownie" from the recordset, and we use GROUP BY to create the aggregations on whatever records remain. After the aggregations are made, the HAVING clause takes effect to exclude order totals less than $100. The bottom line is that in the SQL statement below, the WHERE clause will run first, then the GROUP BY, and finally the HAVING clause.

Code:

```
SELECT LastName, SUM(unitprice*quantity) AS OrderTotal
FROM tbls_customersgr
WHERE productname <> "Chocolate Chip Brownie"
GROUP BY LastName
HAVING SUM(unitprice*quantity)>100
```

Result:

LastName	OrderTotal
Mahoney	210
Martin	121
Spicer	168

Record: 1 of 3

135. The GROUP BY clause with WHERE, HAVING, and ORDER BY

Sorting customer order totals

Discussion:

In this example, we put together all of the statements we learned about GROUP BY up to this point and introduce the ORDER BY clause. When the ORDER BY clause is used with GROUP BY, it takes effect after the database makes the calculations resulting from the GROUP BY clause. Furthermore, in this example, we exclude from the calculations a particular order with orderid=509.

Code:

```
SELECT LastName, SUM(unitprice*quantity) AS OrderTotal
FROM tbls_customersgr
WHERE orderid <> 509
GROUP BY LastName
HAVING SUM(unitprice*quantity)>100
ORDER BY Lastname DESC
```

Result:

136. The GROUP BY clause with NULLS—first example

Calculate customer order averages that might have nulls

Discussion:

For this example, I deleted from the tbls_customersgr table the unit price for one of the products in Mahoney's order with orderid=57. The idea is to demonstrate exactly what happens when nulls exist in data needed for calculations in GROUP BY clauses. Using 12 records, you can check the results manually and learn so that when you deal with 5,000 records, you know exactly what to do.

144

tbls_customersgr					
LastName	**OrderID**	**OrderDate**	**ProductName**	**UnitPrice**	**Quantity**
Mahoney	57	5/29/2008	Dark Chocolate Apricots in 20 oz. Bag		5
Mahoney	57	5/29/2008	Mushrooms Sauce	5	2
Mahoney	57	5/29/2008	Chocolate Chip Brownie	15	1

Let us run two pieces of code:

Code:

SELECT OrderID, Avg(([unitprice]*[quantity])) AS AverageOrderAmount
FROM tbls_customersgr
GROUP BY OrderID

Result:

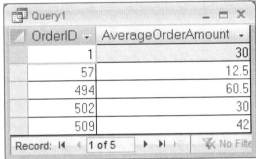

SELECT OrderID, [unitPrice]*[quantity] AS UnitPricexQuantity
FROM tbls_customersgr

Result:

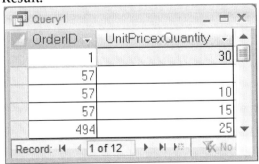

As you can see from the first result set, all of the calculations look right except for orderid = 57. In this case, the database is giving us an average of 12.5. In other words, it takes into consideration only the two products in that order and leaves out the third—the one with the missing quantity. I will not express an opinion whether this is correct or not. I simply want you to know that when missing data exists, aggregate functions will ignore the missing values. Some people might argue that this is correct because if we do not have data for an item, it should not be included in the calculations. Others might say that when missing data exists, aggregate functions should take this into consideration.

We will not miss the forest for the trees in this case. Instead of becoming bogged down by database peculiarities, the most effective action when you make calculations like multiplications or when you use the GROUP BY clause is to first check your fields for missing data and do your calculations. It takes a few seconds to check for nulls (chapter 23), and you will not have to worry how aggregate functions will handle your data.

137.   The GROUP BY clause on multiple columns

Find order totals grouped by customer and order number at the same time
Discussion:
Sometimes, you want to have a more detailed view of your data. For example, you might want to find order totals by customer and OrderID at the same time. You can easily achieve this with GROUP BY in Access 2007. Since you grouped first by last name and then by OrderID, orders will be totaled by OrderID first, followed by last name. You can reverse the order of grouping or add more grouping fields according to the level of the detail you would like to see.

Code:
```
SELECT lastname, OrderID, SUM(([unitprice]*[quantity])) AS OrderTotal
FROM tbls_customersgr
GROUP BY lastname, OrderID
```

Result:

CHAPTER 17
AGGREGATE FUNCTIONS

Aggregate functions like sum(), avg(), count(), count(*), max(), and min() have the main goal of summarizing data and converting this data into useful pieces of information. Aggregate functions process values in a table column to produce a summary value, whether a summation, an average, or a maximum value.

Aggregate functions can and often are used on calculated fields as well (chapter 14) such as fields which are themselves the result of the multiplication, summation, or division of two or more fields.

With aggregate functions, you need to pay attention to any null values in your data. In this chapter, you will understand well the effect of null values on aggregate calculations. However, no matter how much knowledge you have regarding the behavior of aggregate functions with null values, you should have one goal in mind: To eliminate null values from the columns on which you conduct aggregations. In other words, you need to develop a habit or a process so that before you even use an aggregate function, you examine your data for nulls (chapter 23). Of course, advanced developers by design do not allow null values in their tables. They will use default values, constraints, or validation rules to avoid nulls altogether.

Finally, aggregate functions are extremely useful when combined with the GROUP BY clause. We examined GROUP BY in the previous chapter and are now ready to go a step further, using it with aggregate functions to observe the power of the results obtained.

In this chapter, we will use aggregate functions with calculated fields, the GROUP BY clause, the WHERE clause, the HAVING clause, and a few operators so that you learn the combined use of aggregate functions—and not in isolation. For the purposes of this chapter, I have created a special table called tbls_customersag with only 20 records so that you can check the results against the dataset, make calculations manually, and fully understand the effects of aggregate functions. Before you start the examples in this chapter, open this table to understand its structure and have a look at its 20 records.

138. The count() function

Count the number of orders

Discussion:

The count() function, used alone, will calculate the number of records in a dataset as soon as it is used on a field that contains no null values. In practice, the count() function is usually applied on the primary key of the table since it is the one field that is certain not to contain nulls. In this example, we use it on the OrderID field, which is not the primary key, but I use it to show you the different results produced by count() in the subsequent examples. In this case, the count() function returned the number of records in the table, i.e. 20. We can be certain of one thing from this result: The OrderID field does not contain any null values since the number returned from the count() function is equal to the number of records in the table.

Code:

SELECT count(orderid) as NumberofOrders
FROM tbls_customersag

Result:

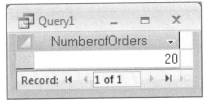

139. The count() function with DISTINCT

Count the number of unique orders from customers

Discussion:

The previous example is fine, but we need to find a way to count the number of unique orders in this table. The proper way to accomplish this task in SQL is to use the COUNT and DISTINCT statements together as:

SELECT Count (Distinct orderid) as NumberofOrders FROM tbls_cusotmersag

This is excellent, but our problem is that it does not work in Access 2007. We need to deviate thematically for a second and use a subquery with DISTINCT to achieve the

149

result we want. (See chapter 30 on subqueries for a detailed explanation of how they work). From the result set below, please notice that the number of orders produced by the count() function is now 15. This is actually the number of unique orders in the table, which is exactly what we need.

Code:
SELECT Count(*) AS NumberofOrders
FROM
(SELECT DISTINCT orderid FROM tbls_customersag)

Result:

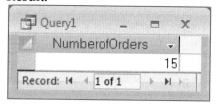

140. The count() function with the GROUP BY clause

Count the number of orders by customer
Discussion:

The objective in this scenario is to calculate how many orders we received from every customer. We can provide an answer very quickly by using the count() function with the GROUP BY clause. From the result set, you obtain two pieces of information. First, you know that you have 9 unique customers in the dataset of 20 records. Second, you have a count of the number of orders by each customer.

Code:
SELECT lastname, count(orderid) as NumberofOrders
FROM tbls_customersag
GROUP BY lastname

Result:

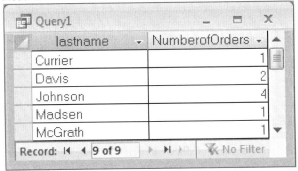

141. The count() and count(*) functions in comparison

Count the number of records in a table using count(*)

Discussion:

In this scenario, the objective is to clearly understand the differences between Count(), Count(*), and count() DISTINCT so that you can take full advantage of them in your data tasks. For this purpose, I have temporarily deleted the name of customer Davis from the table tbls_customersag. Now, we have 20 records in the table with the last name of a customer missing.

tbls_customersag					
PK	LastName	OrderID	ProductID	UnitPrice	Quantity
1		4	55	15	3
2	Sterling	60	56	12	5
3	Sterling	60	21	15	4

Let's use the count() function first. As you can see from the result set, the number returned is 19. This is because we used count() on the lastname field in which a value is missing. Consequently, while the table contains 20 records, we received only 19. You do not need to worry about these intricacies if you follow a simple piece of advice: Any time you work with aggregate functions, calculated fields, or GROUP BY, check your records for null values, and make the necessary edits and replacements (see chapter 23 for details on null values). Then, you do not need to worry about the intricacies of how aggregate functions or calculated fields behave with missing data.

Code:

SELECT count(lastname) as NumberofCustomers
FROM tbls_customersag

Result:

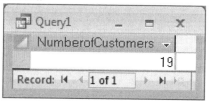

Now, let's use the count(*) function. As you can see from the result set, the count(*) function returned the correct result of 20 records in the table. This does not mean we have 20 unique customers, however, since the count(*) function is generic and not applicable to a particular field.

Code:

SELECT count(*) as NumberofCustomers
FROM tbls_customersag

Result:

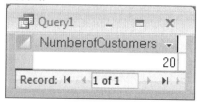

Now, let's use count(*) with a subquery and DISTINCT. As you can see from the result set, the number of unique customers returned is 10. We know already, however, that we have 9 unique customers in the table. This time, the count(*) function returned 10 because it counted the "blank" customer as an additional unique customer.

Code:
SELECT Count(*) AS NumberofCustomers
FROM
(SELECT DISTINCT lastname FROM tbls_customersag)

Result:

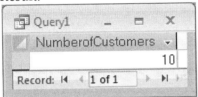

Of course, at this point, we might ask which result is correct: 19, 20, or 10? Well, none of the three numbers is correct. All of them are wrong for a single reason: The existence of a null value in the last name field. You should have two plans of action when it comes to calculated and aggregated fields. First, you eliminate the null values from the dataset. If this plan fails, go to plan B, which is to do aggregations and calculations on fields that do not have null values.

142. The AVG() function

Calculate the average order amount by customer
This example demonstrates how we can calculate the number of orders and the average order amount by customer. In a previous example, we learned how to calculate the number of orders by customer. This is good information but not enough for our business. For example, some customers might have many orders but with minimal order amounts. If we depend on the number of orders only, we might miss some good customers with big orders, and our marketing promotions and resources might be off target. Calculating the average order amount solves this problem.

Code:
SELECT lastname, count(orderid) as NumberofOrders, AVG(unitprice*quantity)
AS AvgOrderAmount
FROM tbls_customersag
GROUP BY lastname

Result:

143. The avg() function with the WHERE clause

Calculate the number of orders and average order amounts for specific customers

Discussion:

We have the flexibility to use the WHERE clause with aggregate functions to manipulate the result set and retrieve the exact pieces of information we need. Using WHERE will cause the database engine to first eliminate records per the WHERE clause and perform any calculations on the remaining ones. In this particular example, we exclude two customers using the NOT IN operator.

Code:

```
SELECT lastname, count(orderid) as NumberofOrders, AVG(unitprice*quantity)
AS AvgOrderAmount
FROM tbls_customersag
WHERE lastname NOT IN ("Johnson", "Madsen")
GROUP BY lastname
```

Result:

lastname	NumberofOrders	AvgOrderAmount
Currier	1	30
Davis	2	60
McGrath	1	10
Miller	2	25
Ming	2	60
Powers	4	31
Sterling	3	50

Record: 1 of 7 — No Filter — Search

144. The sum() function

Calculate the number of orders, average, and total order amounts by customer

Discussion:

Here, we use everything we have written in the previous example and add the sum() function to calculate the total order amount by customer. We are still excluding two customers from the calculations using the NOT IN operator in the WHERE clause.

Code:

```
SELECT lastname, count(orderid) as Num, avg(unitprice*quantity)
AS Avg, sum(unitprice*quantity) AS Total
FROM tbls_customersag
WHERE lastname NOT IN ("Johnson", "Madsen")
GROUP BY lastname
```

Result:

lastname	Num	Avg	Total
Currier	1	30	30
Davis	2	60	120
McGrath	1	10	10
Miller	2	25	50
Ming	2	60	120
Powers	4	31	124
Sterling	3	50	150

Record: I◄ ◄ 1 of 7 ► ►I ► ▼ No Filter

145. The min() function

Calculate the minimum (lowest value) of customer orders

Discussion:

Let's assume that we now have an additional request to find the minimum order amount for each customer. Leaving all of the other aggregated functions in our calculations will not affect the result of the min() function.

Code:

SELECT lastname, count(orderid) as Num, min(unitprice*quantity) AS Min,
avg(unitprice*quantity) AS Avg, sum(unitprice*quantity) AS Total
FROM tbls_customersag
WHERE lastname NOT IN ("Johnson", "Madsen")
GROUP BY lastname

Result:

146. The max() function

Calculate the maximum value of customer orders

Discussion:

The max() function will calculate the value of the biggest order for each customer, and it will report just that in the result set.

Code:

SELECT lastname, count(orderid) as Num, min(unitprice*quantity) AS Min, avg(unitprice*quantity) AS Avg, max(unitprice*quantity) AS Max, sum(unitprice*quantity) AS Total
FROM tbls_customersag
WHERE lastname NOT IN ("Johnson", "Madsen")
GROUP BY lastname

Result:

lastname	Num	Min	Avg	Max	Total
Currier	1	30	30	30	30
Davis	2	45	60	75	120
McGrath	1	10	10	10	10
Miller	2	20	25	30	50
Ming	2	60	60	60	120
Powers	4	15	31	45	124
Sterling	3	30	50	60	150

Record: I◀ ◀ 1 of 7 ▶ ▶I ▶ No Filter   Search

147. The Standard Deviation and Variance functions

Calculate the standard deviation and variance of customer order amounts

Discussion:

Using SQL, we can do much more than the usual arithmetic calculations. Actually, we can even perform some statistical analysis. In this example, we are looking for the standard deviation and variance of order amounts from each customer. In the SQL code, we used the cint() conversion function to avoid multiple decimals for the standard deviation column (chapter 24). In the result set, Currier and McGrath have only one order and, as it is logical, no variance and standard deviation can be calculated. From a business point of view, customers Davis, Sterling, and Powers are prone to making orders that vary a lot in size.

Code:

```
SELECT lastname, count(orderid) as Num, min(unitprice*quantity) AS Min,
avg(unitprice*quantity) AS Avg, max(unitprice*quantity) AS Max,
sum(unitprice*quantity) AS Total, cint(stdev(unitprice*quantity)) As stdev,
var(unitprice*quantity) as var
 FROM tbls_customersag
WHERE lastname NOT IN ("Johnson", "Madsen")
GROUP BY lastname
```

Result:

lastname	Num	Min	Avg	Max	Total	stdev	var
Currier	1	30	30	30	30	#Error	
Davis	2	45	60	75	120	21	450
McGrath	1	10	10	10	10	#Error	
Miller	2	20	25	30	50	7	50
Ming	2	60	60	60	120	0	0
Powers	4	15	31	45	124	15	218
Sterling	3	30	50	60	150	17	300

Record: 1 of 7   No Filter   Search

148.   Aggregate functions with GROUP BY and HAVING

Calculate order amounts and filter records based on results of aggregate functions

Discussion:

This time, our manager wants a report that shows the number of orders, minimum, average, maximum, and total order amounts calculated by customer. In addition, he wants products with productID 13, 56, and 30 to not participate in the calculations. He wants us to exclude from the result set any customers with total order amounts of less than $100. He also wants us to exclude from the calculations any customers with average order amounts of less than $40. Finally, he wants us to exclude from the calculations any customers with a standard deviation in their order amounts of 20 and above, but the standard deviation calculation should not appear in the result set.

The above sounds complicated, and it is complicated to a degree. Still, it is not difficult to achieve. I would like you to learn to follow a process when it comes to complicated SQL statements. This process involves the incremental building of the SQL statement instead of trying to think about everything at once. Essentially, we will build the solution one step at a time.

Our first step in any complicated problem involving SQL is to try to identify the fields. In this example, we need seven fields to do our job, and this step is straightforward. The SELECT statement with the seven fields appears below. We include the type conversion function cint() so that we restrict the number of decimals for the standard deviation field.

SELECT lastname, count(orderid) as Num, min(unitprice*quantity) AS Min, avg(unitprice*quantity) AS Avg, max(unitprice*quantity) AS Max, sum(unitprice*quantity) AS Total, cint(stdev(unitprice*quantity)) As stdev FROM tbls_customersag

Since our manager wants results produced by customer, we add the GROUP BY clause on lastname.

SELECT lastname, count(orderid) as Num, min(unitprice*quantity) AS Min, avg(unitprice*quantity) AS Avg, max(unitprice*quantity) AS Max, sum(unitprice*quantity) AS Total, cint(stdev(unitprice*quantity)) As stdev FROM tbls_customersag GROUP BY lastname

Our next step is to exclude products with productID 13, 56, and 30. For this task, we make use of the WHERE clause with the NOT IN operator (chapter 11) as it appears below:

SELECT lastname, count(orderid) as Num, min(unitprice*quantity) AS Min, avg(unitprice*quantity) AS Avg, max(unitprice*quantity) AS Max, sum(unitprice*quantity) AS Total, cint(stdev(unitprice*quantity)) As stdev FROM tbls_customersag WHERE productID NOT IN (13,56,30) GROUP BY lastname

The next step is to exclude from the result set any customers with total order amounts of less than $100 or any customers with average order amounts of less than $40. Here, we have a problem since we must first perform the aggregate calculations and run the GROUP BY clause to find out who those customers are. How can we do this in one SQL statement? For cases like this one, we make use of the HAVING clause, which is the filtering clause you can use to filter records after aggregate calculations have been performed. The code will now look like this:

SELECT lastname, count(orderid) as Num, min(unitprice*quantity) AS Min, avg(unitprice*quantity) AS Avg, max(unitprice*quantity) AS Max, sum(unitprice*quantity) AS Total, cint(stdev(unitprice*quantity)) As stdev
FROM tbls_customersag
WHERE productID NOT IN (13,56,30)
GROUP BY lastname
HAVING sum(unitprice*quantity) > 100 AND avg(unitprice*quantity) > 40

The final step in building the SQL statement is to exclude from the calculations any customers with a standard deviation in their order amounts of 20 and above but without including the standard deviation calculation in the result set. In the SQL code below, we took out the expression cint(stdev(unitprice*quantity)) from the SELECT statement and put it in the HAVING clause. This way, the filtering happens, but the standard deviation calculations do not appear in the result set.

Code:
SELECT lastname, count(orderid) as Num, min(unitprice*quantity) AS Min, avg(unitprice*quantity) AS Avg, max(unitprice*quantity) AS Max, sum(unitprice*quantity) AS Total FROM tbls_customersag
WHERE productID NOT IN (13,56,30)
GROUP BY lastname
HAVING sum(unitprice*quantity) > 100 AND avg(unitprice*quantity) > 40 AND cint(stdev(unitprice*quantity)) < 20

After all of the filtering, only one customer out of nine satisfied all of the criteria.

Result:

lastname	Num	Min	Avg	Max	Total
Ming	2	60	60	60	120

Record: 1 of 1 No Filter Search

CHAPTER 18
CROSSTAB QUERIES

Crosstab queries have a reputation of being complicated and intricate objects. This should not be the case. You can really work efficiently with crosstab queries once you recognize their basic structure. In essence, to create a crosstab query, you use three fields only. One field will function as the column heading, the second as the row heading, and the third as the value field. The value field is the actual field in which calculations occur using aggregate functions like sum(), avg(), count(), count(*), max(), and min(). From the previous chapter, you know very well how to work with aggregate functions. Let us apply this knowledge in crosstab queries.

Suppose you want to calculate order totals by state and year. In other words, you would like to know how much you sold in every state in every year. Since you know already that to create a crosstab query, you need to have a field as a column heading, a field as a row heading, and a value field, your query will look like this in its basic design:

	Year
State	Value

When you run the query, since you have multiple states and years in your data, your result set will look like this:

	Year1	Year2	Year3
State1	Value	Value	Value
State2	Value	Value	Value
State3	Value	Value	Value

The state row field will expand automatically to include data for as many states as you have in your database. The year field will expand to include as many columns as the number of years you have in your data. The value field will present the sum of order amounts for all of the combinations of year and state.

The above diagram represents the basic structure of a crosstab query in Access 2007. However, you have a couple of bonuses at this point. Now that you understand how crosstab queries work in Access 2007, you also understand how pivot tables work in Excel, you understand how pivot charts summarize their data, and you definitely have an advantage over someone who creates pivot tables and charts without full knowledge of data summaries under the hood. In the following examples, we start with basic crosstab queries and incrementally add techniques that will make your crosstab queries powerful tools for your work. I also provide the design code for all the crosstab queries so that they are easier to understand.

Working with crosstab queries usually involves the joining of multiple tables. We might need a field from the customers table, a field from the orders table, and a field from the products table. Since joins are not the focus of this chapter, I would like to spare you the intricacies of joining tables and focus on the actual crosstab queries themselves. That is why the examples in this chapter are based on a query purposely made for this chapter. Its name is "Qry_Crosstab_Base" from which we will take all of the fields we need to work with. Of course, I also provide chapter 29 toward the end of the book to explain joins inside out so that you can professionally and easily work with joined tables.

149.   A crosstab query with three fields - example 1

Find total sales by state and year

Discussion:

As you can see from the design view and the SQL code, we use three fields to create this very informative crosstab query. The first is the state field, which we use as the row heading. The second is the OrderDate field, which we use for column headings. For the OrderDate field there is a catch: We use the year() function to extract only the year out of the multitude of order dates we have in the database. The third field is the value field, which we call OrderTotal. This is a calculated field that sums the unitprice * the quantity of each product for each of our customer orders.

When you look at the SQL code, you will notice the use of a new statement called TRANSFORM. The TRANSFORM statement relates to the value field in a crosstab query, and it always precedes the SQL statement. Additionally, it is always followed by the aggregate function used for the value field, which in this case is sum(Quantity * UnitPrice). Below is the SQL code for the crosstab query explaining it step by step:

TRANSFORM Sum([unitprice]*[quantity]) AS Ordertotal

The TRANSFORM statement is used for the value field in a crosstab query.

SELECT State FROM Qry_Crosstab_Base

The SELECT statement is used only for the row-heading field of the crosstab query, which in this case is the State field.

GROUP BY State

The GROUP BY clause follows next, and it is applied on the same field used in the SELECT statement. Since we used State for the SELECT statement, we use State for the GROUP BY clause as well.

PIVOT Year([OrderDate])

The PIVOT statement is the last one used in a crosstab query, and it is applied on the column-heading field.

Below is the general structure of a crosstab query in SQL code.

TRANSFORM ValueField
SELECT ColumnField
FROM DataSource
GROUP BY ColumnField
PIVOT RowField

Design Code:

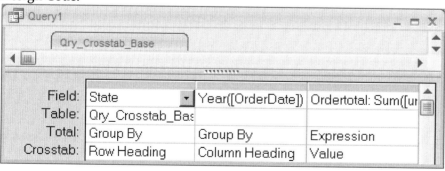

Code:

```
TRANSFORM sum([unitprice]*[quantity]) AS Ordertotal
SELECT State
FROM Qry_Crosstab_Base
GROUP BY State
PIVOT Year([OrderDate])
```

Looking at the results below, we can quickly understand and compare sales volumes by each state and each year. For example, the biggest sales revenues come from California, and they grow year by year. In Florida, we need to have a look at what is happening because sales dropped a lot for 2010. This is the power of crosstab queries. We get summarized results in seconds.

Result:

State	2008	2009	2010
AZ	2849	2386	3460
CA	12216	13879	14404
CO	2166	3121	1937
DC	3020	3351	3102
FL	4439	4736	3413

Record: 10 of 10 — No Filter — Search

150. A crosstab query with three fields—example 2

Find total sales by city and year

Discussion:

Our business manager is very happy with the comprehensive sales report we provided by state and year. Now that she knows what our database can do, she asks for an additional report that will show sales volumes by city and year. We reply that it will take a while to compile it. In about three seconds, however, we replace the state field with the city field in our query, and our new crosstab query is ready. We can then use the rest of the time for a nice cup of coffee!

Design Code:

Code:

TRANSFORM Sum([unitprice]*[quantity]) AS Ordertotal
SELECT City
FROM Qry_Crosstab_Base
GROUP BY City
PIVOT Year([OrderDate])

Result:

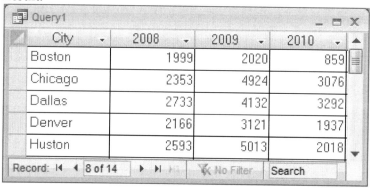

151.   The issue of uniqueness of values in crosstab queries

Find total sales by customer and year

Discussion:

Now, our supervisor asks for additional detail. Specifically, he wants a sales report by customer and year. Again, in a few seconds, we replace the city field from the previous example with lastname and presumably, we are done!

Unfortunately, that isn't the case this time! Our problem is that multiple customers might have the same last names. Since we are grouping on the last name field, all of the customers with the same lastname will be grouped together! This is a very common problem in crosstab queries and when using the GROUP BY clause. Consequently, I would like you to develop a process to think thoroughly about the uniqueness of values when using the GROUP BY clause. For instance, you should think about the possibility of having the same last name in your data for multiple customers. The same is true for city fields since the same city name might refer to multiple distinct cities, as is the case with Portland, Oregon and Portland, Maine. We will see how we can solve this problem in the next example with concatenated fields.

In addition, notice from the result set that there are some blank values. For example, there is a blank value for Ames in 2008 and Andersen in 2009. These blanks mean that Ames and Andersen have not placed any orders in 2008 and 2009 respectively. This is not a problem at all.

Design Code:

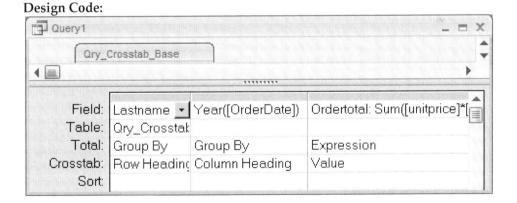

Code:

```
TRANSFORM sum([unitprice]*[quantity]) AS Ordertotal
SELECT lastname
FROM Qry_Crosstab_Base
GROUP BY lastname
PIVOT year([OrderDate])
```

Result:

Lastname	2008	2009	2010
Ackerman	120	32	207
Ames		75	796
Andersen	350		393
Anderson	965	924	1434
Anthopolis	220	240	48

Record: 10 of 171   No Filter   Search

152.   Crosstab queries with concatenated fields

Find total sales by customer and year displaying full customer names

Discussion:

In the previous example, we discussed that the results of the crosstab query were incorrect because multiple distinct customers might have the same last name. In this example, we need to make sure that we summarize sales volumes by unique customers. The knowledge acquired from the concatenated fields chapter (chapter 15) comes in handy here. In this example, we will GROUP BY the field resulting from the concatenation of the last and first name fields of the customers to obtain accurate results.

I know what you are thinking: What if there are customers with the same last and first names? This is a possibility, after all. We have three ways to solve this problem depending on its nature. First, if the two customer entries pertain to the same customer, (there are duplicated records in the data set), read chapter 22 on duplicate and orphaned records to explore a range of solutions.

Second, if the two customer entries pertain to two different customers, we can add middle names, zip codes, and even part of the address information to the concatenated expression to obtain unique results.

Third, to avoid this problem in its conception, we can add to the customer table a unique multiple-field index on the last and first name fields so that values of customers with the same last and first names are not accepted at all in the table. See chapter 2 for the exact syntax of multiple-field indexes.

I have created an additional problem on purpose: When you look at the result set in this example, you will notice that the first record is blank! If this is the case, go immediately to your record set, and check the values of the fields you use in the concatenated expression for blanks. You will notice that customer "Corelli" does not have a first name entry! Add a first name for this customer, and your blank record will disappear when you run your crosstab again.

Design Code:

Code:
```
TRANSFORM Sum([unitprice]*[quantity]) AS Ordertotal
SELECT (Lastname + ' ' + FirstName) AS Customer
FROM Qry_Crosstab_Base
GROUP BY (Lastname + ' ' + FirstName)
PIVOT Year([OrderDate])
```

169

Result:

153. Display row totals in crosstab queries

Find customer sales by state and year and calculate grand totals

Discussion:

There are two ways to calculate grand totals in crosstab queries. The first is to calculate grand totals for column fields. For example, the grand totals of orders in all states for 2008, 2009, and 2010. Grand totals of columns will appear at the bottom of the crosstab grid. To accomplish this task, we can use the $\sum$ command on the ribbon. We can find it at the "Home" tab in the "Records" group. By clicking on $\sum$, an additional row will become available at the bottom of the crosstab query grid where we can select any grand total calculations we want as the following figure shows:

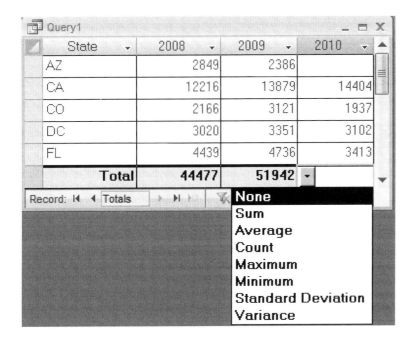

The other way is to calculate grand totals for row fields when we might want to see grand totals from all years for the states of AZ, CA, CO, etc., for example. To accomplish this task, we need to perform a little trick in the design of the crosstab query grid: We take the value field, in this case OrderTotal, and we create an additional column in the design grid that we name Grand Total. We leave the calculated field the same (Sum(Unitprice*quantity)) and assign this new column to be an additional row heading in the query. Check the design of the Grand Total field in the figure below:

Design Code:

If we want to accomplish this task in SQL, the only thing we need to do is to add the value field expression Sum([unitprice]*[quantity]) AS GrandTotal in the SELECT line of the SQL statement as it appears below:

Code:

```
TRANSFORM Sum([unitprice]*[quantity]) AS Ordertotal
SELECT State, Sum([unitprice]*[quantity]) AS GrandTotal
FROM Qry_Crosstab_Base
GROUP BY State
PIVOT Year([OrderDate]);
```

Result:

State	GrandTotal	2008	2009	2010
AZ	8695	2849	2386	3460
CA	40499	12216	13879	14404
CO	7224	2166	3121	1937
DC	9473	3020	3351	3102
FL	12588	4439	4736	3413
MA	4878	1999	2020	859
NY	21861	8584	6344	6933
OH	10353	2353	4924	3076
PA	5044	1525	2036	1483
TX	19781	5326	9145	5310

Record: 10 of 10 — No Filter — Search

154. Limit the number of rows in crosstab queries using WHERE

Find total sales by product and year for certain products only

Discussion:

All of the crosstab queries we have examined up to this point produce summaries counting every record in the underlying database table. Experience shows, however, that in the vast majority of cases, we will make calculations on a subset of data. We can use the WHERE clause to filter the data we want to cross tabulate. The WHERE clause always affects the number of records returned from a query whether this query is a simple SELECT or a crosstab one. In this specific example, the goal is to provide sales volumes by product and year, excluding some products from the calculations. Specifically, the products 'Chocolate Chip Cookies' and 'Chocolate Fudge' should be excluded from the calculations. We can use the WHERE clause in conjunction with the NOT IN operator to get exactly the results we need. The design view of the crosstab query appears below, as well as in the SQL code. When it comes to the result set, the two products we excluded will not appear in the cross-tabulated calculations.

Design Code:

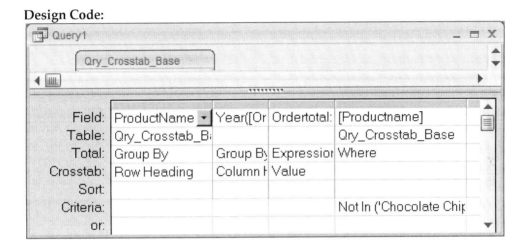

Code:

TRANSFORM Sum([unitprice]*[quantity]) AS Ordertotal
SELECT ProductName
FROM Qry_Crosstab_Base
WHERE ((Productname) NOT IN ('Chocolate Chip Cookies','Chocolate Fudge '))
GROUP BY ProductName
PIVOT Year([OrderDate])

Result:

ProductName	2008	2009	2010
All-Purpose Marinade I	406	546	560
All-Purpose Marinade II	915	750	255
Almonds, Hickory Smoked - 12 oz. Bag	600	180	675
Almonds, Roasted and Salted - 18 oz. Ba	660	975	540
Apple Cinnamon Raisin Cookies	552	540	696
Artichokes in white sauce	420	810	735

Record: 10 of 65 No Filter Search

155. Limit the number of columns in crosstab queries using PIVOT IN

Find total sales by product and year for specific years

Discussion:

In the previous example, we discussed how we can use the WHERE clause to filter the number of products included in the crosstab results. We learned how to limit the number of rows in a crosstab query, but there is a way to limit the number of columns as well.

For instance, what if our dataset contains sales data for the last ten years, and we do not want to include all of them in our crosstab results? We might want to see only the last two or three years. In this scenario, we are looking to control the number of columns appearing in the crosstab results. To achieve this task, we can use the PIVOT IN statement. In this particular example, we only want to see sales volumes for the years 2008 and 2009.

Code:

```
TRANSFORM Sum([unitprice]*[quantity]) AS Ordertotal
SELECT productname
FROM Qry_Crosstab_Base
GROUP BY productname
PIVOT Year([OrderDate]) IN (2008,2009)
```

Result:

productname	2008	2009
All-Purpose Marinade I	406	546
All-Purpose Marinade II	915	750
Almonds, Hickory Smoked - 12 oz. Bag	600	180
Almonds, Roasted and Salted - 18 oz. Ba	660	975
Apple Cinnamon Raisin Cookies	552	540
Artichokes in white sauce	420	810

Record: 10 of 67   No Filter   Search

156.   Filter crosstab queries using any field for criteria

Find total sales by product and year in AZ, CA, and OH

Discussion:

In the previous two examples of filtering crosstab queries, we used the WHERE clause on the productname field and the PIVOT IN on the Orderdate field. Both of these fields are part of the crosstab query. The productname field is used for rows, and the orderdate field for columns. I would like you to know, however, that you can use any field in your dataset to filter records in a crosstab query without this field being an integral part of the crosstab query. You simply designate it as a "WHERE" field as it appears in the design grid below, or you use it in a WHERE clause as it appears in the SQL code. In addition, the state field, used as a "WHERE" field in this example, will not appear in the result set.

Design Code:

Query1

Qry_Crosstab_Base

Field:	ProductName	Year([OrderDate])	Ordertotal:	[State]
Table:	Qry_Crosstab_B			Qry_Crosstab_B
Total:	Group By	Group By	Expressior	Where
Crosstab:	Row Heading	Column Heading	Value	
Sort:				
Criteria:				In ('AZ','CA','OH')

Code:

```
TRANSFORM Sum([unitprice]*[quantity]) AS Ordertotal
SELECT ProductName
FROM Qry_Crosstab_Base
WHERE ((State) IN ('AZ','CA','OH'))
GROUP BY ProductName
PIVOT Year([OrderDate])
```

Result:

ProductName	2008	2009	2010
All-Purpose Marinade	182	70	238
All-Purpose Marinade	450	360	120
Almonds, Hickory Sm	360	45	495
Almonds, Roasted an	225	615	315
Apple Cinnamon Rais	180	108	276
Artichokes in white sau	60	495	465
Banana Bisquits	64	40	224

Record: 10 of 67   No Filter   Search

157. Using parameters with crosstab queries

Find sales by customer and year using state as a parameter

Discussion:

Now, we have a new situation. Corporate managers are ecstatic about our ability to produce such useful results with crosstab queries. However, they call on us constantly to design the queries they need, and we spend a lot of time defining simple criteria. To solve this problem, we can use parameters with crosstab queries. Parameters in crosstab queries need a little attention. We need to enter the parameter twice: First in the query design grid as seen in the figure below:

Design:

Second, we need to enter it in the parameters dialog box that we can find in the "Show/Hide" group of the "Query Design" tab as in the figure below:

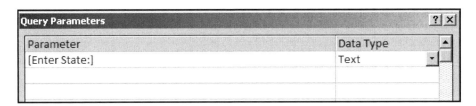

Make sure the parameter data type is the same as the one in the field where you are using it. The items to notice in the SQL code below are the PARAMETERS statement in the first line and the WHERE clause. Notice that the WHERE clause is waiting for a value from the PARAMETERS statement. (For a detailed analysis on parameters, see chapter 19). The result set produced in this example is for the state of NY.

Code:

```
PARAMETERS [Enter State:] Text ( 255 );
TRANSFORM Sum([unitprice]*[quantity]) AS Ordertotal
SELECT (Lastname+' '+FirstName) AS Customer
FROM Qry_Crosstab_Base
WHERE (((Qry_Crosstab_Base.[State])=[Enter State:]))
GROUP BY (Lastname+' '+FirstName)
PIVOT Year([OrderDate]);
```

Result:

Customer	2008	2009	2010
Ames Pindar		75	796
Anderson Peter	484	277	444
Anthopolis Ricky	220	240	48
Aversa Scott	469		
Carr Edward	301	541	
Cindon Barbara	355		641

Record: 10 of 29 — No Filter — Search

158. Conditional processing of crosstab queries using the iif() function

Calculate discounted sales volumes depending on revenue volumes

Discussion:

Our business assignment in the first example of this chapter was to give our manager a print out of total of sales by state and year. We were able to do that successfully and in no time. Now, however, our task is a little bit more complicated. Management wants to know the sales volumes if they gave a 10% discount to customers in states with total sales of more than $10,000. In addition, they want to know the sales volumes if they gave a discount of 5% to customers in states with total sales of less than $10,000. And they want to see all results in one report.

This is not a problem at all. The key here is to use the iif() function with the crosstab query. The expression for the value field in the crosstab query is the expression shown below. We ask the database to apply a 10% discount if total sales are bigger than $10,000 or to apply a 5% discount if total sales are less than $10,000.

178

Sum(iif([unitprice]*[quantity]>10000, ([unitprice]*[quantity])*(0.9), ([unitprice]*[quantity])*(0.95))) AS Ordertotal

Design Code:

Code:

TRANSFORM Sum(iif([unitprice]*[quantity]>10000, ([unitprice]*[quantity])*(0.9), ([unitprice]*[quantity])*(0.95))) AS Ordertotal
SELECT State
FROM Qry_Crosstab_Base
GROUP BY State
PIVOT Year([OrderDate])

Result:

159.   Format output in crosstab queries

Find total sales by product and year and show results as currency

Discussion:

There might be some instances in which we would like to format the results of the value field of a crosstab query as currency so that the dollar sign appears in front of the numbers. This can be accomplished by using the format() or Ccur() functions right in the TRANSFORM statement as it appears below. Both will produce the same output.

Code:

```
TRANSFORM Format(Sum([unitprice]*[quantity]), "Currency") AS Ordertotal
SELECT ProductName
FROM Qry_Crosstab_Base
GROUP BY ProductName
PIVOT Year([OrderDate]);


TRANSFORM Ccur(Sum([unitprice]*[quantity])) AS Ordertotal
SELECT ProductName
FROM Qry_Crosstab_Base
GROUP BY ProductName
PIVOT Year([OrderDate]);
```

Result:

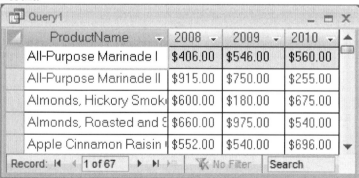

160.   Using the nz() function in crosstab queries

Find total customer orders by customer and year

Discussion:

In the cross-tabbed results below, the many blanks in the grid are immediately noticeable and do not appear very professional.

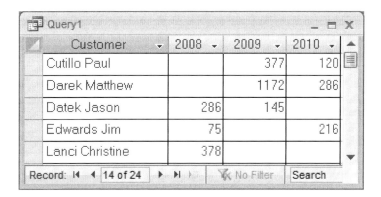

There is a way to replace these blank values with zeros using the nz() function. Notice how we use three functions in the TRANSFORM line to obtain the results we need.

Code:

```
TRANSFORM Ccur(Nz(Sum([unitprice]*[quantity]))) AS Ordertotal
SELECT (Lastname + ' ' + FirstName) AS customer
FROM Qry_Crosstab_Base
WHERE ((State) In ('AZ','CO','MD'))
GROUP BY (Lastname + ' ' + FirstName)
PIVOT Year([OrderDate])
```

Result:

customer	2008	2009	2010
Cutillo Paul	$0.00	$377.00	$120.00
Darek Matthew	$0.00	$1,172.00	$286.00
Datek Jason	$286.00	$145.00	$0.00
Edwards Jim	$75.00	$0.00	$216.00
Lanci Christine	$378.00	$0.00	$0.00
Lareous Angelo	$295.00	$175.00	$193.00

Record: I◄ ◄ 10 of 24 ► ►I ►☆   ✕ No Filter   Search

161.   Conditional crosstab queries

Calculate order totals for "expensive" and "inexpensive" products

Discussion:

This time, management wants to know the contribution to the total sales volume of products selling above $25 per unit and the contribution of products selling below $25 per unit. Depending on the results we will give them, they will change their sales priorities to focus more on products that will generate the most sales for the company. In addition, they would like to have the results by year so that they can also distinguish any trends in sales volumes. We can use the switch function right in the PIVOT statement to create product categories exactly the way management has asked.

Code:

```
TRANSFORM Sum([unitprice]*[quantity]) AS Ordertotal
SELECT Year([OrderDate]) As Year
FROM Qry_Crosstab_Base
GROUP BY Year([OrderDate])
PIVOT
SWITCH(
unitprice >= 25 ,      "ExpensiveProducts",
unitprice < 25,        "InexpensiveProducts"
)
```

Result:

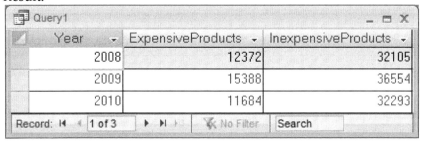

CHAPTER 19
PARAMETER QUERIES

The primary goal of a parameter query is to provide flexibility in criteria expressions. Instead of hard coding criteria values in the query code, it provides users the capability to supply the values that they want to work with. For example, instead of hard coding the value "NY" for the state field, a parameter query allows users to supply any state they want and get the corresponding results.

Parameter queries in their simplest form will include one or two parameterized fields. However, you should know that parameter queries can be used with multiple parameters of any data type, wildcard characters, operators, equality and inequality predicates, and even functions. We will go through examples of all the above in this chapter so that you can make full use of the power and flexibility of parameter queries.

162.   Creating a query with one parameter field
Retrieve order information using state as a parameter
Discussion:
The simplest form of a parameter query is one with a single parameter field. The parameter field always appears in the WHERE clause of the query, and its parameter prompt is enclosed in brackets. In this example, the parameter field is "state", and its prompt will appear as [Enter State:]. The colon at the end of the prompt is optional, and you can omit it if you want. In this specific example, we used the equality predicate "=" in the expression ((State)=[Enter State:]). This is because the parameter in this query is waiting for complete state values like "NY", "AZ", "FL", or "CA". However, you are not restricted to equality or inequality predicates such as (=, <>, <, <=, >, =>). Later, you will learn how you can enter only part of the value you are looking for, in which case you can use an operator such as LIKE. You could also use the BETWEEN operator or even wildcard characters and functions as you will see in this chapter.

Code:

SELECT OrderID, OrderDate, City, State
FROM Qry_Parameters_Base
WHERE ((State)=[Enter State:])

Parameter Prompt:

Result:

163.   Creating a query with two parameter fields

Retrieve order information using state and city as parameters

Discussion:

Creating multi-field parameter queries is a possibility in Access 2007. In this example, we use the state and city as parameter fields using the AND operator. This means that we force our users to select a state first and then, a city within that state like NY and New York City. We can just as easily use the OR operator so that our users can select any state and any city they want.

Code:

SELECT OrderID, OrderDate, City, State
FROM Qry_Parameters_Base
WHERE ((((State)=[Enter State:]) AND (City)=[Enter City:]))

Result:

OrderID	OrderDate	City	State
43	5/1/2009	New York	NY
115	1/22/2008	New York	NY
264	2/4/2008	New York	NY
642	3/11/2009	New York	NY

Record: ◄ ◄ 10 of 118 ► ►◄ ▼ No Filter   Search

164. Creating a query with three parameter fields, one of them an expression

Retrieve order information using state, city, and ordertotal as parameters

Discussion:

In this example, we use three parameters for the State, City, and TotalOrder fields. Notice the third parameter ">[Enter Amount Bigger Than:]" for the TotalOrder field. Here, we use the ">" greater than inequality predicate to retrieve orders from NY and New York City, which are bigger than $200 in this example. Of course, we could have used any amount for order totals to retrieve the orders we want. Equality and inequality predicates allow amazing flexibility in parameter queries. For a review of equality and inequality predicates, review chapter 9.

Code:

```
SELECT OrderID, OrderDate, City, State
FROM Qry_Parameters_Base
WHERE ((((State)=[Enter State:]) AND (City)=[Enter City:]) AND
(totalorder)>[Enter Amount Bigger Than:])
```

Result:

OrderID	OrderDate	City	State
341	4/19/2008	New York	NY
411	8/24/2010	New York	NY
429	3/23/2010	New York	NY
447	4/16/2008	New York	NY

Record: ◄ ◄ 10 of 30 ► ►◄ ▼ No Filter   Search

165.   Define the order of the parameter prompts

Retrieve order information using orderdate, state, and ordertotal as parameters
Discussion:
Using multiple parameters might present a problem if we enter them directly in the query design grid in Access 2007. In this case, Access will present the parameters from left to right according to the lineup of the columns in the grid. Some sources suggest entering parameters in the "Parameters" sheet in the "Show/Hide" group of the "design" tab to force order. It is really not necessary to type our parameters a second time. In our SQL statement, we just type our parameters in the order we would like them to appear. However, always think about the logic behind the parameter lineup. In this example with the AND operator, the order will not make a difference in the result set since all three parameter values will apply concurrently on the fields for which they are specified. However, there might be cases in which we want a certain date range to be specified first and then, use operators to search for data within that range using operators different from AND.

In this example, the parameters are: NY, 1/1/2009, and $200.

Code:
```
SELECT OrderID, OrderDate, City, State
FROM Qry_Parameters_Base
WHERE ((((State)=[Enter State:]) AND (orderdate)>[Enter Date Later Than:])
AND (totalorder)>[Enter Amount Bigger Than:])
```

Result:

187

166.   Using wildcard characters in parameter Queries

Find customers by supplying only part of the name

Discussion:

If we want to give your users the ability to search orders by customer name but without remembering the exact last name of the customer, we can use a wildcard character with a parameter field. In this example, we use the * wildcard character and lastname as the parameter field. Of course, we can use our creativity and employ any wildcard character we want (see chapter 7) with any kind of equality or inequality predicates to achieve amazing results. In this example, we will look for all customer names starting with "Ba". As you might expect, the same customer will come up multiple times since each customer might have multiple orders. That is why the name Balfur appears multiple times.

Code:

```
SELECT lastname, firstname, city, state
FROM Qry_Parameters_Base
WHERE ((lastname) LIKE [Enter last name:] + "*")
```

Result:

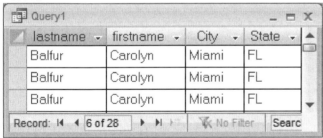

167.   Using numeric ranges in parameter queries

Find sales volume ranges from customer orders

Discussion:

Suppose we have a request to provide managers the ability to retrieve sales volumes. They would like to do it themselves without our hard coding the criteria in the query every time. This is easy with a parameter query. As you can see from the result set, there are 159 orders between $200 and $300. In this example, we used the "<" and ">" inequality predicates instead of the BETWEEN operator. The lower and upper limits of our boundaries ($200, $300) will not appear in the result set. However, if we used

BETWEEN (chapter 10), which is inclusive, the boundaries would have been included in the result set. The same would happen if we used the "<=" and "=>" inequality predicates.

Code:
SELECT OrderID, OrderDate, City, State, TotalOrder
FROM Qry_Parameters_Base
WHERE ((((TotalOrder)>[Enter Min Order Amount:]) AND (totalorder)<[Enter Maximum Order Amount:])

Result:

OrderID	OrderDate	City	State	TotalOrder
507	4/27/2009	Huston	TX	225
517	6/30/2010	Huston	TX	240
508	10/16/2010	Orlando	FL	211

Record: 18 of 159   No Filter   Search

168. Using date ranges in parameter queries

Find total order amounts between specific dates

Discussion:
This time, our goal is to retrieve order amounts between specific dates. For example, we might want to retrieve sales volumes only for a period of five days, ten days, a few months, or years. In this example, we are looking for orders between 1/1/2009 and 1/7/2009. It was a bit slow in the beginning of the year with only two orders!

Code:
SELECT OrderID, OrderDate, City, State, TotalOrder
FROM Qry_Parameters_Base
WHERE ((((OrderDate)>[Enter Min Date:]) AND (OrderDate)<[Enter Max Date:])

189

Result:

OrderID	OrderDate	City	State	TotalOrder
719	1/2/2009	Denver	CO	193
529	1/6/2009	New York	NY	75

Record: 1 of 2   No Filter   Search

169.   Using functions in parameter queries

Find orders for a specific month for any range of years

Discussion:

Now, we have a very peculiar request from our company. Management wants to do some decision-making, and they have asked us for a way to run multiple scenarios such as: What were the sales volumes in the months of May for the last two years? Or June for the last three years? Or for any month for any range of years? They want to be able to perform these scenarios at will. For this, we tell them that we need a day or so to set up the scenario, but it will only take about 15 seconds with the use of functions. We use the month() function to extract the month out of the OrderDate field, the year() function to extract years out of the OrderDate field, and the BETWEEN operator!

In this example, we used May (5) for the month and 2009 to 2010 for the year range. As you can see from the result set, we only retrieved orders for May of 2009 and May 2010.

Code:

```
SELECT OrderID, OrderDate, City, State, TotalOrder
FROM Qry_Parameters_Base
WHERE (((Month([OrderDate])=[Enter Month Number:]) AND
((Year([OrderDate])) BETWEEN [ Enter Min Year:] And [Enter Max Year:])));
```

Result:

OrderID ▾	OrderDate ▾	City ▾	State ▾	TotalOrder ▾
73	5/14/2009	Miami	FL	90
841	5/17/2010	New York	NY	156
398	5/17/2010	Los Angeles	CA	162
670	5/27/2009	Los Angeles	CA	259
692	5/3/2009	Huston	TX	327

Record: ◄ ◄ 1 of 39 ► ►► ▾ No Filter Search

170.   Calculations and functions in parameter queries

Find fulfillment cycle times for customer orders for specific periods

Discussion:

Management now wants to find fulfillment cycle times for customer orders for internal efficiency indicators. They would like us to retrieve the amount of time it took the company to ship an order from the time it received the order and for any range of dates. This is not as bad as it sounds. In this example, we measure the lag time in days for the period of 1/1/2009 to 1/30/2009. We use twice the day() function to construct a calculated field (lagTimesInDays) and then, two parameters for the OrderDate field.

Code:

```
SELECT OrderID, (day(ShippedDate) - day(OrderDate)) AS LagTimeInDays,
TotalOrder
FROM Qry_Parameters_Base
WHERE ((((OrderDate)>[Enter Min Date:]) AND (OrderDate)<[Enter Max Date:]))
```

Result:

OrderID ▾	LagTimeInDays ▾	TotalOrder ▾
649	5	45
317	5	30
599	5	228

Record: ◄ ◄ 10 of 19 ► ►► ▾ No Filter Search

CHAPTER 20
CONDITIONAL DATA
MANIPULATION

The iif(), switch(), and partition() functions are the most useful and practical functions for conditional data manipulation in Access 2007. Keep in mind that CASE does not work in Access 2007, so do not bother wasting your time looking for it.

What exactly do we mean by conditional data processing? Let's assume we have a customer database that we use for promotional campaigns. We might decide that we want to provide different discount levels for customers in the Northeast, Midwest, West, Southeast, and Southwest states. Since we do not have region information in our database, we need to create multiple SELECT queries for these categories and apply the appropriate discount for each region. Using conditional data processing, on the other hand, will enable us to do our job in just one query.

You are probably thinking at this point that it does not bother you to create four queries to do your job. What matters in the end is getting the job done. I totally agree. However, what will happen after a couple of years at work is that you will end up with several hundred queries. In the end, you will not remember what was what, and you will be afraid to delete even one of them since you no longer know what it was used for. During the last 15 years, I have seen this happen countless times with departmental databases.

To encourage you to use conditional processing, let me give you another example. Let's say we have a database in which we store our products, along with the corresponding suppliers. Every now and then, our suppliers send us updated prices, and we need to update our own product catalog as well. We have only 20 suppliers and 200 products in our database, and we need to update our prices every few weeks.

Of course, thinking logically, suppliers will provide us with different price updates. Some of them will increase their prices by 3%, some by 5%, some by 3.5%, some by 4%, ending up with 12 clusters in this example. Still, we will have to create 12 update queries and include the specific calculated fields for the updates and specific criteria so that the appropriate supplier products are updated and with the correct percentages.

Furthermore, every time we have price updates, we will need to modify our current update queries, create new ones, modify their criteria, and calculate new prices for the updates. We will end up with an unmanageable number of queries even for this simple scenario. Using conditions, on the other hand, we can do the job very effectively using just one single query!

A final point on conditional statements: Those who understand conditional statements well will produce much better database designs and entity relationship diagrams since they know in advance what needs to be stored and what can be produced automatically by the database. We will start with simple examples and increase their complexity as we go on.

171.   Using the iif() and switch() functions with two simple conditions

Produce a product catalog with special discounts for one product only

Discussion:

We received an urgent message from the inventory department saying that we have a large quantity of Chocolate Fudge which needs to go out into the market fast. We only have a few hours to produce a new product catalog for this week and send to our customers. All of the product prices in the catalog should remain the same except for Chocolate Fudge, which will be reduced by 50%. We must not make this percentage change right in the table because this price will be valid only for a week.

Solution 1: using the iif() function

We can solve the problem above using an iif() function. The translation of the iif() function in this example says: For the product with productid = 14, change the value of the field ProductUnitPrice by 50%, and for the rest of the products in the catalog, leave the price as is in the table. In addition, notice that a second function is used, cCur(), to display numbers with the dollar sign in front of them. Notice also that we changed the title of the ProductUnitPrice field to appear as "ProductPrice" in this week's catalog. Finally, notice in the result set that the price of Chocolate Fudge is now $20.50 in the query, while it remains $41 in the products table.

Code:

SELECT ProductID, ProductName, QuantityPerUnit,
cCur(iif([productid]=14,[productunitprice]*0.5,[productunitprice])) AS
ProductPrice
FROM Products

Result:

ProductID	ProductName	QuantityPerUnit	ProductPrice
14	Chocolate Fudge	28	20.5
15	Chocolate Blueberries	28	24
16	Chocolate Almonds in	25	25
17	Dark Chocolate Aprico	35	46

Record: 1 of 70   No Filter   Search

Solution 2: using the switch() function

There is no need to use the switch function in this case since the conditions are very simple. However, I would like to show you its syntax and how it works with respect to an iif() function. In this example, we again used the Ccur() function in front of the switch function to obtain the dollar sign in front of the product prices. There is no doubt that the switch() function is much cleaner and comprehensible than the iif() function. This becomes more evident as the number of conditions goes up.

Code:

SELECT ProductID, ProductName, QuantityPerUnit,
SWITCH(
productid = 14,   productunitprice*0.5,
productid <>14,   productunitprice
)
AS ProductPrice
FROM Products

Result:

ProductID	ProductName	QuantityPerUnit	ProductPrice
14	Chocolate Fudge	28	20.5
15	Chocolate Blueberries	28	24
16	Chocolate Almonds in	25	25
17	Dark Chocolate Aprico	35	46

Record: ◄ ◄ 1 of 70 ► ►I ►≡ No Filter Search

172. Using the iif() and switch() functions with two conditions but multiple criteria

Provide discounts for customers in NY, TX, and CA only

Discussion:

This time, management initiates a new promotional campaign. They want to offer a 20% discount to customers in large states such as NY, TX, and CA and 10% to everyone else around the country. They want a list of customers and their corresponding discount rates for review.

Solution 1: using the iif() function

Using the iif() function becomes a bit more complicated this time and requires two OR operators. The iif() function translates to: If the customer is in NY, CA, or TX, provide him or her with a discount of 20%. Otherwise, provide the customer with a discount of 10%.

Code:

SELECT State, lastname, firstname, OrderTotal,

IIf([state]= 'NY' Or [state]= 'CA' Or [state]= 'TX',"20%","10%")

AS Discount

FROM Qry_Conditions

Result:

Solution 2: using the switch() function

The use of the switch function with two conditions and multiple criteria is again more legible than using the iif() function and, therefore, easily editable if we need to update our criteria later on.

Code:

```
SELECT State, lastname, firstname,  OrderTotal,
SWITCH(
[state]= 'NY' Or [state]= 'CA' Or [state] = 'TX',      "20%",
[state] <> 'NY' Or 'CA' Or 'TX',                       "10%"
)
AS Discount
FROM Qry_Conditions
```

Result:

173.   Working with multiple conditions and criteria

Determine discount amounts based on customer sales volumes

Discussion:

Our sales manager wants to provide order discounts to customers based on their historical sales volume with the company. Thus, if a customer has a certain recorded sales volume, the next time she orders, she will get a predetermined discount rate regardless of her new order amount.

If the total orders amount for a customer is less than $200, that customer will receive no discounts. If it is between $200 and $300, the customer will get a 5% discount. If it is between $300 and $500, the customer will get a 10% discount. For anything above that, our manager will offer a generous 25% discount to the customer. Our job is to create a datasheet that will list customers and show the corresponding discount rate for each customer.

Solution 1: using nested iif() functions

Our first option is to use a series of nested iif() functions as shown below—four iif() functions, one inside the other to accomplish our goal. However, the use of nested iif() functions is a convoluted process. In addition, if we need to change the business logic behind our statement by adding additional categories, the task is not a clear and clean preposition. The problem originates from the fact that the iif() function takes only two arguments. For more outcomes or categories, we need to nest, which, in turn, results in complicated statements.

Code:

```
SELECT lastname, firstname, OrderTotal,
IIf([ordertotal]<200,0,IIf([ordertotal]>=200 And
[Ordertotal]<300,'5%',IIf([ordertotal]>=300 And
[ordertotal]<500,'10%',IIf([ordertotal]>500,'25%')))) AS Discount
FROM Qry_Conditions;
```

Result:

Solution 2: using the switch() function

In this example, the first observation is that the switch() function does not limit the number of expressions we can use, so we need no nesting. In addition, our logic becomes immediately apparent to both us and anyone else who will need to edit the SQL statement later on. The cleanliness of the SQL statement is obvious:

Code:

```
SELECT lastname, firstname, ordertotal,
SWITCH(
ordertotal < 200,                          "0" ,
ordertotal>= 200 and ordertotal < 300,     "5%" ,
ordertotal> 300 and ordertotal <= 500,     "10%" ,
ordertotal> 500 ,                          "25%"
)
AS Discount
FROM qry_conditions
```

Result:

lastname	firstname	OrderTotal	Discount
Riegert	Joanne	30	0
Read	Lisa	210	5%
Moore	Gerald	231	5%
Davis	Catherine	45	0

Record: ◄◄ ◄ 10 of 919 ► ►► | No Filter | Search

174. An effective trick with the switch() function

Calculate customer discounts based on location

Discussion:

This time, the task is to provide customer discounts in specific states. At the same time, a general discount percentage should be extended to all customers in states not included in the specific state list. We can achieve this task by using the TRUE keyword as part of the last expression in a switch() function. This last expression will evaluate true for every state not included in the specific state list, and we will extend the 10% discount to all of the customers in states different from NY, AZ, CO, FL, and MA.

Code:

```
SELECT State, lastname, firstname,  OrderTotal,
SWITCH(
[state]= 'NY',    "20%",
[state] ='AZ',    "15%",
[state] ='CO',    "12%",
[state] ='FL',    "18%",
[state] ='MA',    "18%",
TRUE,          "10%",
)
AS Discount FROM Qry_Conditions
```

Result:

175. Using switch() with WHERE, IN, and ORDER BY

Calculate discounted order totals based on customer sales volume

Discussion:

Our goal now is to calculate sales totals for specific customer categories. These categories are obtained by calculating customer total order amounts. We only offer discounts to customers with order totals between $200 and $500. No one else receives discounts. In addition, we want to extend these discounts only to customers in AZ, CO, TX, and FL. After the switch function ends, we can absolutely use the WHERE clause with the IN operator to define the exact records for which our calculations will apply.

Code:
```
SELECT OrderID, lastname, firstname, State,
SWITCH(
ordertotal>= 200 and ordertotal < 300,    Ordertotal*(1-0.1) ,
ordertotal> 300 and ordertotal <= 500,    OrderTotal*(1-0.15) ,
ordertotal> 500 ,                         OrderTotal*(1-0.2),
TRUE,                                     OrderTotal
)
as DiscountedOrders
FROM qry_conditions
WHERE state in ('AZ', 'CO', 'TX', 'FL')
ORDER BY ordertotal DESC
```

Result:

OrderID	lastname	firstname	State	DiscountedOrders
944	Corelli		TX	459.2
308	Darek	Matthew	CO	409.6
404	Crandil	Joseph	TX	408
932	Weinberger	Fred	FL	386.75

Record: 10 of 301   No Filter   Search

176.   Using switch() with calculated fields

Produce product categories based on product prices

Discussion:

This time, the request we have from management is to provide a product list categorized arbitrarily by price. They want to see a product list that specifies each product as "economical", "moderate", and "expensive" based on its price. Although we carry no such field in the database, we can absolutely create the list in seconds by using a switch() function combined with calculated fields. In essence, we calculate the unit price times its quantity per unit to get the total price we pay, and we then assign categories based on price. For instance, if the price falls between $500 and $1000, we designate these products as "moderately" priced. We can save this query and update it at will if management wants more, less, or otherwise defined categories.

Code:

```
SELECT ProductName, UnitsInStock, UnitsOnOrder,
SWITCH(
ProductUnitPrice*QuantityPerUnit < 500,    "Economical",
ProductUnitPrice*QuantityPerUnit >= 500 AND
ProductUnitPrice*QuantityPerUnit<1000,    "Moderate",
ProductUnitPrice*QuantityPerUnit >= 1000,  "Expensive",
)
as PricingCategory
FROM Products
ORDER BY  ProductUnitPrice*QuantityPerUnit DESC
```

Result:

177. Using switch() with aggregate functions

Calculate employee commissions and bonuses based on their sales volume

Discussion:

There are multiple tasks in this example. First, we need to calculate employee commissions as a percentage of their sales. Second, we need to calculate employee bonuses based again on sales volumes. Third, we need to add commission and bonus amounts. Fourth, we need to make these calculations only for 2010. Fifth, we need to present the results as currency.

Do not be intimidated by the long SQL statement. It is long but not as tough as it looks. In two minutes, you will have a total grasp of it. First, notice we use only three fields in this SQL statement: lastname, orderdate, and CommissionAndBonus. We use the lastname field as is. For the orderdate field, we use the function year() to extract only the year part of the date. The CommissionAndBonus field will be the result of the switch function calculations.

Next, notice that we use three functions, sum(), Ccur(), and switch(), one after the other. We use the sum() function to obtain the total order amounts sold by our salesperson. Since we do not have a field for order totals in the database (correctly, since we can calculate it), we need to multiply the quantity of each product sold by its price in every order and sum() the results. Then, we use the Ccur() function to convert the data type of the CommissionAndBonus field to appear as currency. Finally, we use the switch function to assign commissions and bonuses according to sales volumes.

Next, we have a FROM statement but do not pay attention to the joins since Access will create the joins automatically when we paste this code in a query and look at its design. However, we devote a whole chapter on joins (chapter 29).

In the final part of the SQL statement, we group by employee and year since we need to have commissions and bonuses shown by employee. We filter the year by using the HAVING clause as we examined in our "GROUP BY" chapter.

In the end, the whole query is reduced to three fields: lastname and year by which we group by and the commissionandbonus field on which we apply the sum() aggregate function.

Code:
```
SELECT LastName,  Year([OrderDate]) AS [Year],

SUM(CCur(SWITCH(
([UnitPrice]*[quantity]) < 5000,         ([UnitPrice]*[quantity])*(0.1) + 500 ,
([UnitPrice]*[quantity]) >= 5000 and  ([UnitPrice]*[quantity]) <10000,
([UnitPrice]*[quantity])*(0.15) + 1000,
([UnitPrice]*[quantity]) >= 10000 and  ([UnitPrice]*[quantity]) <15000,
([UnitPrice]*[quantity])*(0.2) + 3000,
([UnitPrice]*[quantity]) >= 15000 ,     ([UnitPrice]*[quantity])*(0.25) + 5000,
)))
as CommissionAndBonus

FROM SalesReps INNER JOIN (Orders INNER JOIN ProductsOrders ON
Orders.OrderID = ProductsOrders.OrderID) ON SalesReps.SalesRepID =
Orders.SalesRepID

GROUP BY LastName, Year([OrderDate])
HAVING (((Year([OrderDate]))=2010))
ORDER BY Sum([UnitPrice]*[quantity]) DESC
```

Result:

LastName	Year	CommissionAndBonus
Bernstein	2010	$50,068.30
Simmons	2010	$48,512.70
Vanderback	2010	$43,506.50
Anderson	2010	$40,452.10

Record: ◄ ◄ 10 of 10 ► ►► ► No Filter Search

178. Using partition() for data visualization

Calculate sales volume intervals and count orders included

Discussion:

What if we encounter a request for a visualization of the distribution of our orders? We would want to know how many orders fall between 0 and $50, how many between $50 and $100, how many between $100 and $150, etc. We can provide an answer using the partition() function.

The partition() function has the syntax: Partition(field, beginning number, ending number, interval). For instance, if we want to categorize orders in $50 increments starting at $0 and ending at $500, we can write: Partition(ordertotal, 0, 500, 50).

In this example, we use two fields: "Range" and "Count". Both of these fields are calculated fields. The contents of the Range field are produced by the partition function, and the contents of the Count field are produced by counting the number of orders in each partition according to their order total amount. We can change the parameters of the partition function at will to produce any intervals we want.

A fact to keep in mind about the partition function is that in this example, we defined the boundaries between $0 and $500 with intervals of $50. This does not mean that the partition function will stop at $500. It will stop producing intervals at $500, and from $501 and above, it will put all remaining orders in the same category. We will still know how many orders we have above $501.

Code:

SELECT DISTINCTROW Partition([ordertotal],0, 500, 50) AS Range,

Count(ordertotal) AS Count
FROM Qry_Conditions
GROUP BY Partition([ordertotal],0, 500, 50)

Result:

179. Using switch() with update queries

Update multiple product prices from multiple suppliers conditionally
Discussion:
Now, this is an occasion where a switch() function will show its true and unique power. When we combine it with update statements, we can produce highly effective updates that otherwise would have required multiple update queries to obtain.

In this example, we update about 70 products from ten suppliers, and for each supplier, we apply different update percentages. Those percentages start from 2% all the way up to 11%, as you can see from the SQL code below. By combining the switch() function with the UPDATE statement, we can do everything in one single query. We can save this query and use it every time we need to update our prices. Even if we do not receive price updates for one or some of the suppliers, we can leave the query as is and simply do not use any percentage updates for that supplier. We can just write: ProductUnitPrice = ProductUnitPrice.

Code:

```
UPDATE tbls_Products_Upd
SET ProductUnitPrice =
SWITCH (
supplierid=1,    ProductUnitPrice*(1.1) ,
supplierid=2,    ProductUnitPrice*(1.08),
supplierid=3,    ProductUnitPrice*(1.07) ,
supplierid=4,    ProductUnitPrice*(1.05) ,
supplierid=5,    ProductUnitPrice*(1.03) ,
supplierid=6,    ProductUnitPrice*(1.02) ,
supplierid=7,    ProductUnitPrice*(1.03) ,
supplierid=8,    ProductUnitPrice*(1.07) ,
supplierid=9,    ProductUnitPrice*(1.11) ,
supplierid=10,   ProductUnitPrice*(1.08) ,
)
```

Result:

180.   Using switch() with crosstab queries

Create a crosstab query that calculates order totals for "big" and "small" cities

Discussion:

This time, we have a request from management to calculate sales volumes by year and, at the same time, categorize results by small and big cities in the country. They told us specifically that they want to see combined sales volumes for big cities like New York and Los Angeles and combined sales volumes for every other city in which we do business. This is an excellent occasion to combine the power of the switch function with the flexibility of crosstab queries. Instead of pivoting by the city field as we did in the crosstab queries chapter, we use the switch function right in the PIVOT statement to create city categories of our own imagination and creativity.

Code:
```
TRANSFORM Sum([unitprice]*[quantity]) AS Ordertotal
SELECT Year([OrderDate]) As Year
FROM Qry_Crosstab_Base
GROUP BY Year([OrderDate])
PIVOT
SWITCH(
[city]= 'New York' Or [city]= 'Los Angeles' ,        "BigCities",
[city] <> 'New York' Or 'Los Angeles',               "SmallCities"
)
```

Result:

Year	BigCities	SmallCities
2008	13110	31367
2009	14215	37727
2010	15180	28797

Record: 1 of 3   No Filter   Search

CHAPTER 21
UNION OPERATIONS

The primary goal of the UNION statement is to combine records from multiple data sets. In this respect, you can merge records from two or more SQL statements, from a SQL statement and a table, or from two or more tables. In contrast to popular belief, you can combine records with fields of different data types and sizes in Access 2007. In addition, the fields do not have to be similar in content or name! The number of fields, however, does need to be the same. The UNION operator will return no duplicate records, while the UNION ALL operator will return all records from the combined data sets.

The UNION operator is not just a dull SQL statement that we use to combine records from multiple tables. You will see throughout this chapter that you can combine it with clauses like WHERE, ORDER BY, and GROUP BY, operators like IN, NOT IN, and BETWEEN, and even subqueries for powerful results. Understanding the UNION operator will enable you to perform operations and achieve results that other database users could not even imagine possible.

In this chapter, we will work with two customer tables under the assumption that we have two distribution centers with one as our main center and the other as a regional center. For the most part, customers order from one of the two distribution centers. However, just to complicate our scenario a bit, we do have customers who will order from both. Consequently, we need to pay attention to how customer records are merged in order to exclude duplicate ones.

We will use two tables: The customers table with 201 records and the tbls_customers_un table with 20 records. Fifteen of the customers in the tbls_customers_un table are identical to the customers table, while five are different. The similarities or dissimilarities of data among tables are important for UNION statements, as we shall see in a second.

181. The UNION operator with similar fields

Combine unique customer records from two datasets

Discussion:

In this example, we use a simple UNION statement to combine customer records from the two distribution centers. Notice that the number of customers returned is 206. This is because we combined 201 customers from the first table and 20 from the second. Since 15 customers are identical in both tables, and we use the UNION operator, however, we will only get 206 unique customers. If we used the UNION ALL operator, we would get 221 records.

Code:

```
SELECT lastname, firstname, city, state, zip
FROM customers
UNION
SELECT lastname, firstname, city, state, zip
FROM tbls_customers_un
```

Result:

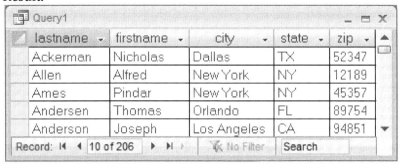

182. The UNION operator with dissimilar fields

Combine customer and supplier records from two different tables

Discussion:

Here, we demonstrate the ability of the UNION statement to combine data from two dissimilar tables. Notice the different field names from the customer and supplier tables. In addition, check the numbers. We get all of the customers from the customers table (201) and all of the suppliers (10) from the suppliers table.

Code:

SELECT lastname, firstname, city, state, zip

FROM customers

UNION

SELECT companyname, contactname, city, state, zip

FROM suppliers

Result:

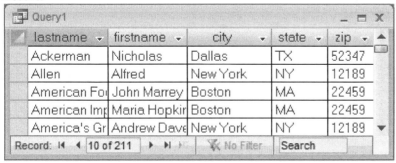

183.   The UNION operator with tables and SQL statements

Combine all customer records from a table and some from a SQL statement

Discussion:

In this example, we will combine all of the records from the customers table with some of the records from the tbls_customers_un table. Essentially, we merge a table and a SQL statement. Notice the absence of a SELECT statement for the customers table and the use of the WHERE clause in the code below:

Code:

TABLE [customers]

UNION

SELECT *

FROM tbls_customers_un

WHERE state='TX'

Result:

184. Using multiple UNION operators

Combine records from two customer tables and a supplier table

Discussion:

We can use UNION to merge records from multiple data sources. In this example, we employ two UNION statements to merge data from three data sources. Notice that while the first two SELECT statements contain identical fields, the third one uses different ones. Also, we must pay attention to our numbers. The first table (customers) contains 201 records, the second (tbls_customers_un) 20, and the third (suppliers) 10. We have a total of 231 records, but our result set contains only 216. This is correct since we have 15 identical customers. Consequently, the final result is 231-15 = 216 records.

Code:

SELECT lastname, firstname, city, state, zip

FROM customers

UNION

SELECT lastname, firstname, city, state, zip

FROM tbls_customers_un

UNION

SELECT companyname, contactname, city, state, zip

FROM suppliers

Result:

lastname	firstname	city	state	zip
Ackerman	Nicholas	Dallas	TX	52347
Allen	Alfred	New York	NY	12189
American Foi	John Marrey	Boston	MA	22459
American Imp	Maria Hopkir	Boston	MA	22459
America's Gr	Andrew Dave	New York	NY	12189

Record: 10 of 216   No Filter   Search

185.   The UNION ALL operator

Combine customer records from two data sources and allow duplicates to appear

Discussion:

The UNION operator will exclude duplicate records. Suppose we want to combine two lists, but we also want to include duplicates. For this purpose, we need to use the UNION ALL operator. Have a look at the number of records returned. In this case, it should be 201 + 20 for a total of 221, and this is exactly what we get. (Remember that we have 201 records in the customer table and 20 in the tbls_customers_un).

Code:

```
SELECT lastname, firstname, city, state, zip
FROM customers
UNION ALL
SELECT lastname, firstname, city, state, zip
FROM tbls_customers_un
```

Result:

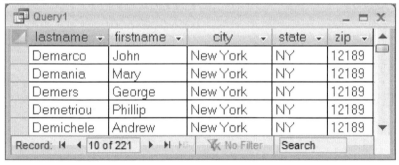

lastname	firstname	city	state	zip
Demarco	John	New York	NY	12189
Demania	Mary	New York	NY	12189
Demers	George	New York	NY	12189
Demetriou	Phillip	New York	NY	12189
Demichele	Andrew	New York	NY	12189

Record: 10 of 221   No Filter   Search

186.   Using UNION with ORDER BY

Sort customer records correctly when using UNION

Discussion:

The ORDER BY clause should be used at the end of the whole SQL statement when using UNION operators, not after the individual SQL statements.

Code:

```
SELECT lastname, firstname, city, state, zip
FROM customers
UNION
SELECT lastname, firstname, city, state, zip
FROM tbls_customers_un
ORDER BY lastname
```

Result:

lastname	firstname	city	state	zip
Ackerman	Nicholas	Dallas	TX	52347
Allen	Alfred	New York	NY	12189
Ames	Pindar	New York	NY	45357
Andersen	Thomas	Orlando	FL	89754
Anderson	Joseph	Los Angeles	CA	94851

Record: 10 of 206   No Filter   Search

187.   Using UNION with WHERE

Create customer lists with filtering criteria using WHERE

Discussion:

In this example, notice the use of the WHERE clause in each individual SELECT statement. We can absolutely use multiple WHERE clauses to get exactly what we need from the individual data sets. In this example, we wanted to get only customers from New York from the first and customers from Texas from the second.

Code:

SELECT lastname, firstname, city, state, zip

FROM customers

WHERE state = 'NY'

UNION

SELECT lastname, firstname, city, state, zip

FROM tbls_customers_un

WHERE state ='TX'

ORDER BY state

Result:

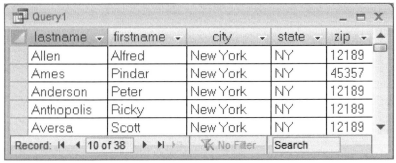

188. Using UNION with IN and NOT IN

Create customer lists with filtering criteria using IN and NOT IN

Discussion:

We can perform detailed filtering using the WHERE clause and the IN or NOT IN operators within each individual SELECT statement in this UNION operation. Notice that we can apply criteria with different operators on different fields. We might have used the WHERE clause with the AND operator in the first SELECT and the IN operator in the second. In addition, we could have applied some criteria on the city field in the first SELECT and some criteria on the state field in the second.

Code:

```
SELECT lastname, firstname, city, state, zip
FROM customers
WHERE city IN('New York', 'Los Angeles')
UNION
SELECT lastname, firstname, city, state, zip
FROM tbls_customers_un
WHERE city IN('Dallas', 'Miami', 'Orlando', 'Ontario')
ORDER BY lastname
```

Result:

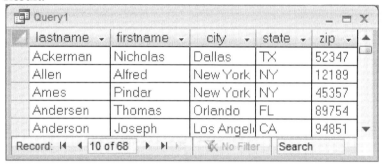

lastname	firstname	city	state	zip
Ackerman	Nicholas	Dallas	TX	52347
Allen	Alfred	New York	NY	12189
Ames	Pindar	New York	NY	45357
Andersen	Thomas	Orlando	FL	89754
Anderson	Joseph	Los Angeli	CA	94851

Record: 10 of 68

189.   Using UNION with BETWEEN

Find customers in a certain zip code range who ordered from multiple distribution centers

Discussion:

We can use the BETWEEN clause to filter results in UNION statements. As soon as we satisfy the basic requirements of a UNION statement, we can filter records as we please using any filtering clauses such as LIKE, "=", or BETWEEN. Notice in this example that we must use the cLng() number conversion function (chapter 24) to convert zip codes to numbers since in the original table, they are stored as text. Otherwise, the BETWEEN operator will not work since it cannot find text ranges. We can use any conversion functions we want, however, with no problems in UNION statements.

Code:

```
SELECT lastname, firstname, city, state, zip
FROM customers
WHERE cLng(zip) BETWEEN 12000 AND 12999
UNION
SELECT lastname, firstname, city, state, zip
FROM tbls_customers_un
WHERE cLng(zip) BETWEEN 12000 AND 12999
ORDER BY lastname
```

Result:

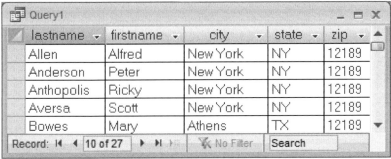

190. A trick with UNION and the aggregate function count()

Display total customer numbers dynamically

Discussion:

Here, we use a trick to display all of the customer records from the customers table and a total row at the end of the recordset. We can do this by using a single SQL statement and UNION. Notice that in the second SQL statement we use quotes instead of fields to satisfy the UNION requirement of same field numbers in both statements. In addition, notice that we start the name of the first field of the second SQL statement with a "z", which has no other meaning but to force the total row to appear last in the recordset. Finally, for our trick to succeed, we need to use the ORDER BY clause on the first field of the first SQL statement.

Code:

SELECT lastname, firstname, city, state, zip, CustomerID
FROM customers
UNION
SELECT
'zTotal customer count', '', '', '', '', Count(CustomerID)
FROM customers
ORDER BY lastname ASC

Result:

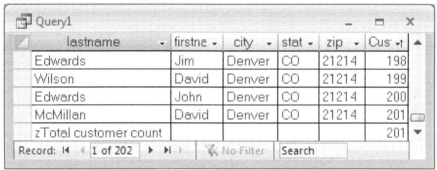

191. Using UNION with SELECT INTO

Combine customer data from multiple tables and save the combined dataset dynamically in a different table

Discussion:

This is a useful trick to get data from multiple data sources and save it in a different table. We can use SELECT INTO to pull this off, but we must pay attention! The first SQL statement may naturally come to mind, but it will not work. We need to use a subquery (chapter 30) as can be seen in the second SQL statement. Pay attention to the number of records. It has to be 206 (201 from the first table and 5 from the second) since we are asking for unique records to be moved. If we want to move everything, we can use UNION ALL.

Code:

Will not work

SELECT lastname, firstname, city, state, zip INTO UnionTable

FROM customers

UNION

SELECT lastname, firstname, city, state, zip

FROM tbls_customers_un

Will work

SELECT lastname, firstname, city, state, zip INTO tempTable

FROM

(SELECT lastname, firstname, city, state, zip

FROM customers

UNION

SELECT lastname, firstname, city, state, zip

FROM tbls_customers_un

)

Result:

192.   Using UNION with INSERT INTO

Combine records from multiple data sources, filter them, and append them into an existing table

Discussion:

There are occasions in which we need to combine data from multiple tables and append it in an existing table. We can use INSERT INTO and UNION to accomplish these tasks. The table "tempTable_un" used in this example needs to exist before we run the SQL statement. Also, notice the use of the WHERE clause through which we can transfer the records we want.

Code:

```
INSERT INTO tempTable_un (lastname, firstname, city, state, zip)
SELECT lastname, firstname, city, state, zip
FROM
(SELECT lastname, firstname, city, state, zip
FROM customers
WHERE state = 'NY'
UNION
SELECT lastname, firstname, city, state, zip
FROM tbls_customers_un
WHERE state = 'NY'
)
```

Result:

193.   Using UNION with GROUP BY within each SELECT statement

Combine customer data from all distribution centers, count the totals, and designate in the query the center they came from

Discussion:

Here, we use a number of tricks and functions to arrive at the result we need. First, notice that we use a GROUP BY clause in both SQL statements in the query. Second, we use the count() function to get the number of customers by state. Third, we create a field of our own ("Main" and "Regional") in the beginning of each of the two SQL statements so that we can show customer numbers according to distribution center. Finally, we use the ORDER BY clause to present results by state for easy comparison of numbers.

Code:

```
SELECT "Main" As DisCenter, state, count(CustomerID) AS Customers
FROM customers
GROUP BY state
UNION
SELECT "Regional" As Center, state, Count(CustomerID) AS Customers
FROM tbls_customers_un
GROUP BY state
ORDER BY STATE
```

Result:

DisCenter	state	Customers
Main	CO	13
Main	DC	12
Main	FL	21
Regional	FL	5
Main	MA	14
Main	NY	31
Regional	NY	4

Record: 11 of 14   No Filter

194. Using UNION with GROUP BY outside each SELECT statement

Combine customer data from all distribution centers, count the totals, and group results by state

Discussion:

In this example, the GROUP BY clause produces combined results from each state regardless of distribution center. Unlike what we did in the previous example, we first combine the data and then, use the GROUP BY clause. Notice the use of the subquery with the UNION operator that enables us to GROUP results from the two data sets.

Code:

SELECT state, count(customerid) as Customers
FROM

(SELECT state, CustomerID
FROM customers
UNION
SELECT state, CustomerID
FROM tbls_customers_un
)

GROUP BY state
ORDER BY STATE

Result:

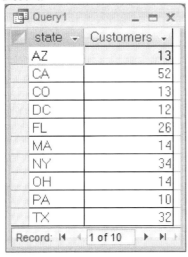

state	Customers
AZ	13
CA	52
CO	13
DC	12
FL	26
MA	14
NY	34
OH	14
PA	10
TX	32

Record: 1 of 10

195. Using UNION with two subqueries to filter records for aggregations

Compare customer data from two tables only for states existing in both tables

Discussion:

Our goal this time is to compare customer numbers from both distribution centers, but we only want to see customer states from the "Main" center for which a corresponding state exists in the "regional" center. We need a subquery in the first SELECT statement to achieve the desired output. The subquery in the first SELECT statement will search for matching records in the table in the second SELECT statement.

Code:
SELECT "Main" As DisCenter, state, count(CustomerID) AS Customers
FROM customers
WHERE State in (SELECT state from tbls_customers_un)
GROUP BY state
UNION
SELECT "Regional" As Center, state, Count(CustomerID) AS Customers
FROM tbls_customers_un
GROUP BY state
ORDER BY STATE

Result:

DisCenter	state	Customers
Main	CA	48
Regional	CA	4
Main	FL	21
Regional	FL	5
Main	NY	31
Regional	NY	4
Main	TX	25
Regional	TX	7

Record: ⏮ ◀ 8 of 8 ▶ ⏭ ▸ No Filter

CHAPTER 22
DUPLICATE, ORPHANED, and UNRELATED RECORDS

This chapter focuses on four specific learning goals: The identification of duplicate, orphaned, related, and unrelated records. Orphaned and duplicate records will affect your database integrity, while related and unrelated records will affect your business decisions.

Orphaned records occur when there are no primary key values for corresponding foreign key values in a one-to-many relationship. For example, in a relationship between customers and orders, you might have orders without corresponding customers in the customers table. This scenario can occur if referential integrity for this relationship is off (chapter 3). This will allow a user to delete a customer without any warning that there are existing orders for this customer. Alternatively, it might allow a user to enter order information without first entering a customer.

We need to have referential integrity on in order to avoid the occurrence of orphaned records. Yet, what happens when we already have orphaned records in the database? There are two solutions with orphaned records. The first is to delete orphaned records from the database. However, to eliminate orphaned records, we first need to find them. In this chapter, there will be plenty of examples to locate orphaned records.

The second solution is to keep orphaned records such as orders in the database, but in this case, we need to enter their corresponding customer information. In any case, we must be able to retrieve orphaned records.

A second common occurrence in business databases is duplicate records. In this chapter, you will learn several techniques to isolate and deal with duplicate records, which are not, by the way, synonymous with identical records. Two customer records might be duplicates even if they have the same name but different address information. So, you will learn how to find duplicate records based on the values of one, two, or multiple fields.

A third case involves unrelated records. For example, we might have customers in the database who have not placed an order for quite some time. These customers have no relations in the orders table. This is a business and not a database problem. However, we need to act, and we have two choices for inactive customers. The first is to use a marketing campaign to entice them to start buying again. If this is not feasible, we might want to delete them from the database or move them to a historical customer table. To delete or move these records, we need to be able to find them first. We will explore how to find unrelated records such as customers without orders in general or without orders for a specific period.

The fourth scenario is related records. We might want to know how many customers placed orders over a period of a year, month, or quarter. In other words, we want to know how many customers have related order entries in the orders table. In this chapter, you will learn how to quickly identify these customers to increase the effectiveness of your business operations.

Finally, so that you can check your numbers, you will use the table named tbls_orders, which contains a number of orphaned and duplicate records. Specifically, the records with OrderDd = 8, 45, 254, 820, 993 are duplicate records. In addition, there are two records with null OrderIDs, which I put in to make our work a bit more complicated.

SECTION 1 – DUPLICATE RECORDS

196.   Find duplicate records in a table based on the values of one field

Find duplicate customer orders based on the value of the orderID
Discussion:
In this example, we are looking for records in the tbls_Orders table that have the same value for the OrderID field. In addition, we use the count(*) function to calculate the number of instances of duplicate records. We can use the code below to look for duplicate values for any field. We will just replace the OrderID field with the field on which we want to search for duplicate values. Remember that this example will give us duplicate field values and not necessarily duplicate records. Though the OrderID values are the same, the rest of the fields in the returned records might have different values. Still, it is very useful to know how to search for duplicate values on one field. As you can see from the result set, two records have null values for the OrderID. In addition, there

are two instances of duplicate records for OrderIDs with values 8, 45, 254, and 820. Finally, the OrderId with value 993 appears in three records in the table.

Code:

SELECT OrderID, Count(*) AS NumberofDuplicates
FROM tbls_Orders
GROUP BY OrderID
HAVING count(*)>1

Result:

197.   Find duplicate records in a table based on the values of two fields

Find duplicate customer orders based on the values of OrderID and CustomerID

Discussion:

In this example, we are looking for duplicate records based on the values of OrderID and CustomerID. If the values of the OrderID and CustomerID are the same for at least two records, they will appear in the result set as duplicates. In addition, the count(*) function is used to calculate the number of records with identical OrderID and CustomerID values. We can replace the two fields used in this example with any fields on which we would like to look for duplicate values. Keep in mind that while two records might have matching values for two fields, this does not necessarily mean that they have identical values for the rest of their fields. This code will allow us to locate potential duplicate records based on the values of two fields. We need to examine the individual records to verify that they are indeed duplicates.

Code:

```
SELECT OrderID, CustomerID, Count(*) AS NumberofDuplicates
FROM tbls_Orders
GROUP BY OrderID, CustomerID
HAVING count(*)>1
```

Result:

OrderID	CustomerID	NumberofDuplicates
8	71	2
45	93	2
254	198	2
820	46	2
993	99	3

Record: 1 of 5 — No Filter — Search

198.   Find duplicate records in a table based on the values of multiple fields

Find duplicate customer orders based on the values of multiple fields

Discussion:

In this example, we are looking for duplicate records based on the values of eight fields. In other words, if the values of eight fields of at least two records are identical, those records will appear as duplicates. Of course, with eight identical values, two records will most probably be duplicate entries. Notice that there are two identical records for each OrderID with values 8, 45, 254, and 820, while there are three identical records with OrderID = 993.

Code:

SELECT Count(*) AS NumberofDuplicates, OrderID, CustomerID, SalesRepID, ShipperID, OrderDate, RequiredDate, ShippedDate, ShippingCost

FROM tbls_Orders

GROUP BY OrderID, CustomerID, SalesRepID, ShipperID, OrderDate, RequiredDate, ShippedDate, ShippingCost
HAVING count(*)>1

Result:

Numbe ▾	OrderID ▾	CustomerID ▾	SalesRepID ▾	ShipperID ▾	OrderDate ▾
2	8	71	3	1	4/1/2010
2	45	93	1	3	10/23/2008
2	254	198	3	2	7/15/2008
2	820	46	8	1	9/4/2010
3	993	99	10	2	10/14/2008

Record: ◄ ◄ 5 of 5 ► ►► ▾ No Filter   Search

199.   Find and display all duplicate records in a table

Find and display all duplicate records in the Orders table
Discussion:

In the previous examples, we were able to find duplicate records in the table but display only one instance from each in the result set. There are cases, however, in which we will want to display all instances from all duplicate records. We can achieve this goal by using a subquery. In this example, we will display all instances of all duplicate records based on the values of the OrderID field, or put another way, based on the values of one field.

Code:

```
SELECT *
FROM tbls_Orders WHERE OrderID IN(
SELECT OrderID
FROM tbls_Orders
GROUP BY OrderID
HAVING count(*)>1)
ORDER BY OrderID
```

Result:

OrderID	CustomerID	SalesRepIC	ShipperID	OrderDate
8	71	3	1	4/1/2010
8	71	3	1	4/1/2010
45	93	1	3	10/23/2008
45	93	1	3	10/23/2008
254	198	3	2	7/15/2008
254	198	3	2	7/15/2008
820	46	8	1	9/4/2010
820	46	8	1	9/4/2010
993	99	10	2	10/14/2008
993	99	10	2	10/14/2008
993	99	10	2	10/14/2008

Record: 1 of 11   No Filter   Search

SECTION 2 – ORPHANED RECORDS

200.   What are orphaned records and how to deal with them

In the figure below, there are five orders in the Orders table with OrderIDs from 1 to 5. For the first four orders, there are corresponding customers in the Customers table. For orders with OrderID=5, there does not exist a corresponding customer in the database. This is an order that belongs to no one. The record in the Orders table with OrderID=5 is called an orphaned record.

CUSTOMERS	
CustID	Name
1	John
2	Mary
3	George
4	Stacy

ORDERS		
OrderID	CustID	OrderDate
1	2	9/10/2009
2	2	10/10/2010
3	1	11/10/2010
4	3	11/11/2010
5	7	11/15/2010

A reason for this might be that when the database was created and relationships established, referential integrity was not turned on. The immediate consequence is that a user of the database deleted the customer with CustomerID=7 either by mistake or on purpose. Although the customer record is gone, his or her orders are still in the database, useless and compromising data integrity. Another reason might be that a user received an order from a new customer. The correct process would be to check if the customer exists and if it does not, enter the customer information first. Then, enter order data for that particular customer. If referential integrity is off, this scenario is possible. To avoid orphaned records, referential integrity should be on for a relationship between two tables.

201. Find orphaned records using a subquery

Find orders for which there are no customers using a subquery
Discussion:
Let us assume that we want to turn on referential integrity for the relationship between the Customers and Orders tables (chapter 3, 23). If Access 2007 does not allow us to do this, our first action should be to look for orphaned records in the Orders table or in the table in general in the many side of the relationship. We can use the code below to do just that. In this example, we use the tbls_Orders table since in the original Orders table, there are no orphaned records. As you can see in the result set, there are three orders (OrderID= 1500, 1501, and 1502) that came up as orphaned records. This in turn means that the customers with CustomerID values of 250, 251, and 252 do not exist in the Customers table. If we open the customers table, we will not find any customers with these CustomerID values.

Code:

```
SELECT *
FROM tbls_Orders
WHERE CustomerID
NOT IN (SELECT CustomerID from Customers)
```

Result:

OrderID	CustomerID	SalesRepl	ShipperID	OrderDate
1500	250	11	2	1/20/20
1501	251	12	2	11/18/20
1502	252	14	3	2/5/20

Record: 1 of 3   No Filter   Search

202.   Find orphaned records using a join

Find orders for which there are no customers using a join

Discussion:

There is a second and faster way to locate orphaned records in a table. Specifically, we can use a LEFT join (chapter 29, **Error! Reference source not found.**) between Customers and tbls_Orders to locate any orphaned records in the tbls_Orders table. As you can see, the result set is identical to the one using a subquery in the previous example.

Code:

```
SELECT *
FROM tbls_Orders
LEFT JOIN Customers ON tbls_Orders.[CustomerID] = Customers.[CustomerID]
WHERE (((Customers.CustomerID) Is Null));
```

Result:

OrderID	CustomerID	SalesRepl	ShipperID	OrderDate
1500	250	11	2	1/20/20
1501	251	12	2	11/18/20
1502	252	14	3	2/5/20

Record: 1 of 3   No Filter   Search

203.   Delete orphaned records using a subquery

Delete orders for which there are no customers using a subquery

Discussion:

We can use a subquery to find and delete orphaned records in one step. In the code below, we use the DELETE statement to delete orders in the tbls_Orders table for which there are no customers in the customers table. The subquery will isolate CustomerID values in the tbls_Orders table for which there are no corresponding CustomerID values in the Customers table. Notice that the CustomerID is the primary key in the Customers table and the foreign key in the tbls_Orders table.

Code:

```
DELETE
FROM tbls_Orders
WHERE CustomerID
NOT IN (SELECT CustomerID FROM Customers)
```

Result:

204.   Delete orphaned records using a join

Delete orders for which there are no customers using a join

Discussion:

We can also use a LEFT join to isolate and delete orphaned records in the tbls_Orders table. Notice the WHERE clause in the code below which looks for CustomerID values in the LEFT JOIN with a null value, i.e. CustomerID or foreign key values in the tbls_Orders table for which no primary key values exist in the customers table. Joins work faster than

231

subqueries especially on indexed fields, and while they are more complicated, their use might well be justified in cases with many records. However, this does not mean that a join will always be faster than a subquery. The bottom line is that we have the option to isolate and delete orphaned records using joins.

Code:
DELETE tbls_Orders.*
FROM tbls_Orders
LEFT JOIN Customers ON tbls_Orders.[CustomerID] = Customers.[CustomerID]
WHERE (((Customers.CustomerID) Is Null))

Result:

SECTION 3 – UNRELATED RECORDS

The knowledge to locate unrelated records is fundamental in database applications. It allows us to reply to questions such as: How many customers have not placed any orders? How many students have not taken classes this semester? What sales reps did not have sales last week? As you might have realized, these questions refer to records at the one part of the relationship between two tables. So, we are looking for customers who have no orders (maybe over a period of time) knowing that there is a one-to-many relationship between customers and orders. Keep in mind that finding customers without orders is not a problematic situation when it comes to database integrity; it is simply a business fact. However, finding orders without customers represents a database integrity problem, and we call these orphaned records. The conclusion is that we are looking for unrelated records between two tables for business purposes and for orphaned records for database integrity purposes.

205. Find unrelated records using a subquery

Find customers for whom there are no orders using a subquery

Discussion:

In this example, we use a subquery with the NOT IN operator to find customers who do not have any orders. We are looking for records in the customers table that have no related records in the Orders table. In other words, we are looking for CustomerID values (1, 2, 3 etc.) in the Customers table, which do not exist in the Orders table. Put in yet another way, we are looking for primary key values (CustomerID) in the customers table with no corresponding foreign key values (CustomerIDs) in the Orders table. The code appears below:

Code:

```
SELECT *
FROM Customers
WHERE CustomerID
NOT IN (SELECT CustomerID from tbls_Orders)
```

Result:

206. Find unrelated records using a subquery and criteria

Find customers for whom there are no orders using date criteria

Discussion:

In the previous example, you learned how to identify customers without orders for all sales years in the database. This is excellent knowledge, but in actual business practice, you will need some additional criteria to derive insightful pieces of information. For example, we might want to know what customers have not placed any orders in the last year, quarter, month, or even week. Alternatively, we might want to know what

233

customers from NY have not placed any orders in the last two months. It is possible to use criteria to extract these amazing pieces of information fast and efficiently. In this example, we are looking for customers who have not placed any orders in 2010. As you can see from the result set, we have 44 such customers. Of course, we can use the vast arsenal of date functions in the upcoming chapter 26 to extract any period we feel we need to look into.

Code:
```
SELECT *
FROM Customers
WHERE CustomerID NOT IN
(SELECT CustomerID
FROM tbls_Orders
WHERE OrderDate BETWEEN #1/1/2010# AND #12/31/2010#)
```

Result:

CustomerID	FirstName	LastName	Address
1	John	Demarco	11 Lark Street
5	Andrew	Demichele	14 Glandel Ave
6	Michael	Demizio	23 Grove Rd
19	Erin	Erin	28 Karrie Terrace

Record: 10 of 44

SECTION 4 – RELATED RECORDS

207.   Find related records using a subquery

Find customers who placed orders

Discussion:

There will be occasions in your work in which you will need to find related records. In other words, you might want to find customers who placed orders, suppliers who sent raw materials, or products that sold some units. We can achieve this task by using a subquery. In this example, we are looking for customers who placed orders, such as which of the 201 customers in the customers table actually placed orders. Since we know from previous examples that out of the 201 customers, 11 never placed any orders, we would expect to retrieve 190 records. This is exactly the result from the following code.

Remember that we can add additional criteria to identify customers who placed orders in certain periods such as years, quarters, or months, as we will see in the next example.

Code:

```
SELECT *
FROM Customers
WHERE CustomerID
IN (SELECT CustomerID from tbls_Orders)
```

Result:

CustomerID	FirstName	LastName	Address
1	John	Demarco	11 Lark Street
2	Mary	Demania	12 Madison Ave
3	George	Demers	23 New Scotlan Ave
4	Phillip	Demetriou	22 Academy Road

Record: 10 of 190   No Filter   Search

208.   Find related records using a subquery and criteria

Find customers who placed orders during the 4th quarter of 2010
Discussion:

In this scenario, we are looking for customers who placed orders in the 4th quarter of 2010. Notice that we use two date functions, datepart() and year(), to extract the quarter and year out of the OrderDate field respectively. Using the subquery and the two date functions, we are able to extract exactly the information we need about our customers. This list of customers can definitely help in our marketing and promotional campaigns, and we can retrieve it in seconds.

Code:

```
SELECT *
FROM Customers
WHERE CustomerID
IN (SELECT CustomerID from tbls_Orders WHERE
DatePart("q",[OrderDate]) = 4 AND  year(OrderDate) = 2010)
```

Result:

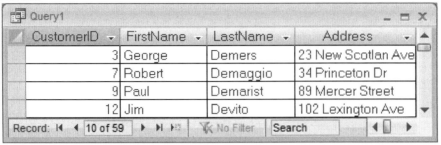

CHAPTER 23
WORKING WITH NULLS

There are three concepts you need in order to understand null values in full: First, a zero (0) value is not a null value. It means that there is a value, and it is zero. Second, a zero-length string, also called an empty string, is not a null value. It means that there should be a value, but there is none. Third, a null value means that we do not know whether there should be a value or not.

Zero-length strings and null values appear as empty cells in Access 2007. We have no way of distinguishing which cell actually has a null value and which one has an empty string in it; they both appear empty. Do not be concerned about this because in our examples, we will see how to take care of this situation. The best way to avoid tricky and problematical situations with nulls and zero-length values is to avoid them altogether. When designing a new database, we can assign default values to fields that users might leave blank. For example, for a customer middle name, we can set a default value of "NA" when none is entered. For existing databases, we can run effective update statements (chapter 27 in this book) to replace null and empty string values with default values.

Null values will affect your calculations in aggregate functions, searching expressions, union operations, and will leave doubts about the validity of your results. Let us explore in detail all of the scenarios around nulls and the ways to eliminate them. For this chapter, so that you can verify the effects of null values and zero-length strings, I have created a table called "ProductsN" which contains only ten records. Using these ten records, you will be able to verify your calculations and learn to work with nulls effectively. Then, you will be able to apply the same techniques for thousands or hundreds of thousands of records.

209.   Looking for nulls using criteria

Find products whose stock keeping unit codes (SKUs) are null

Discussion:

Our task is to find all products for which the SKU code is missing. Of course, with only ten products, we can just eye the table and tell right away that there are four SKU codes missing. Let us try to write the code to retrieve them and see if the database agrees. In this example, we are looking for null values using the criterion "is null" in the WHERE clause, and as you can see, the SQL statement returned four records.

Code:

```
SELECT productID, productname, productunitprice, SKU
FROM tbls_ProductsN
WHERE SKU IS NULL
```

Result:

210.   Looking for nulls using the IsNull() function

Display all products to find the ones whose SKU is null

Discussion:

The isnull() function provides us with additional functionality in looking for nulls. Specifically, it will produce a true or false value for all of the entries in the field we are inspecting. In this example, we use isnull() to check the SKU field for nulls. For every value in the SKU field, we will get a true or false response from the database. In Access 2007, the value 0 means false, and the value -1 means true. In the following datasheet, we will get -1 for the four records with null values.

Code:

SELECT ProductID, productname, productunitprice, IsNull(SKU) AS SKUCheck
FROM tbls_ProductsN

Result:

211.   Looking for nulls using the iif() function

Display the word "null" for products with null SKUs

Discussion:

You can use the iif() function to find nulls in a field and obtain more readable results. The iif() function in this example will display the word "null" for every null value it finds in the SKU field. In this particular example, we indicate null values by the word "null", but we could have used "unknown", "empty", or anything else we would have liked.

Code:

SELECT ProductID, productname, productunitprice, IIf(IsNull([SKU]),"NULL",
[SKU]) AS SKUCheck
FROM tbls_ProductsN
ORDER BY SKU

Result:

ProductID ▾	productname ▾	productunitpri ▾	SKUCheck ▾
3	Banana Chips (Z	30	NULL
4	Berry Cherry (Zer	30	NULL
71	Almonds (Null)		NULL
72	Almonds Roaste		NULL

Record: ◄ ◄ 10 of 10 ► ►I ►☐ ☒ No Filter Search

212.   Calculations with nulls

Calculate product inventory subtotals where some values are nulls
Discussion:
In this example, we want to multiply the ProductUnitPrice with the QuantityPerUnit to calculate the value of our inventory by product. In the ProductsN table, there are blank values for both the ProductUnitPrice and the QuantityPerUnit fields. Let's see how our result set will come up.

Code:

SELECT productID, productname, (productunitprice*quantityperunit) As
Subtotal
FROM tbls_ProductsN
ORDER BY subtotal DESC

Result:
As you can see, for the records with null values for either one of the two multiplied fields, there will be no result. This will have consequences in our inventory results since at least for productid=72, we know that we do have 25 units on hand. Since their price is missing, the inventory report will be erroneous. To avoid this situation, we need to make it a habit to look for nulls before we do any calculations.

productID	productname	Subtotal
3	Banana Chips (Zero-Length)	360
4	Berry Cherry (Zero-Length)	450
5	California Original Pistachio	435
6	Choice Apricots - 16 oz. Bag	800
7	Cran Raisin Mix in 17 oz. Ba	372
8	Dried Blueberries - 1 lb. Ba	280
9	Dried Cranberries - 34 oz.	525
10	Raw Sunflower Seeds in 19	625
71	Almonds (Null)	
72	Almonds Roasted (Null)	

Record: 10 of 10   No Filter   Search

213.   Using sum() with null values

Calculate the total inventory value

Discussion:

The situation becomes even worse when we use aggregate functions since we cannot see the empty field values to realize we have missing data. When aggregate functions encounter null values, they will leave them out of the calculations altogether and report only on known values.

In this case, products with productID 71 and 72 will be missing from the calculations. For productid=72, we have no quantity or price data, and we do not know if this is correct or not. For productid=71, we know that we have a quantity on hand = 25 but no price, and our results are definitely wrong. The best way to avoid the above situations is to check the data for nulls and make every effort to complete the values that are missing.

Code:

SELECT SUM(productunitprice*quantityperunit) As Total
FROM tbls_ProductsN

Result:

214.   Using count() with nulls

Count the number of products in the inventory correctly

Discussion:

As I have mentioned countless times in this book, our primary goal is to rid the database of nulls by replacing them with concrete values in our tables such as "NA" for text fields or zeros for numeric ones. Now, our goal is to calculate the number of products in our inventory table. If we apply the count() function on the SKU field, we will get six records. This is because the four null values in the SKU field have not been counted!

Code:

```
SELECT Count(SKU) As CountSKUs
FROM tbls_ProductsN
```

Result:

Discussion:

My recommendation to this problem is to use count() or other arithmetic functions on fields that, by default, do not allow nulls in their values. For example, we could use count() on the ProductID field which is the primary key of the table.

Code:

```
SELECT Count(ProductID) As CountSKUs
FROM tbls_ProductsN
```

Result:

Discussion:

Another solution for correct counts is to use the count(*) function, which will return the actual number of records in the table independently of any null values in any field.

Code:

SELECT Count(*) As CountRecords
FROM tbls_ProductsN

Result:

215. Leaving nulls out of the result set

Find products for which the SKU code is not null

Discussion:

We can obtain a list of products that do not contain null values in the SKU field by using the IS NOT NULL clause. The IS NOT NULL clause is not a panacea to null values problems. The real solution would be to use UPDATE statements to replace null values with concrete values such as "NA" for text or zeros for numeric fields. As we expected, the SQL statement returned six records with non-null values for the SKU field.

Code:

SELECT productID, productname, productunitprice, SKU
FROM tbls_ProductsN
WHERE SKU IS NOT NULL

Result:

```
┌──────────────────────────────────────────────────────────────────┐
│ ▦  Query1                                              _  ▢  X    │
├──────────────────────────────────────────────────────────────────┤
│ ▨  productID ▾  productname ▾  productunitprice ▾    SKU    ▾  ▲  │
│        5  California Original            29  PDK-2347          ▤  │
│        6  Choice Apricots -              32  PDK-2347            │
│        7  Cran Raisin Mix in             31  PDKLS-1889          │
│        8  Dried Blueberries              28  PDKLS-1889        ▼  │
├──────────────────────────────────────────────────────────────────┤
│ Record: ◄ ◄ │6 of 6│  ► ►I ►☰   ▼ No Filter   │Search│           │
└──────────────────────────────────────────────────────────────────┘
```

216.   Using the NZ() function to deal with null values

Calculate inventory replenishment amounts

Discussion:

Our task this time is to replenish our inventory. We need to know how many units of a product we need to order so that we will have enough to operate. We must take into consideration the units we have on hand, how many we have already ordered, and the reorder level that will trigger more orders. All of this information is available in the "tbls_ProductsN" table.

We need to add the units in stock to the units we have already ordered and subtract the result from the reorder level amount which is preset. This is easier said than done because the awful null values will get in the way again. Of course, with ten records in the table, we can easily check for null values, but with 10,000 product records, we will not be able to tell. If we try to do the calculations while ignoring the presence of nulls, we will end up with the database unable to produce results for 40% of our products—four out of ten!

Code:

SELECT ProductID, (ReorderLevel-(UnitsInstock+UnitsOnOrder)) AS
UnitsToOrder
FROM tbls_ProductsN

Result:

Some people resort to sorting as a way of dealing with null values. This is impractical and amateurish for solid business databases, as well as an obstacle to automation. Even if you find them, what are you going to do with them? Thankfully, in Access 2007, there is a function for situations like this one, and it is called the nz() function. The nz() function has two arguments as shown below:

Nz(field, value of field if it is null)

For the "value of field if it is null" argument, we can put any value we want to like 0, 1, 2, etc. for numeric fields or "hi my name is John" for text fields. In this particular example, the nz() function will replace the null values of the fields unitsinstock and unitsonorder with zeros so that the calculations can go ahead. Please notice from the result set that the database was now able to produce results for 100% of our records.

Code:

SELECT ProductID, (ReorderLevel-(nz(UnitsInstock,0)+nz(UnitsOnOrder,0))) AS UnitsToOrder

FROM tbls_ProductsN

Result:

217.   Permanently replace nulls using an update statement

Use UPDATE to replace null values in the SKU field

Discussion:

We can replace the null values in the SKU field by using the UPDATE statement with the WHERE clause and the IS NULL expression. As you can see from the result set, the database is asking to replace the four existing null values in the SKU field. (Check chapter 27 for an in depth look at the update statement).

Code:

```
UPDATE tbls_ProductsN
SET SKU = "NA"
WHERE SKU IS NULL
```

Result:

Microsoft Office Access   ☒

⚠   **You are about to update 4 row(s).**

Once you click Yes, you can't use the Undo command to reverse the changes.
Are you sure you want to update these records?

[Yes]   [No]

CHAPTER 24
TYPE CONVERSION FUNCTIONS

Type conversion functions are an excellent tool in the arsenal of the database power user and developer. Unfortunately, they usually go underneath the radar screen of even advanced users because their functionality is not apparent or because they use other methods to accomplish the same result. For instance, to convert a column from a text data type to a column of number data type, some users go to the table design view and force a change there.

There are three problems with this approach: First, by changing the field data type forcefully, data might be lost. Second, if something goes wrong, there is no turning back to the original data. Third, Access might function as the front-end to enterprise databases like MSSQL, Oracle, or IBM DB2, in which case the administrators will not allow a change to the design of the back-end database.

The solution is to use type conversion functions to change data types on the fly without affecting table design. In Access 2007, the range of type conversion functions at our disposal are: CBool(), CByte(), CCur(), CDate(), CDbl(), CInt(), CLng(), CSng(), and CStr(). We will start by examining the conversion functions CByte(), CInt(), CLng(), CSng(), and CDbl(). All of these functions relate to the number data type in Access 2007, and we use them for two purposes: First, to change numeric data from one format to another such as to change a numeric field from an integer to a double size. Second, to convert text data to numeric data. For instance, suppose a developer created a table and assigned the "Quantity" as a text field. If we later need to make calculations on this field, we first need to convert it to a numeric data type.

Let's say we have a table field called "PartWeight": Although the data type is number, you can see from the figure below that you have various choices for its size. Shifting dynamically between these choices of Byte, Integer, Single, Double, or Decimal is exactly the job of conversion functions like CByte(), CInt(), CLng(), CSng(), and CDbl().

218. The CByte() function

Convert numbers to byte size

Discussion:

The CByte() function will convert any numbers with decimals such as doubles to a number between 0 and 255, which is one byte according to extended ASCII. There are few occasions when we need this transformation. Suppose, however, that we have a column or a number that we want to convert to a byte.

Code:

SELECT cbyte(245.2346) as Number_Byte

Result:

If we try to use cbyte() on a number bigger than 255, we get an overflow error, and the conversion is not possible. Of course, we can dynamically use the cbyte() function on a column without affecting the table design as the code indicates below:

Code:

SELECT cbyte(unitprice) as ByteNumber
FROM ProductsOrders

Result:

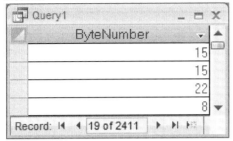

219.   The CInt() function

Convert numbers to integer size

Discussion:

An integer number size will hold numbers between -32,768 to 32,767 and with no decimals. Consequently, if we want to convert the number 234.2345 to an integer value, we can write:

Code:

SELECT cint(234.2345) as Number_Integer

Result:

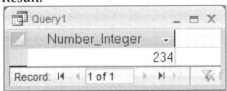

220.   The CLng() function

Convert expressions to long integer numbers

Discussion:

A long integer number size will hold numbers between -2,147,483,648 to 2,147,483,647 with no decimals. If we want to convert the number 50,234.2345 to a long integer value, we will write clng(50234.2345). Notice that we cannot convert to an integer in this case since this number exceeds the integer's capabilities.

Code:

SELECT clng(50234.2345) as Number_Long

Result:

221.   The CSng() and CDbl() functions

Convert numbers to Single or Double sizes
Discussion:

We can use the Single and Double number sizes when working with high precision floating numbers. Both single and double sizes are high precision field sizes, and we can store a lot of detail using them. Specifically, we can use the Single size for floating values between -3.4×10^{38} and $+3.4 \times 10^{38}$. Single number field sizes can have up to 7 digits. We can use the double size for floating values between -1.797×10^{308} and $+1.797 \times 10^{308}$. Double number field sizes can have up to 15 digits. Let us go through two examples working with the number 1500345.45349345. Notice this number has 15 digits in total.

If we convert it to a single number, we write:

Code:

SELECT csng(1500345.45349345) as Number_Single

Result:

Notice the resulting number contains only 7 digits, and the decimal has been rounded to one digit.

If we convert the same number to a double, we write:

Code:

SELECT cdbl(1500345.45349345) as Number_Double

Result:

As you can see, converting to a double number, we have not lost any of the digits either before or after the decimal since double numbers can hold up to fifteen digits.

222.   The CBool() function

Compare customer first and last name values

Discussion:

The cbool() function will return a true or false value. To demonstrate its usefulness, let us assume that a coworker comes to our office and says that something is wrong with the mailing labels they are producing. On certain occasions, the last and first name fields print the same. Obviously, someone typed in the same value as both first and last name in the database. We can use the cbool() function to find the records for which this occurs.

Code:

SELECT CustomerID, cbool([lastname]=[firstname]) As TrueFalse
FROM customers

Result:

Whenever you see 0 in Access 2007, this means the result is false, or, in other words, the last and first names have different values since you checked for equality. If you see -1, the result is true, which means that the first and last names have identical values. As you scroll through the records, you will notice that you get a -1 for customerid = 19 and an error for 106.

This is cause for investigation. For record 19, last and first names are the same, while for record 106, the first name value is missing! Consequently, with one function, we found two errors that would mess up our coworker's job. Now, we can correct them and send him on his way to produce correct mailing labels.

223. The cCur() function

Convert numbers to currency
Discussion:
If we open the ProductsOrders table in design view, we notice that both the UnitPrice and Quantity fields are of the number data type and specifically long integers. We might want to create a report that shows their multiplication as currency since we want to calculate order subtotals. We can easily accomplish this task by using the ccur() conversion function.

Code:
SELECT OrderID, CCur(UnitPrice*Quantity) as OrderSubtotal
FROM ProductsOrders

Result:

224. The CDate() function

Convert text to a date data type

Discussion:

We might have inherited or imported date data in text format like "November 21 2011" or even "21 November 2011". Since we want to properly store this text data in a date field, we can conveniently use the cdate() function to achieve our goal.

Code:

SELECT cdate("November 21 2011") as DateType

You will achieve the same result if you use:

SELECT cdate("21 November 2011") as DateType

Result:

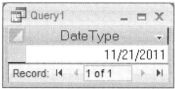

Of course, we can combine the cdate() conversion function with a date function like year() to concurrently extract the year out of our text data. (Check chapter 26 in this book for many tips on dates).

Code:

SELECT year(cdate("November 21 2011")) as FormattedDate

Result:

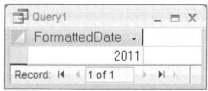

225.   The CStr() function

Convert numeric data to text

Discussion:

This is a very useful function on many occasions. Let us assume that the previous DBA used two fields to store zip codes—one for the five-digit zip code and one for the four-digit extended zip code. Since zip codes are numbers, he chose to use number fields for both of them. Now, we need to create labels and concatenate the two zip fields since orders arrive faster to our customers if we use the extended zip. If we try:

Code:

SELECT (12456 + 2345) As ZipCode

Result:

We will get the sum of the two numbers, which is not what we need.

If, however, we convert to a string, we will get the actual concatenation that we need.

Code:

SELECT cstr(12456 + 23458) As ZipCode

Result:

CHAPTER 25
WORKING WITH STRINGS

It is now time to enter the amazing world of string functions and text manipulation. String functions produce output that is difficult or impossible to generate without them. They should be in the toolbox of every database user since lack of such knowledge has direct effects on database and table design. In other words, extra fields might be inserted in tables when not needed. In this chapter, we will explore more than 25 examples of how to use string functions.

226.   Use the Ucase() function to capitalize field values

Capitalize the first and last names of customers using ucase()
Discussion:
The general syntax of the ucase() function is shown below. It takes just one argument, and it will capitalize the contents of the field on which it is applied. Ucase() will capitalize all of the lowercase characters in the field, leaving the existing capital characters unchanged.

ucase(field name)

In this example, notice the [Last] and [First] field titles in brackets because they are reserved words in Access 2007.

Code:
SELECT UCase(lastname) AS [Last], UCase(firstname) AS [First], city, state, zip
FROM customers

Result:

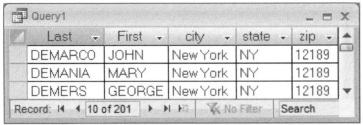

227.   Use the strConv() function to capitalize fields

Capitalize the first and last names of customers using strConv()
Discussion:
We can also use the strConv() function to capitalize field values. The strConv() takes two arguments from which the second is a constant. Its general syntax appears below:

strConv (field, constant)

Depending on the value of the constant, the strConv() function will produce different outputs. The table below shows the three possibilities for the constant:

Constant Value	Output Result
1	Converts field value to uppercase characters.
2	Converts field value to lowercase characters.
3	Converts the first letter of every word in the field to uppercase.

As you can see in the code below, the value of the constant is 1, and all of the field contents will be converted to uppercase.

Code:
SELECT strConv(lastname, 1) AS [Last], strConv(firstname, 1) AS [First], city, state, zip
FROM customers

Result:

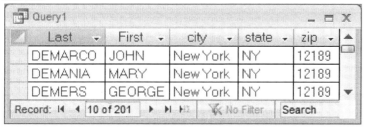

228.   Use the format() function to capitalize fields

Capitalize the first and last names of customers using format()

Discussion:

The format() function is the third function we can use to manipulate the case of characters in a field.   The general syntax of the format() function with respect to text manipulation appears below.   We will use the format() function again and again in date and number fields.   For the purposes of string manipulation, however, we will concentrate on this syntax:

Format(field, constant)

Constant Value	Output
<	Force all characters to lowercase.
>	Force all characters to uppercase.

Code:

SELECT format(lastname, '>') AS [Last], format(firstname, '>') AS [First], city, state, zip

FROM customers

Result:

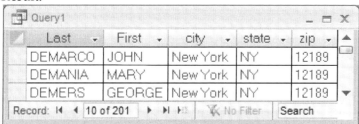

229. Use the strConv() function to capitalize first characters only

Capitalize the first letters of the first and last names of our customers
Discussion:
As we have seen, before the strConv() function takes two arguments, the second is a constant with the possible values of 1,2, or 3. Its general syntax appears below:

$$strConv \ (field, \ constant)$$

Constant Value	Output Result
1	Converts field value to uppercase characters.
2	Converts field value to lowercase characters.
3	Converts the first letter of every word in the field to uppercase.

In this example, we will use the value 3 for the constant because we want to capitalize only the first character of each word in the last and first name fields.

Code:
SELECT strconv(lastname, 3) AS Last_Name, strConv(firstname, 3) AS
First_Name, customers.city, customers.state, customers.zip
FROM customers

Result:

230.   Use the Lcase() function to convert field values to lowercase

Convert the first and last names of our customers to lowercase

Discussion:

The lcase() function takes only one argument—the field name—and results in converting all characters of a field value to lowercase. Its general syntax is:

$$Lcase(field\ name)$$

In this particular example, we use it to convert both the first and last names of our customers to lowercase as you can see in the example below:

Code:

```
SELECT Lcase(lastname) AS Last_Name, Lcase(firstname) AS First_Name,
customers.city, customers.state, customers.zip
FROM customers
```

Result:

Last_Name	First_Name	city	state	zip
demarco	john	New York	NY	12189
demania	mary	New York	NY	12189
demers	george	New York	NY	12189

Record: 10 of 201   No Filter   Search

231.   Use the strConv() function to convert field values to all lowercase

Convert the first and last names of customers to lowercase

Discussion:

Again, we can use the strConv() function which takes two arguments to convert the characters of a field value to lowercase. We know that the second argument of a strConv() function is a constant with the possible values of 1,2, or 3. Its general syntax appears below:

$$strConv\ (field,\ constant)$$

Constant Value	Output Result
1	Converts field value to uppercase characters.
2	Converts field value to lowercase characters.
3	Converts the first letter of every word in the field to uppercase.

In this example, we will use the value 2 for the constant because we want to convert the values of the last and first name fields of our customers to lowercase.

Code:

SELECT strconv(lastname, 2) AS Last_Name, strconv(firstname, 2) AS First_Name, customers.city, customers.state, customers.zip FROM customers

Result:

Last_Name	First_Name	city	state	zip
demarco	john	New York	NY	12189
demania	mary	New York	NY	12189
demers	george	New York	NY	12189

Record: 10 of 201   No Filter   Search

232.   Use the len() function to count the number of characters in a field

Count the number of characters in the SKU field

Discussion:

There are occasions in which we would like to count the actual number of characters for a field in every record in the database. This is especially useful when we want to change the data type of a field or when we want to decrease its length. If we work with extraction, transformation, and loading (ETL) tools, this function is particularly useful to know exactly what is happening instead of making guesses and ending up with truncated values. The len() function is especially easy to use, it takes just one argument, and its general syntax appears below:

Len(field name)

In this particular example, we count the number of characters in the product name field of the products table. Notice from the output that the result of the function for each record is different. We can then sort ascending or descending to display the smallest or lengthiest entries first in the output.

Code:

SELECT productid, productname, len(sku) AS CountSKUChars
FROM Products

Result:

productid	productname	CountSKUChars
1	Almonds, Hickory Smoke	10
2	Almonds, Roasted and Sa	11
3	Banana Chips - 20 oz. Bag	11
4	Berry Cherry in 8 oz. Bag	8

Record: 10 of 70 No Filter Search

233. Use the instr() function to find the position of a character in a string evaluating from the beginning of a string

Find the number of characters occurring before the "-" character in the SKUs field

Discussion:

In business, we use stock keeping unit codes (SKU) to assign a unique code to products. In our products table, we do have an SKU field. This code consists of some letters and a hyphen followed by some numbers like PDKLS-3483. The letter part of the code before the hyphen signifies some larger category, and we might be required to create a report listing only the letter part of the SKU codes. Our problem is that the number of letters in the SKU code might not always be the same. At least this is what happened in my own experience. So, how can we get the string part of the SKU independent of the number of characters it consists of? To complete this task effectively, we first use the instr() function to determine the position of the hyphen in the string (PDKLS-3483). Its general syntax appears below:

instr(starting character, field, character to find)

In this example, we use inStr(1,sku,"-") to look for the "-" character in the SKU field starting from the first character.

Code:

SELECT productid, productname, sku, InStr(1,sku,"-") AS PartSKU
FROM Products

Result:

234.   Use the instr() function to find the position of a blank space evaluating from the beginning of a string

Find the number of characters occurring before a blank space in the SKU field
Discussion:

For this example, I have purposely created an additional problem for us: Some of the hyphens separating the letter code of the SKU from the number code are missing because they were not typed correctly during data entry. We can still use the instr() function to find the position of those blanks. Notice the WHERE clause, which is there so that the result set includes only SKU codes with spaces between letter and number codes and not those with hyphens.

Code:

SELECT productid, productname, sku, InStr(1,sku," ") AS PartSKU
FROM Products
WHERE InStr(1,sku," ") <> 0

Results:

productid	productname	sku	PartSKU
41	Banana Bisquits	ADSE 2345	5
42	Chocolate Bisqu	ADST 2345	5
43	Cocoa and Haze	ADSD 2345	5
44	Cream and hone	ADSL 2345	5

Record: I◄ ◄ 8 of 8 ► ►I No Filter | Search

235. Use the instr() and left() functions to extract a substring from the beginning of a string

Extract the letter part of the SKU field

Discussion:

Now, we are at the essence of the matter, which is how we can dynamically extract a substring from within a string. In other words, how can we extract what we want from part of a field? To do this, we use the left() and instr() functions together. First, we use the instr() function on the SKU field to obtain the numeric value of the exact position of the "hyphen" in the SKU field. Then, we use the left() function, which takes two arguments. The first is the field, and the second is the number of characters to be returned. If we apply the left() function on the string "Hello there" as Left("Hi There", 5), it will return "Hi th".

$$left(sku, InStr(1,sku,"-")-1)$$

What is the -1 doing in the instr() function? When we apply the instr() function alone, it will return the numeric position of the hyphen including the hyphen. Thus, we apply the instr() function minus one character, which, in the end, will result in the string only ("PDKLS")! The cool part of this process is that it happens dynamically. We do not care about the number of letters in the first part of the SKU code. They can be any number, and we will be able to retrieve the string we need.

Code:

SELECT productid, productname, sku, left(sku, InStr(1,sku,"-")-1) AS PartSKU
FROM Products

Result:

236. Extract a substring before a space in the string evaluating from the beginning of a string

Extract the letter part of the SKU field just before a blank space

Discussion:

This example is the same as the previous one, but this time, we extract the letter code of the SKU before a space.

Code:

```
SELECT productid, productname, sku, left(sku, InStr(1,sku," ")-1) AS PartSKU
FROM Products
WHERE InStr(1,sku," ") <> 0
```

Result:

237. Use the Ltrim() function to remove spaces from the beginning of a field

Remove blank spaces from the beginning of the product name field

Discussion:

The ltrim() function takes only one argument and is extremely easy and useful. It will simply eliminate any blank spaces from the beginning of the values of a field. For instance, in this example, we are not certain if there are blank spaces at the start of the field for some product names. We can simply use the ltrim() function to make certain there are not. The ltrim() function will eliminate any blank spaces if they exist. If there are no blank spaces for this field in some records, it will leave those values unchanged. Besides, blank spaces affect how other functions such as instr() work. We can use the ltrim() function to make sure we count correctly from the beginning of the field.

Code:

SELECT productid, Ltrim(productname) AS LeftTrimmedName, sku
FROM Products

Result:

productid	LeftTrimmedName	sku
1	Almonds, Hickory Smoke	PDKLS-2332
2	Almonds, Roasted and S	PDKLSD-2344
3	Banana Chips - 20 oz. Ba	PDKLSD-2347
4	Berry Cherry in 8 oz. Bag	PDK-2589

Record: 10 of 70 — No Filter — Search

238.   Use the Rtrim() function to remove spaces from the end of a field

Remove blank spaces from the end of the product name field
Discussion:

The Rtrim() function takes one argument, and its main job is to eliminate any blank spaces from the end of a field. Why is this so useful? First, let us suppose in this example that we are not certain if there are blank spaces at the end of the field for some product names. We can use the Rtrim() function to make certain there are not. Second, the Rtrim() function will eliminate any blank spaces if they exist. If there are no blank spaces for a field in some records, it will leave those values unchanged. Third, blank spaces affect how other functions work like right(). Using the Rtrim() function, we make sure we count correctly from the end of the field.

Code:

SELECT productid, Rtrim(productname) AS RightTrimmedName, sku
FROM Products

Result:

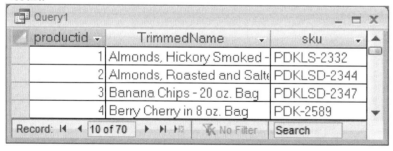

239. Trim blank spaces both at the end and beginning of a string

Remove blank spaces from the beginning and end of the product name field
Discussion:
The role of the trim() function is to eliminate blank spaces from the beginning and end of
a field simultaneously. The trim() function takes only one argument as you can see in the
example below:

Code:

```
SELECT productid, trim(productname) AS TrimmedName, sku
FROM Products
```

Result:

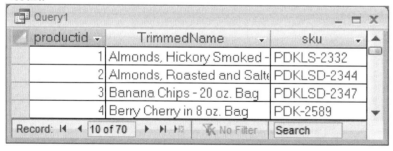

240. Insert one space dynamically before or after a field

Insert one blank space in the beginning and end of the product name field
Discussion:
This time, we have the opposite task. Instead of using the ltrim(), rtrim(), or trim()
functions to remove blank spaces from the beginning, end, or both ends of a field
respectively, we want to add spaces. To achieve this task, we use concatenation

characters like '+' to add a space in the beginning and end of the productname field. I have devoted a whole chapter in this book on concatenation, which you can consult for multiple concatenation techniques.

Code:

SELECT productid, (' ' +productname + ' ') AS SpacedName, sku
FROM Products

Result:

productid	SpacedName	sku
1	Almonds, Hickory Smoked - 12 oz. Bag	PDKLS-2332
2	Almonds, Roasted and Salted - 18 oz. B{	PDKLSD-2344
3	Banana Chips - 20 oz. Bag	PDKLSD-2347
4	Berry Cherry in 8 oz. Bag	PDK-2589

Record: ⏮ ◀ 10 of 70 ▶ ⏭ ▶⁺ 🗙 No Filter Search

241. Use the space() function to insert any number of spaces dynamically before or after a field

Insert ten blank spaces in the beginning and end of the product name field
Discussion:

In some cases, we might want to add any number of blank spaces in the beginning or at the end of the same field. Using concatenation characters to achieve this task will be a very messy affair. Instead, we can use the space() function to achieve the same outcome as we do in the example below:

Code:

SELECT productid, (space(10)+ productname + space(10)) AS SpacedName, sku
FROM Products

Result:

productid	SpacedName	sku
1	Almonds, Hickory	PDKLS-2332
2	Almonds, Roaste	PDKLSD-2344
3	Banana Chips - 20	PDKLSD-2347

Record: I◄ ◄ 10 of 70 ► ►I ►⁚ No Filter Search

242. Use the left() function to retrieve any number of characters from the beginning of a field

Retrieve the first four characters of the SKU code

Discussion:

In some situations, the data in our database is well formatted, and we do not have to resort to combinations of functions such as left() and instr() to retrieve a substring from a string in a field. For example, if the letter part of the SKU code in our products table is always of length 4 (PDKS-2345), we can use the left function to retrieve the first four characters in this field. The left() function takes two arguments—the field name and the number of characters we would like to retrieve.

left(fieldname, number of characters to retrieve)

Code:

SELECT productid, productname, left(sku,4) AS 4SKU
FROM Products

Result:

productid	productname	4SKU
1	Almonds, Hickory Smoke	PDKL
2	Almonds, Roasted and Sa	PDKL
3	Banana Chips - 20 oz. Bag	PDKL
4	Berry Cherry in 8 oz. Bag	PDK-

Record: I◄ ◄ 10 of 70 ► ►I ►⁚ No Filter Search

243. Use the right() function to retrieve any number of characters from the end of a field

Retrieve the last four characters of the SKU code

Discussion:

In this example, instead of retrieving the first four characters of the SKU code, we would like to get the last four, which, by the way, represent the number part of our SKUs (PDKS-2345). If the SKU field is well formatted, we can use the right() function to achieve this task very easily. By well formatted, I mean that the number part of the SKU will always have four digits. Otherwise, we will run into trouble with the right() function. The right() function takes two arguments—the field name and the number of characters we would like to retrieve.

right(fieldname, number of characters to retrieve)

Code:

SELECT productid, productname, right(sku,4) AS SKU4
FROM Products

Result:

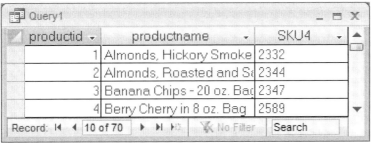

244. Use the mid() function to retrieve any number of characters from any part of a field

Retrieve the first five characters of the product name field starting at character 1

Discussion:

The mid() function is practically an improved left() function, and we can use it instead of left for greater flexibility. The mid() function takes three arguments as they appear below:

Mid(field name, character to start, number of characters to get)

In this example, we use the mid() function to retrieve five characters from the productname field starting at character one or, in other words, at the beginning of the field. We could also have written mid(productname, 5, 5) to retrieve five characters starting with the fifth character in the field.

Code:

SELECT productid, mid(productname, 1, 5) As TrimmedName, sku
FROM Products

Result:

245.   Use the string() function to repeat any number of characters from the beginning of a field

Retrieve the first character of the product name field repeated five times
Discussion:

The string() function will return the first character of a field value any number of times we wish. It takes two arguments.

String(number of times character repeats, field name)

The string function might look simplistic, and you might wonder about its purpose. Alone, it might not be very useful, but we can always use it in combination with other functions to repeat characters in the middle or at the end of a field. In addition, we can use the string() function in concatenated fields to create categories like AAA, BBB, CCC, etc. In this particular example, we repeat the first letter of the productname field five times.

Code:

SELECT productid, string(5, productname) As Name, sku
FROM Products

Result:

246. Use the replace() function to update field values

Replace part of supplier's SKU codes dynamically

Discussion:

The replace() function is amazingly useful, and it provides us with great flexibility for doing our work. Let us suppose that one of our suppliers has recently updated the SKU coding they use, and we need to do the same for their products in our own database. From now on, products with the SKU letter codes "PDK" need to be updated to "PDS". Keep in mind that PDKSs and PDKRs need to remain as they are untouched. In addition, the number part of the SKU code needs to remain untouched. So, "PDK-2389" needs to become "PDS-2389". Consequently, we need to isolate the exact letter code "PDK", replace it with PDS, and leave the trailing numbers untouched. This is a job for the replace function. Is basic syntax appears below:

replace(field name, string to search for, string to replace with, at what character to start)

For example the expression

replace(sku, "pdk-", "pds-")

will replace "pdk-" with "pds-". Notice that the fourth argument (at what character to start) is optional, and if we leave it out, the replace function will start the evaluation at the first character of the field. We could start at any character, however.

The way I work when it comes to updates is to isolate the records to be updated first. I write a SELECT SQL statement to isolate the records to be updated. Then, I write the update statement against those records only. This way, just in case something goes sideways, I know which records are affected. This logic is demonstrated below with two consecutive SQL statements:

Code:
SELECT productid, productname, sku
FROM Products
WHERE left(sku, 4) = 'PDK-'

Result:

Code:
SELECT productid, productname, replace(sku, "pdk-", "pds-") As skuUpdated
FROM Products
WHERE left(sku, 4) = 'PDK-'

Result:

247.   Use the strComp() function to compare the length of two fields

Compare the length of the first and lastname fields for all customers
Discussion:
Let us suppose that we want to compare the length of two fields in one of our tables. We can accomplish this task by using the Len() function on both fields and then, compare the

results. However, there is another quick way to achieve the same task by using the strComp() function. The general syntax of the strComp() function appears below:

strComp(field1, field2)

The strComp() function will return (-1, 0, 1, or Null) according to the table below:

Comparison Result	Output
field1 is less than field2	-1
field1 is equal to field2	0
field1 is greater than field2	1
field1 or field2 is Null	Null

In this example, we compare the length of the first name and last name fields of the customers table.

Code:
SELECT lastname, firstname, strcomp(firstname, lastname) As CompResult
FROM Customers

Result:

248. Use the strReverse() function to reverse the order of characters in a field
Reverse the order of characters in the SKU field in the products table
Discussion:
The strReverse() function is easy to use, and it takes only one argument as its syntax shows below. It will return a string in which the character order is reversed.

strReverse(field)

In this example, we apply it on the SKU field in the products table, and we see from the output that the number part of the SKU now appears first. Of course, this happens dynamically, and the actual data in the table will not be affected.

Code:

SELECT productid, strReverse(sku) As ReverseSKU
FROM Products

Result:

CHAPTER 26
WORKING WITH DATES

Date functions are practical tools that will enable you to perform a superior level of work in multiple database tasks. For instance, you can create advanced reports by extracting the year or month out of a date field, and then, you can summarize data based on those years or months. Second, you can extract the quarters out of a date range and create a crosstab query showing your data by quarter. Third, you can create projected order fulfillment cycle times by adding, say, two business days to the order date field and comparing your projections with the actual shipped dates for quality control. Fourth, you can use date functions as default field values to a table field to record the exact date and time a record was inserted. Fifth, with date functions, you can convert numerical date values such as 9/20/2010 to actual named values such as September 20, 2010. Sixth, you can combine date functions with aggregate functions for exceptional data calculations and summaries. Seventh, your level of knowledge on date functions will have a direct effect on the quality of your database design since you can avoid date fields that you can create automatically from other date fields. These examples are just a small part of what you can do with date functions. The main point is that date functions do not just represent additional knowledge; they are required for truly exceptional work.

249.   Use the year(), datepart(), or format() functions to extract the year from a date field

Calculate order totals by year
Discussion (year function):
On many occasions, we will want to extract the year out of a date field to create aggregate summaries of your data. One way to achieve this task is to use the year() function, which takes only one argument. Its general syntax is:

Year(date)

In this example, we want to calculate order totals by year. We use the year() function to extract the year out of the OrderDate field in combination with the sum() aggregate function to calculate order totals.

Code:

SELECT year(OrderDate) AS Year, sum(unitprice*quantity) AS OrderTotal
FROM Qry_Invoices
GROUP BY Year(OrderDate)

Result:

Year	OrderTotal
2008	44477
2009	51942
2010	43977

Record: 1 of 3

Discussion (datepart function):

We could also extract the year from a date field using the datepart() function. The datepart() function has four arguments, but for practical situations, we can use only two of them. Its simplified syntax appears below:

$$datepart(interval, datefield)$$

The interval argument is just a string indicating the date part that we want to extract from the date field. For example, we would use "yyyy" to extract the year or "q" to extract the quarter. Do not forget the quotes in the code since without them, it will not work. Check table 1 at the end of this chapter for a list of all possible values for the interval arguments for the datepart() function for amazing flexibility in extracting date parts from years all the way down to seconds.

Code:

SELECT datepart("yyyy", OrderDate) AS Year, SUM(unitprice*quantity) AS
OrderTotal
FROM Qry_Invoices
GROUP BY datepart("yyyy", OrderDate)

Result:

Discussion (format function):

The format function is the most flexible, and it offers more choices than the year() and datepart() functions. Officially, it takes four arguments, but again, for practical purposes, we need only two. Its simplified version appears below:

format(datefield, interval)

The interval argument is a string expression like "yyyy" for years or "mmmm" for months. Unlike the datepart() function, however, it will give us multiple choices for displaying years or months. Using format, we can display the full month name, the month number with or without leading zeros, or the abbreviated month name if we want. Please check table 2 at the end of this chapter for a full list of the available choices with the format() function.

Code:

SELECT format(OrderDate, "yyyy") AS Year, sum(unitprice*quantity) AS
OrderTotal
FROM Qry_Invoices
GROUP BY format(OrderDate, "yyyy")

Result:

Year	OrderTotal
2008	44477
2009	51942
2010	43977

Record: 1 of 3

Discussion (format function):

In this example, we use the format function to extract only the last two digits of the years on which we provide summary statistics. Notice that we use the "yy" argument to achieve this task.

Code:

```
SELECT format(OrderDate, "yy") AS Year, sum(unitprice*quantity) AS
OrderTotal
FROM Qry_Invoices
GROUP BY format(OrderDate, "yy")
```

Result:

Year	OrderTotal
08	44477
09	51942
10	43977

Record: 1 of 3

250. Use the datepart() and format() functions to extract quarters from a date field

Calculate order totals by quarter for a specific year

Discussion (with datepart):

The business goal in this example is to create a quarterly sales report for the year 2009. To achieve this task, we need to use two date functions. First, we will use the year() function to extract the year from the orderdate field and use this expression in the WHERE clause with an equality predicate "=". This way, we make certain that our resulting recordset contains orders only for the year 2009. Then, we can use the datepart() function to group by our order totals by quarter. Of course, we could use the format function to extract quarters, which is demonstrated in the second part of this example.

Code:

```
SELECT datePart("q",[OrderDate])  AS Quarter, sum(unitprice*quantity) AS OrderTotal
FROM Qry_Invoices
WHERE Year(orderdate) = 2009
```

GROUP BY DatePart("q",[OrderDate])

Result:

Quarter ▾	OrderTotal ▾
1	10052
2	10575
3	17221
4	14094

Record: ◀ ◀ 1 of 4 ▶ ▶ ▶ ✗ No

Discussion (with format):

In this second part of the same example, we use the format() function to extract quarters from a date field. The results will be identical with those of the datepart() function.

Code:

SELECT format(OrderDate, "q") AS Quarter, sum(unitprice*quantity) AS
OrderTotal
FROM Qry_Invoices
WHERE Year(orderdate) = 2009
GROUP BY format(OrderDate, "q")

Result:

Quarter ▾	OrderTotal ▾
1	10052
2	10575
3	17221
4	14094

Record: ◀ ◀ 1 of 4 ▶ ▶ ▶ ✗ No

251. Use the month(), monthname() datepart(), or format() functions to extract the month from a date field

Calculate monthly order and discount totals for a specific year

Discussion (with month):

The business goal in this example is to calculate order and discount totals by month for the year 2010. Management wants to have a look at the numbers to check the discount percentages forwarded by the sales reps. There are four different ways to achieve this result depending on the date function we want to use. Notice that in all four examples, the rational is the same. We will use the year() function to isolate the year from the orderdate field and use this expression in the WHERE clause. Then, we need to use a function to isolate the month from the orderdate field so that we can group by month within the year 2010. Finally, notice that we will use two calculated fields (OrderTotal and TotalDiscount) to calculate the order and discount totals for each month.

In this first alternative, we will use the month function to extract the month from the orderdate field. The month() function has only one argument, and its syntax is below:

$$\text{month(datefield)}$$

Code:

```
SELECT month(OrderDate) AS [Month], Sum(unitprice*quantity) AS
OrderTotal, Sum(([unitprice]*[quantity])*[Discount]) AS TotalDiscount
FROM Qry_Invoices
WHERE year(orderdate) = 2010
GROUP BY month(OrderDate)
```

Result:

Month	OrderTotal	TotalDiscount
1	3369	567.65
2	4320	663.2
3	5208	809.9
4	4438	644.15

Record: ◄ ◄ 12 of 12 ► ►► No Filter Se

Discussion (with monthname):

Suppose that management was not very happy with our first report because the month numbers confused them, and they could not quickly discern the corresponding month name. They now ask us to provide them with another report showing actual month names. We can do this immediately using the monthname() function in conjunction with the month() function. Notice that we cannot use the monthname() function by itself. We have to use it with the month() function to work as it is in the code below:

Code:

```
SELECT monthname(month(OrderDate)) AS [Month], sum(unitprice*quantity)
AS OrderTotal, sum(([unitprice]*[quantity])*[Discount]) AS TotalDiscount
FROM Qry_Invoices
WHERE year(orderdate) = 2010
GROUP BY monthname(Month(OrderDate)), month([OrderDate])
ORDER BY month([OrderDate])
```

Result:

Discussion (with datepart):

We can also use the datepart() function to achieve the same result except that we will get numerals instead of month names. In other words, the result will be identical with that of the month() function. The only real difference is that the month function is much simpler, and we do not need to remember the "m" argument of the datepart() function.

Code:

```
SELECT datepart("m", OrderDate) AS [Month], sum(unitprice*quantity) AS
OrderTotal, Sum((([unitprice]*[quantity])*[Discount]) AS TotalDiscount
FROM Qry_Invoices
WHERE year(orderdate) = 2010
GROUP BY datepart("m", OrderDate), month([OrderDate])
ORDER BY datepart("m", OrderDate)
```

Result:

Month	OrderTotal	TotalDiscount
1	3369	567.65
2	4320	663.2
3	5208	809.9
4	4438	644.15

Record: 12 of 12   No Filter

Discussion (with format):

Finally, we can use the format() function with the "mm" argument to put a leading zero in front of the month for sorting purposes.

Code:

```
SELECT format(OrderDate, "mm")  AS [Month], sum(unitprice*quantity) AS OrderTotal,
sum((([unitprice]*[quantity])*[Discount]) AS TotalDiscount
FROM Qry_Invoices
WHERE year(orderdate) = 2010
GROUP BY format(OrderDate, "mm")
ORDER BY format(OrderDate, "mm")
```

Result:

252. Use the datepart() or format() functions to extract the week from a date field

Create a crosstab report showing product sales by week for a six-month period

Discussion (with datepart):

This time, management wants a report listing product sales by week within a six-month period and within a specific year. To create this crosstab query, we need to use three date functions in combination. First, we will use the month() function to extract the month number from the orderdate field and use this as a criterion in the WHERE clause. Notice how the IN operator is used with the WHERE clause to get the first six months of the year. Since, however, we have multiple years of sales in the database, we need to include a criterion in the WHERE clause to isolate the year we want. We can use the year function on the orderdate field to achieve this task. Finally, in the PIVOT part of the crosstab query, we can use the datepart() function with the "ww" argument to produce a column for each week. (For a detailed overview of crosstab queries, check chapter 18). As you can see from the result set, we can now examine detailed total product sales by week for a period of 27 weeks within the six-month period that we defined in our WHERE clause.

Code:

```
TRANSFORM Sum([unitprice]*[quantity]) AS Ordertotal
SELECT ProductName
FROM Qry_Invoices
WHERE month(orderdate) IN (1,2,3,4,5,6) AND year(orderdate) = 2010
GROUP BY ProductName
PIVOT datePart("ww",[OrderDate])
```

Result:

Discussion (with format):

We could use the format function to achieve the same task, but notice in the result set that the weeks are not in order this time.

Code:

```
TRANSFORM Sum([unitprice]*[quantity]) AS Ordertotal
SELECT ProductName
FROM Qry_Invoices
WHERE month(orderdate) IN (1,2,3,4,5,6) AND year(orderdate) = 2010
GROUP BY ProductName
PIVOT format([OrderDate], "ww")
```

Result:

ProductName	1	10	11	12	13	14	15
All-Purpose Marinade			42			56	
All-Purpose Marinade				45			15
Almonds, Hickory Sm		15		90	45		
Almonds, Roasted an		60		15		60	
Apple Cinnamon Rais		24	60		96	48	
Artichokes in white sa				60			15

Record: I4 ◄ 10 of 67 ► ►I ► | No Filter | Search

253. Use the day(), datepart(), weekday() and weekdayname() functions to extract the day from a date field

Create a crosstab report showing product sales by day within a month.

Discussion (day function):

Management is impressed by our detailed reports, and they now ask for a report of daily product sales for the month of May in the year 2010. Again, we need to use three date functions—two for criteria and one to pivot our results. In this example, we will use the month() and year() functions to isolate the year and the month in the WHERE clause and the day() function to pivot or display product sales by day. Notice that only days with product sales appear as columns in the result set.

Code:

TRANSFORM Sum([unitprice]*[quantity]) AS Ordertotal
SELECT ProductName
FROM Qry_Invoices
WHERE month(OrderDate) = 5 AND year(orderdate) = 2010
GROUP BY ProductName
PIVOT day(OrderDate)

Result:

Discussion (datepart function):

We can achieve the same result using the datepart() function with the "d" (day) argument. For a full list of possible arguments for the datepart() function, see table 1 at the end of this chapter.

Code:

```
TRANSFORM Sum([unitprice]*[quantity]) AS Ordertotal
SELECT ProductName
FROM Qry_Invoices
WHERE month(OrderDate) = 5 AND year(orderdate) = 2010
GROUP BY ProductName
PIVOT datepart("d",OrderDate)
```

Result:

ProductName	4	8	9	13	17	23	26	27
Almonds, Roasted		75						
Apple Cinnamon R				60				36
Chili Salsa								75
Chocolate Almond:					60			
Chocolate Blueber		20						

Record: I◀ ◀ 10 of 30 ▶ ▶I ▶ | No Filter | Search | ◀ □ ▶

Discussion (weekday function):

In this example, we will create a report of daily product sales within a week. Specifically, management asks for a report of product sales, by day, within the 25th week of the year 2010. This time, we will use the datepart() and year() functions in the WHERE clause to extract the week and the year respectively from the orderdate field. In addition, we will use the weekday() function to display product sales by day within the week. The general syntax of the weekday() function appears below. It takes two arguments, datefield and firstdayofweek, and the second is optional. With the firstdayofweek argument, we can define which day we want to be the first day of the week. We can choose any day between Sunday and Saturday as the table indicates below. In this example, we left the second argument blank, which defaults the first day of the week to Sunday. From the result set, you can see that we had sales only for the sixth and seventh day of the week — Friday and Saturday.

weekday (datefield, [firstdayofweek])

Argument value	First day of week
1	Sunday (default)
2	Monday
3	Tuesday
4	Wednesday
5	Thursday
6	Friday
7	Saturday

Code:

```
TRANSFORM Sum([unitprice]*[quantity]) AS Ordertotal
SELECT ProductName
FROM Qry_Invoices
WHERE datePart("ww",[OrderDate]) = 25 AND year(orderdate) = 2010
GROUP BY ProductName
PIVOT weekday([OrderDate])
```

Result:

Discussion (weekdayname function)

The previous example is fine, but it will confuse management and anybody else who tries to understand what day of the week corresponds to numbers 6 or 7. To solve this problem, we can use the weekdayname() function to provide the actual day name. Notice that we cannot use the weekday() function alone because we will receive an error from Access 2007. We need to use it in conjunction with the weekday() function to retrieve the day names. As you can see in the result set, the names of the days appear now as column headings.

Code:

```
TRANSFORM Sum([unitprice]*[quantity]) AS Ordertotal
SELECT ProductName
FROM Qry_Invoices
WHERE datePart("ww",[OrderDate]) = 25 AND year(orderdate) = 2010
GROUP BY ProductName
PIVOT weekdayname(weekday([OrderDate]))
```

Result:

ProductName	Friday	Saturday
All-Purpose Marinade I		28
All-Purpose Marinade II		60
Artichokes in white sauce	75	
Biscuits with cream	45	

Record: 9 of 9   No Filter   Search

254. The Now() function

Use the now() function for default field values

Discussion:

The now() function takes only one argument, and its general syntax appears below:

$$now(datefield)$$

It will output the system date and time, and it is frequently used as the default value for a date field. For example, if we open the SalesReps table, we will notice that there is a field called DateInserted with a default value of now(). This means that every time a record is inserted in this table, the system date and time will be recorded in this field. We can also use now() in a SQL statement or a report to capture the date and time as in the statement below:

Code:

```
SELECT now() as CurrentTimeAndDate
```

Result:

255.   The Date() function

Use the date() function for default field values

Discussion:

The date() function is often used as the default value of a date field in case you do not want to capture the time. It takes just one argument, and its general syntax appears below:

date(datefield)

You can also use it in a SQL statement in a query or in a report to capture the current date:

Code:

SELECT date() as CurrentDate

Result:

256.   Use the DateDiff() function to subtract date intervals

Calculate order processing cycle times with the DateDiff() function

Discussion:

Customer service has reported to management that customers are complaining about shipping. Specifically, they complain that it takes a lot of time to receive their orders after they complete the ordering process. Management is trying to determine the cause, and they need our help. They want to know if the problem is internal as a result of packaging and payment processing or if the problem is external as a result of the shipping company. They suspect the problem is internal, and they tell us to produce a report immediately that lists how many days it takes for an order to ship from the time it has been received.

We can do this in no time by using the datediff() function. The datediff() function takes five arguments, but for most practical scenarios, we only need to use the first three. The general syntax of the function appears below. The interval argument is a string that will determine in what interval we want to find the difference between date1 and date2. For instance, we might want to calculate the difference in days, weeks, months, or years. (Please refer to table 3 at the end of this chapter for a full list of values for the interval argument). In addition, date2 should be a later date than date1. Otherwise, the result will be negative. As you can see from the code below, we calculate the difference between orderdate and shippeddate in days. In other words, how many days elapsed between receiving and shipping an order? The results are not good at all. It takes a full five days to get the order out from our factory for the month of September 2010, which is a very long order processing cycle time.

$$DateDiff(interval, date1, date2[, firstdayofweek[, firstweekofyear]])$$

Code:
```
SELECT OrderID, datediff("d", orderdate, shippeddate) AS CycleTime
FROM Orders
WHERE year(orderdate) = 2010 AND month(orderdate) = 9
```

Result:

257. Use the DateAdd() function to add date intervals

Establish corporate policies on expected shipping dates with the dateadd() function
Discussion:
Management is not very happy to see that it takes five days to ship an order. This means that customers will receive their orders in about ten to fifteen days total. This is unacceptable because we are in the food industry, and our products need to arrive fresh. So, management asks for our help again to produce a timetable that will list the expected shipping dates for orders. Management has determined that it should take two days at most for any order to ship, and they have established a corporate policy to be strictly enforced. We can produce target shipping dates using the dateadd() function. It takes three arguments, and its general syntax appears below:

dateadd(interval, number, datefield)

The interval argument is a string like "d", "m", or "y" determining the time interval we want to add. For instance, if we want to add days to a date, we use the "d" value. If we want to add years, we use the "y" value for the interval argument. (For a full list of the values for the interval argument, please refer to table 3 at the end of this chapter). The number argument is the actual number of time intervals we want to add. If we want to add 15 days, for example, we use the number 15. Finally, the date argument is the date field to which we want to add a number of days, months, or years. In the code below, we add 2 days to the orderdate field:

Code:
```
SELECT OrderID, dateadd("d", 2, orderdate) AS  PolicyShipmentDate
FROM Orders
WHERE year(orderdate) = 2010 AND month(orderdate) = 7
```

Result:

OrderID	PolicyShipmentDate
93	7/30/2010
127	7/13/2010
129	7/25/2010
141	7/11/2010

Record: 10 of 32   No Filter

Table 1: Datepart() function settings	
Character	**Description**
"yyyy"	Year
"q"	Quarter
"m"	Month
"y"	Day of year
"d"	Day
"w"	Weekday
"ww"	Week
"h"	Hour
"n"	Minute
"s"	Second

Character	Description (The following are tested and working. You might find more settings, but they did not work correctly when tested)
"s"	Returns the second as a number without leading zeros
"ss"	Returns the second as a number with leading zeros
"h"	Returns the hour as a number
"hh"	Returns the hour as a number with leading zeros
"d"	Returns the day without a leading zero
"dd"	Returns the day with a leading zero
"ddd"	Returns the day as an abbreviation
dddd	Returns the full name of the day
"m"	Returns the month without a leading zero
"mm"	Returns the month with a leading zero
"mmm"	Returns the abbreviation of the month
"mmmm"	Returns the full name of the month
"q"	Returns the quarter as a number
"y"	Returns the year as number (0-9) without leading

	zeros
"yy"	Returns the year as number (0-9) with leading zeros
"yyyy"	Returns the year in four-digit numeric format

Table 3: DateDiff and DateAdd interval argument values	
Value	**Description**
yyyy	Year
q	Quarter
m	Month
y	Day of year
d	Day
w	Weekday
ww	Week
h	Hour
n	Minute
s	Second

CHAPTER 27
UPDATE SQL STATEMENTS

Update statements are powerful tools for the advanced user, administrator, and developer. They provide astonishing flexibility and control to complete a task in minutes for which you would otherwise need hours. For example, suppose you have a database of 100 suppliers and a few thousand products associated with each supplier. Every week, due to promotional campaigns, pricing strategies, or replenishment costs, your suppliers might change their prices, so you need to update yours since their products constitute your own raw materials. After all, the only constant in business is change. Change will affect your operations, and, in the end, your data. Since this is true, you must be ready for lightning speed changes in your operational data.

Your suppliers will never update their product prices at the same time and at the same percentage rates. This scenario is valid only for theoretical books. What actually happens is that suppliers will send you a price update when their business operations dictate, and this update will most probably be different from everyone else's. So, how do you account for situations like this? Of course, you use flexible update statements that you can reuse effectively. This chapter starts with simple examples and ends up with powerful conditional updates for manipulating your data.

Keep in mind that you cannot undo the results of update statements or update queries. Consequently, my advice and my own policy is to first use a SELECT statement to check the records to be updated and then, run the update itself. This is actually common industry practice. We never run an update statement in the blind.

The general syntax of an update statement is shown below:

UPDATE table
SET fieldvalue1 = value1, fieldvalue2 = value2, fieldvalue3 = value3…
[WHERE condition]

We can also run updates on queries (updateable ones). We might construct a dataset having data from multiple tables and run the update against the query. (I have examples of this in the chapter). In addition, we can update a table based on the values of another table or query. We can easily achieve this by using subqueries. Update statements are highly efficient for operations. Before we delve into examples, let's make sure we understand what cascade updates are and how they work in Access 2007.

258. What are cascade updates, how to use them, and what they mean

There are cases in which we have to update the values of primary keys in your tables. Usually, these changes are mandated by entities external to the organization, such as the government. For example, up until now, we might have used the social security number of an employee as the primary key for the employees table. As a result, SSN functioned as the foreign key to record all related activities for that employee (sales, HR records etc.) Now, the government steps in and says that we cannot do that anymore. This means that we have to change the SSN value for the employee in the employees table, and, most importantly, we need to change all of its occurrences in related tables. So, if this employee worked for us for 10 years, he might have 260 paystub records in the database. We might actually have thousands of references that we need to update for this employee.

Doing so manually is an impossible task, especially if we have several thousand employees. This is where cascade updates come in. Cascade updates will allow us to change the value of the primary key in the primary table, and the database engine will change all of its occurrences automatically, as a foreign key, in related tables. Let's go through a simple graphical example using a customer database to see how cascade updates work.

Customers	
CustID	Name
1	John
2	Mary
3	George
4	Stacy

Orders		
OrderID	CustID	OrderDate
1	2	9/10/2009
2	2	10/10/2010
3	1	11/10/2010
4	3	11/11/2010

Products_Orders		
OrderID	ProductID	Quantity
1	2	2
2	2	5
3	1	3
4	2	4

Products	
ProductID	ProductName
1	A
2	B
3	C
4	D

In the figure above, let's assume that we need to change Mary's primary key value from 2 to 222. First, we need to turn cascade updates on for the relationship between customers and orders. Then, we can simply change the primary key value 2 to the value 222. The database will ask us to confirm the action, and once the updates are completed, this is how the same tables will look:

Customers	
CustomerID	Name
1	John
222	Mary
3	George
4	Stacy

Orders		
OrderID	CustomerID	OrderDate
1	222	9/10/2009
2	222	10/10/2010
3	1	11/10/2010
4	3	11/11/2010

Products_Orders		
OrderID	ProductID	Quantity
1	2	2
222	2	5
3	1	3
4	2	4

Products	
ProductID	ProductName
1	A
2	B
3	C
4	D

Notice how the database automatically changed all of the references of CustomerID=2 to 222 in the Orders and ProductsOrders tables. I strongly recommend having cascade updates turned off except when you actually want to make changes to primary key values. This is a precaution in case an end user changes the value of a primary key by accident. So, how you can use cascade updates in Access 2007?

1. Click on the "Database Tools" tab. Then, in the group "Show/Hide", click on "Relationships".

This will open up the relationships window as shown below:

2. Double click on the relationship line between customers and orders. The following screen will appear. Click on "Cascade Update Related Fields", and click "OK".

Now, we are ready to open the customer table and change the value of the primary key for any customer. Our change will be propagated throughout the database where the database finds a foreign key value that is equal to the primary key we changed. Remember to edit the relationship again and turn off "Cascade Updates" once the records are updated.

259. Update a single field value in a single record

Update address information for a single customer

Discussion:

In this example, our goal is to update the address information for one of our customers. Notice the criteria in the query. They need to uniquely identify the customer we want to update. We will use a SELECT statement beforehand just to make sure that we do not have another customer with the same first and last names.

```
SELECT *
FROM customers
WHERE lastname = "Demizio" AND firstname = "Michael"
```

Code:

```
UPDATE tbls_Customers_Upd
SET Address = "12 Lark Street"
WHERE lastname = "Demizio" AND firstname = "Michael"
```

Result:

260. Update multiple field values in a single record

Update address and city information for a single customer

Discussion:

Our job now is to update both the address and city information for a customer. In other words, we will update two fields of the same record. The criteria remain the same, but notice how the two fields that we are updating are separated by a comma in the SET part of the code.

```
SELECT *
FROM customers
WHERE lastname = "Demizio" AND firstname = "Michael"
```

Code:

UPDATE tbls_Customers_Upd
SET Address = "12 Lark Street", city = "Albany"
WHERE lastname = "Demizio" AND firstname = "Michael"

Result:

261. Update a field value in multiple records

Update zip codes for all customers in a certain city

Discussion:

Our job request is to update zip code values for all of our customers in Dallas, Texas. It might look simple, but please pay attention. We do not update zip codes for all of the records in the customer table. In addition, we need to make sure the city of Dallas does not exist in other States. If it does, we need to add one more criterion in the WHERE clause to identify the state as well. Always run a SQL statement in advance to make sure your operation will affect the correct records.

SELECT *
FROM customers
WHERE city = "Dallas"

Code:

UPDATE tbls_Customers_Upd
SET zip = "54156"
WHERE city = "Dallas"

Result:

LastName	Address	City	State	Zip	Country
Saliba	9 4th Street	Dallas	TX	54156	USA
Tinons	34 Franklin Stree	Dallas	TX	54156	USA
Wells	28 Vine Street	Dallas	TX	54156	USA
Williams	7 Cherry Hill Roa	Dallas	TX	54156	USA

Record: 95 of 201   No Filter   Search

262. Update multiple field values in multiple records

Update city, zip, and address information for all customers in Dallas, Texas

Discussion:

Because of erroneous data entry or importing, customers that show up from Dallas, Texas are actually from Tucson, Arizona. Consequently, we have to update their zip, city, and state information. We need to update multiple field values in multiple records in the database. This is possible by using multiple update values in the SET clause of the update statement. We must always check our criteria in the WHERE clause to make sure they identify the records we want to update.

```
SELECT *
FROM customers
WHERE city = "Dallas"
```

Code:

```
UPDATE tbls_Customers_Upd
SET zip = "54156", city = "Tucson", state = "AZ"
WHERE city = "Dallas"
```

Result:

LastName	Address	City	State	Zip	Country
Saliba	9 4th Street	Tucson	AZ	54156	USA
Tinons	34 Franklin Stree	Tucson	AZ	54156	USA
Wells	28 Vine Street	Tucson	AZ	54156	USA
Williams	7 Cherry Hill Roa	Tucson	AZ	54156	USA

tbls_Customers_Upd

Record: 95 of 201   No Filter   Search

263. Update using calculated values

Update product prices increasing them by a certain percentage

Discussion:

One of our suppliers has sent us updated prices, and we need to increase our own product prices by 5% for the products from this supplier. Notice the calculated field in the SET clause. In the WHERE clause, notice that instead of the supplier name, we will use the supplier ID to make sure we identify the correct product records for this supplier. This is common practice in databases for criteria in the WHERE clause because primary key values are unique. Therefore, we do not need to worry if we have two suppliers with the same name in the database. Finally, notice in this example that we work with the query "Qry_SupplierPrices" which combines the information of suppliers and their products. Running update statements against queries is fine and sometimes desirable because they provide us with just the information we need rather than looking at huge tables. In this particular example, our supplier, "Home of Snacks", has increased prices by 5%, and we will increase our own prices by the same amount.

```
SELECT *
FROM Qry_SupplierPrices
WHERE supplierID = 1
```

Code:

```
UPDATE Qry_SupplierPrices
SET ProductUnitPrice = ProductUnitPrice * (1+0.05)
WHERE supplierID = 1
```

Result:

Sup| ▾	CompanyNam ▾	State ▾	ProductNam ▾	Produc ▾
1	Home of Snacks	MA	Almonds, Hickc	38.5
1	Home of Snacks	MA	Almonds, Roas	24.2
1	Home of Snacks	MA	Banana Chips -	29.7
1	Home of Snacks	MA	Berry Cherry in	33

Record: 10 of 10 — No Filter — Search

264. Update conditionally using the switch() function

Update product prices using different update conditions for every supplier

Discussion:

I know that in everyday work scenarios, our suppliers, customers, students, or partners do not set up meetings to send us uniform and standardized information just so that we can have a nice time with our operations. Most probably, they send us their own percentage increases and not at the same time. So, what can we do to take care of this business fact in minutes instead of making it an operational and administrative nightmare? We can combine the powers of the update statement and the switch() function. As you can see below, our suppliers sent us percentage updates ranging from 2% all the way up to 15%. Using the update statement with the switch() function, we obtain the following: First, using just one statement, we can take care of all of the particular updates in minutes. Second, the statement is so clean that it is reusable the next time we need to do the same job. Third, suppose that some of our suppliers have not sent us any updates. We can leave the statement below as is and update the ProductUnitPrice with itself as is the case with supplierID=5 where nothing is updated.

303

Code:

```
update Qry_SupplierPrices
SET ProductUnitPrice =
SWITCH (
supplierid=1,    ProductUnitPrice*(1.1) ,
supplierid=2,    ProductUnitPrice*(1.05),
supplierid=3,    ProductUnitPrice*(1.1) ,
supplierid=4,    ProductUnitPrice*(1.05) ,
supplierid=5,    ProductUnitPrice ,
supplierid=6,    ProductUnitPrice*(1.02) ,
supplierid=7,    ProductUnitPrice *(1.03),
supplierid=8,    ProductUnitPrice*(1.05) ,
supplierid=9,    ProductUnitPrice*(1.15) ,
supplierid=10,   ProductUnitPrice*(1.1) ,
)
```

Result:

Sup	CompanyNam	State	ProductNam	ProductUnitPrice
1	Home of Snacks	MA	Almonds, Hicko	38.5
1	Home of Snacks	MA	Almonds, Roas	24.2
1	Home of Snacks	MA	Banana Chips -	29.7
1	Home of Snacks	MA	Berry Cherry in	33

Record: 9 of 70   No Filter   Search

265.   Update records in a table using criteria from another table

Update the products table using criteria from the suppliers table

Discussion:

In this example, our goal is to update prices in the tbls_products_Upd table using criteria from the suppliers table. We can achieve this using a subquery. The subquery will retrieve supplier ids from the suppliers table and will update the corresponding product prices in the tbls_products_Upd table. Specifically, the subquery will retrieve supplier ids for suppliers in Boston or Dallas and feed those ids in the WHERE clause of the main update statement.

Let me explain this point a bit more. The business request is to update product prices for suppliers in Boston and Dallas. We might be facing increased shipping costs from those locations, and since management does not understand supplier ids, they tell us to increase prices by 20% for everything coming from that direction. Our problem is that the tbls_products_Upd table does not contain any city information. We can satisfy management and our technical needs by using the subquery below:

Code:

UPDATE tbls_Products_Upd

SET ProductUnitPrice = ProductUnitPrice * (1+0.20)

WHERE SupplierID IN

(SELECT SupplierID FROM Suppliers

WHERE city= "Boston" or city = "Dallas")

Result:

CHAPTER 28
DELETE STATEMENTS

The principal role of delete statements is to remove multiple records in one operation. Instead of deleting table rows manually, we can use a delete statement to delete many of them with one SQL statement. The general syntax of a delete statement appears below, and while it looks simple, it can become an amazing tool when coupled with criteria and subqueries.

```
DELETE
FROM table
WHERE criteria
```

As with update statements, we cannot undo the results of delete statements. Thus, once we delete a set of records, there is no way to get them back. Consequently, we should always backup data or keep the deleted records in a temporary or historical table just in case we made a mistake. In this chapter, I will show you how to easily move records to other tables before deleting them. Furthermore, it is professional practice to run a SELECT statement first to determine if its result set contains the records we want to delete and then, run the delete statement. Before we run any code in this chapter, we should learn about the role of cascade deletes. For all of the examples in this chapter, cascade deletes are off, and we should keep them off in our databases as well unless we specifically want to take advantage of their functionality in specific situations.

266.   What are cascade deletes, how to use them, and what they mean

In order to understand cascade deletes in full, let's work with the record of a customer from five years ago who is no longer in business. We want to delete this customer from the database so that it does not come up in queries and does not take up space.

We could simply go to the customers table and try to delete this record. However, if there are associated orders with this customer, the database will not allow us to delete it since we would then end up with orphaned records in the orders table. Referential integrity rules do not allow this to happen, and we would not be able to delete the customer. (For a full explanation of referential integrity, please check chapter 3. Understanding referential integrity is a must for all database professionals and users). To delete this customer manually, we should first go to the orders table and delete all of the orders associated with this customer. However, since we also have a many-to-many relationship between Orders and Products, we first need to go to the Products_Orders table and delete the associations (records) of Orders and Products for that customer. If we need to delete the customer Mary from the database, we need to do the following in the order provided:

- Delete from the Products_Orders table all of the records with orderid 353, 538, 609, and 982. For example, order 353 contains products 1, 2, 11, 20, 27, 31, and 51.
- Delete from the Orders table the orders with orderid = 353, 538, 609, and 982 since they all belong to Mary.
- Finally, delete Mary's record with CustomerID = 2 from the Customer table.

Even in this simple scenario, deleting a customer is an involved process. Imagine the scenario where you have hundreds of customers with thousands of associated orders. It would be humanly impossible to remove customers manually.

This is where cascade deletes come in. By using cascade deletes, we can delete a customer in the primary table, and the database itself will delete all references to that customer in all related tables. In this example, if cascade deletes are on, when we delete Mary from the customers table, the database will automatically delete all of Mary's references in the Orders and Product_Orders tables reliably and at once. To turn cascade deletes on, follow these steps:

1. Click on the "Database Tools" tab. Then, in the group "Show/Hide", click on "Relationships".

2. This will open up the Relationships window as shown below:

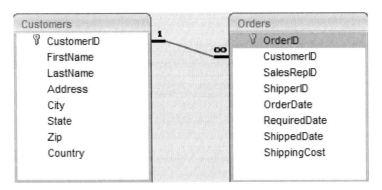

3. Double click on the relationship line between customers and orders. The following screen will appear. Click on "Cascade Delete Related Fields", and click "OK".

4. Repeat step two for the relationship between the tables Orders and Products_Orders, and enable cascade deletes as well.

5. At this point, if we open the customers table and delete Mary's record, all of Mary's orders will be deleted from the Orders table, and all respective associations between Orders and products will be deleted from the Products_Orders table.

For the purposes of this chapter, cascade deletes are off. In addition, we will be working on the tbls_Orders_DEL table, which is just a copy of the Orders table which we can delete at will.

267.   Delete a single record in a table

Delete a specific customer's order
Discussion:

The goal in this example is to delete a customer's order. Notice how we use the OrderID as the criterion in the WHERE clause. The OrderID is the primary key of the Orders table, and it will uniquely identify the record for deletion. Try to use primary key values for criteria instead of fields such as customer names, which might have duplicates in the table with the result of deleting records you do not want to delete. In addition, always run a SELECT beforehand or a SELECT INTO so that you can identify or backup your data respectively. I will show you how you can use the SELECT INTO to make a temporary table for deleted data.

In this example, you will use the tbls_Orders_DEL table, which is just a copy of the Orders table, and the DELETE statement will work very well for demonstration purposes since the tbls_Orders_DEL table does not participate in any relationships. However, I wrote this book for real situations, so I outline all of the steps in each example that you need to follow to delete a customer's order. You need to follow four steps:

Step 1: Run a SELECT statement to uniquely identify and verify records for deletion. Never run a delete statement directly.

SELECT *
FROM tbls_Orders_Del
WHERE orderid = 20

Step 2: Turn on cascade deletes for the relationship between the tables Orders and ProductsOrders.

Step 3: Run the DELETE statement

DELETE
FROM tbls_Orders_Del
WHERE orderid = 20

Result:

Step 4: Turn off cascade deletes for the relationship between the tables Orders and ProductsOrders so that nobody can delete any orders by mistake. If cascade deletes are left on, the database will go ahead with the deletion. If they are off, the database will give a referential integrity warning. We can open the Orders table and try to delete any

310

record to have a look at the referential integrity message. (Check chapter 3 for a full explanation of referential integrity consequences).

268. Delete multiple records in a table

Delete all orders for a specific customer

Discussion:

In this example, we want to delete all orders for customerid= 2, i.e. Mary. To achieve this task, we will use the CustomerID field in the WHERE clause, which is the primary key in the customers table and the foreign key in the orders table. Our task involves four steps as they appear below:

Step 1: Run a SELECT statement to uniquely identify and verify records for deletion.
SELECT *
FROM tbls_Orders_Del
WHERE customerid = 2

Step 2: Turn on cascade deletes for the relationship between the tables Orders and ProductsOrders. We do not need to turn cascade deletes on for the relationship between the tables customers and orders since we are not deleting the customer herself in this case—just her orders.

Step 3: Run the DELETE statement
DELETE
FROM tbls_Orders_Del
WHERE customerid = 2

Result:

Step 4: Turn off cascade deletes for the relationship between the tables Orders and ProductsOrders so that nobody can delete any orders by mistake.

269.   Delete records in a certain date range

Delete multiple orders from multiple customers within a date range
Discussion:
This is an example of how we can use date criteria to delete orders within a specified date range. In this date range, we might have multiple orders from multiple customers.

Our four steps to delete all orders for a specific date range appear below:

Step 1: Run a SELECT statement to uniquely identify and verify records for deletion.
SELECT *
FROM tbls_Orders_Del
WHERE orderdate BETWEEN #10/15/2010# AND #10/17/2010#

Step 2: Turn on cascade deletes for the relationship between tables Orders and ProductsOrders.

Step 3: Run the DELETE statement
DELETE
FROM tbls_Orders_Del
WHERE orderdate BETWEEN #10/15/2010# AND #10/17/2010#

Result:

Step 4: Turn off cascade deletes for the relationship between tables Orders and ProductsOrders so that no one can delete any orders by mistake.

270.   Delete duplicate records while controlling if you want to delete the earliest or the latest ones

Delete earliest or latest duplicate customer orders

Discussion:

Let's discuss the setup of this example so that you can understand it in detail. First, in the table tbls_Orders_DEL, records with orderid 1001, 1002, and 1003 are duplicates. Specifically, the record with orderid = 1 is identical to 1001, the record with orderid = 988 is identical to 1002, and the record with orderid = 990 is identical to 1003. Keep in mind that these records have identical field values but different primary keys values.

The burning question is which records should we delete? The earliest ones or the latest ones? We know that a record with a smaller orderid value was entered before a record with a bigger orderid value since the primary key is an autonumber. In the following example, we discuss both alternatives in detail. In any case, the four steps to follow appear below:

Step 1: Run a SELECT statement to uniquely identify and verify records for deletion.
The SQL statement below will SELECT the records with smaller orderid values. Notice that we use a subquery to obtain what we need. In the main SELECT statement, we select all orders from the tbls_Orders_Del table that do not belong in the subquery. Consequently, we need to check what the subquery will fetch. The subquery itself will fetch the duplicate records with the maximum orderid values in the tbls_Orders_Del table. From the six duplicated records, it will select the three with the maximum orderID values (1001, 1002, and 1003). The main SELECT statement will fetch what is left from the six duplicated records, i.e. 1, 988, and 990. We can also use the NOT IN operator instead of the "<>" inequality predicate to obtain the same results. I know it is counter intuitive to use max() to get the earliest records, but max() is used in the subquery to identify duplicates with maximum primary key values. Then, the main SELECT statement will fetch all duplicates not in the subquery. The logic is the same the other way around for the next example:

313

SELECT *
FROM tbls_Orders_Del AS T2
WHERE OrderID <>
(SELECT Max(OrderID)
FROM tbls_Orders_Del AS T1
WHERE T2.CustomerID = T1.CustomerID AND T2.SalesRepID = T1.SalesRepID
AND T2.ShipperID = T1.ShipperID AND T2.OrderDate = T1.OrderDate)

OrderID	CustomerID	SalesRepID	ShipperID	OrderDate
1	139	2	2	11/6/2009
988	145	10	1	3/21/2010
990	160	10	1	5/17/2008

Record: 1 of 3   No Filter   Search

This SQL statement will select the latest duplicate records:
SELECT *
FROM tbls_Orders_Del AS T2
WHERE OrderID <>
(SELECT Min(OrderID)
FROM tbls_Orders_Del AS T1
WHERE T2.CustomerID = T1.CustomerID AND T2.SalesRepID = T1.SalesRepID
AND T2.ShipperID = T1.ShipperID AND T2.OrderDate = T1.OrderDate)

OrderID	CustomerID	SalesRepID	ShipperID	OrderDate
1001	139	2	2	11/6/2009
1002	145	10	1	3/21/2010
1003	160	10	1	5/17/2008

Record: 1 of 3   No Filter   Search

Step 2: Turn on cascade deletes for the relationship between the tables Orders and ProductsOrders

Step 3: Run the DELETE statement

DELETE
FROM tbls_Orders_Del AS T2
WHERE OrderID <>
(SELECT Min(OrderID)
FROM tbls_Orders_Del AS T1
WHERE T2.CustomerID = T1.CustomerID AND T2.SalesRepID = T1.SalesRepID
AND T2.ShipperID = T1.ShipperID AND T2.OrderDate = T1.OrderDate)

Result:

Step 4: Turn off cascade deletes for the relationship between the tables Orders and ProductsOrders so that nobody can delete any orders by mistake.

271. Delete ALL duplicate records (originals plus duplicates) that have the same field values and same primary key values

Delete all duplicate customer orders including original and duplicate orders
Discussion:
In this example, our goal is to delete all duplicate orders, including the original orders. We are working on a scenario where six records are identical such as below in records with orderids 1, 3, and 5. The records with orderid = 2 and 4 are unique and should not be touched. Notice that for this example, I have created a new table named tbls_Orders_Del2.

OrderID	CustomerID	SalesRepID	ShipperID	OrderDate
1	139	2	2	11/6/2009
1	139	2	2	11/6/2009
2	184	2	1	7/25/2009
3	137	2	2	6/29/2009
3	137	2	2	6/29/2009
4	165	2	1	12/14/2010
5	123	2	2	11/14/2008
5	123	2	2	11/14/2008

Record: 1 of 8   No Filter   Search

The four steps to run in a real situation are the following:

Step 1: Run a SELECT statement to uniquely identify and verify records for deletion.
SELECT *
FROM tbls_Orders_DEL2
WHERE orderid IN(
SELECT OrderID
FROM tbls_Orders_DEL2
GROUP BY OrderID, CustomerID, ShipperID, OrderDate
HAVING count(*)>1)

Step 2: Turn on cascade deletes for the relationship between the tables Orders and ProductsOrders.

Step 3: Run the DELETE statement
DELETE
FROM tbls_Orders_DEL2
WHERE OrderID IN(
SELECT OrderID
FROM tbls_Orders_DEL2
GROUP BY OrderID, CustomerID, ShipperID, OrderDate
HAVING count(*)>1)

Result:

Step 4: Turn off cascade deletes for the relationship between the tables Orders and ProductsOrders.

272. Use SELECT INTO to back up records before deleting them

Create a temp table to back up customers orders before deleting them

Discussion:

In this example, we will use SQL code to create a table, which will store all of the records we want to delete. If we might need the records we delete later, we can easily back them up on the fly in a new table using a SELECT INTO statement. In addition, if we want to append the deleted records in a historical table, we can easily do so by using the INSERT INTO statement, which has the functionality of an append query. The bottom line is that the code of both SQL statements for SELECT INTO or INSERT INTO will be exactly the same with the code of the DELETE statement changing only its first line.

Code:

```
SELECT * INTO TempTable
FROM tbls_Orders_Del
WHERE orderdate
BETWEEN #10/15/2010# AND #10/17/2010#
```

DELETE
FROM tbls_Orders_Del
WHERE orderdate
BETWEEN #10/15/2010# AND #10/17/2010#

Result:

CustomerID	SalesRepID	ShipperID	OrderDate	RequiredDat
82	1	1	10/16/2010	10/31/201
88	3	2	10/15/2010	10/30/201
56	5	2	10/16/2010	10/31/201
42	7	2	10/16/2010	10/31/201

Record: 1 of 4 — No Filter — Search

273. Delete records in a table based on values in a different table using a subquery

Delete records from the orders table using criteria from the customers table

Discussion:

This time, we have a request from management to delete all orders which came in from Los Angeles for a customer with a last name Orlando. They do not care about table relationships and the fact that we do not have a state field and a last name field in the orders table. This is not a problem for us since we can use a subquery to easily delete records in one table based on criteria in a different table. In a production environment, follow the steps below:

Step 1: Run a SELECT statement to uniquely identify and verify records for deletion.

SELECT *
FROM tbls_Orders_DEL
WHERE CustomerID IN
(SELECT CustomerID FROM Customers
WHERE city= "Los Angeles" AND lastname = "Orlando")

Step 2: Turn on cascade deletes for the relationship between the tables Orders and ProductsOrders.

Step 3: Run the DELETE statement
DELETE
FROM tbls_Orders_DEL
WHERE CustomerID IN
(SELECT CustomerID FROM Customers
WHERE city= "Los Angeles" AND lastname = "Orlando")

Result:

Step 4: Turn off cascade deletes for the relationship between the tables Orders and ProductsOrders.

274. Delete records in a table based on calculations in a different table

Update address information for a single customer
Discussion:

This time, the request from management is to delete all orders with a grand total of more than $500, which will be processed by a different distribution center. We need to resort to the Products_Orders table for criteria, make calculations on this table, and use the calculated fields as criteria. It sounds like a big deal, but it is not.

A sample dataset from the ProductsOrders table appears below. Notice the pairs of OrderIDs and ProductIDs so that you know what product is included in what order. For example, order 2 contains products 32 and 70. Order 3 contains products 26, 27, 43, and 51.

To be able to comply with the request of management, we first need to calculate order subtotals or, in other words, total amounts for each product. To put it yet another way, we multiply unitprice*quantity. (We should calculate discounts too, but I left them out for simplicity). Once we have the order subtotals, we need to calculate order totals. To do this, we use the SUM() function and the GROUP BY clause. Finally, since we only want order totals which exceed $500, we insert the criterion ">500". Please note that we use HAVING instead of WHERE since HAVING is applied after the records are grouped while WHERE is applied before they are grouped. Since we deal with calculations, in this case, we use HAVING to filter records after they are grouped and summed, and we know the total amounts.

OrderID	ProductID	UnitPrice	Quantity	Discount
2	32	15	3	0
2	70	15	6	0.15
3	26	22	3	0.2
3	27	15	2	0.15
3	43	15	5	0.15
3	51	15	4	0.2

ProductsOrders — Record: 1 of 2411 — No Filter — Search

For this example, we will use the tbls_Orders_Del table so that we can delete as we please. In a production environment, where we use the actual Orders table, follow the steps below:

Step 1: Run a SELECT statement to uniquely identify and verify records for deletion.
SELECT
FROM tbls_Orders_DEL
WHERE OrderID IN(
SELECT Sum([unitprice]*[quantity]) AS totalOrder
FROM ProductsOrders
GROUP BY OrderID
HAVING ((((Sum([unitprice]*[quantity]))>500)))

Step 2: Turn on cascade deletes for the relationship between the tables Orders and ProductsOrders.

Step 3: Run the DELETE statement
DELETE
FROM tbls_Orders_DEL
WHERE OrderID IN(
SELECT Sum([unitprice]*[quantity]) AS totalOrder
FROM ProductsOrders
GROUP BY OrderID
HAVING (((Sum([unitprice]*[quantity]))>500)))

Result:

Step 4: Turn off cascade deletes for the relationship between the tables Orders and ProductsOrders.

CHAPTER 29
WORKING WITH JOINS

The power of joins is a bit of a hidden jewel in the world of databases and data analysis. Developers and power users alike stay away from a good understanding of joins, mostly because they perceive them as complicated and impractical concepts. Both beliefs are false. You must understand joins to understand databases, and they are actually easy to use. They just look complicated. Devoting some time to understanding the remarkable muscle of joins will transform the way you work and give you amazing flexibility in your everyday work tasks. In this chapter, we will look at practical applications of joins through realistic scenarios. This is the only way someone could convince me to use joins: Show me what they can actually do in practice.

Joins represent the very essence of relational databases. Not using them handicaps your ability to retrieve sensible data from a dataset. This is because in relational databases, we keep data in separate tables. We keep supplier information in the suppliers table, customers in the customer table, and orders in an orders table. This is what we call the physical structure or design of the database. This is done so that normalization rules apply in the database where we keep our business transactions (orders, quotations, invoices). What we are interested in, however, is the conceptual invocations from a relational database. We would like to generate and send out information, such as invoices, in a way that makes sense for our customers and for us. In this respect, joins are links that we establish between or among tables with the goal of retrieving related information.

In this chapter, we will explore the use of inner, left, and right joins. Among these three, inner joins are the most commonly used in practical applications. Left joins are useful in certain business scenarios, while right joins can be used to check the integrity of the database and identify any orphaned records.

275.   Inner Joins

Find customers who actually have some orders

Discussion:

Let us assume that our supervisor has a very simple request: She wants a report of customers who actually ordered something from us. By the way, the customers table might include people who asked for quotations or leads, or it might include customers who have not ordered anything for some time. How can we answer this request? Of course, we can go back to the chapter about duplicate, orphaned, and related records and use a subquery such as:

Code:

```
SELECT *
FROM Customers
WHERE CustomerID
IN (SELECT CustomerID from tbls_Orders)
```

Result:

Notice that the number of customers returned is only 190. However, in the customers table, there are 201 customers. So, 11 customers have not had any orders at all for the historical data we have.

Why, however, should be use a subquery since we can do the same thing in no time using a join? Let's create a new query in design view and add the customers and orders tables. There is a one-to-many relationship between customers and orders. For one customer, there might be multiple orders, but each order definitely belongs to one customer.

Double-click on the relationship line between customers and orders. The following dialog box comes up. By default, Access 2007 will join two tables through an inner join or, in other words, include records from each table where there is a common CustomerID field. The CustomerID field is the primary key in the customers table and the foreign key in the orders table.

This is the case of an inner join. Notice that an inner join will give us the customers who have orders. If there are any customers without orders, they will not appear in the result set. In addition, if there are any orders without associated customers, they will not appear either. Only where the two tables match on the CustomerID will records be returned. The SQL code for the inner join appears below. Notice that the database returned 1000 records. This is because there are 1000 cases in which the CustomerID in the customers table has an associated CustomerID in the orders table. The eleven customers without a CustomerID in the orders table will not appear in the result set of this inner join.

Code:
SELECT FirstName, LastName, Address, OrderDate, ShippingCost
FROM Customers
INNER JOIN Orders ON Customers.CustomerID = Orders.CustomerID

Result:

FirstName ▾	LastName ▾	Address ▾	OrderDate ▾	ShippingCost ▾
John	Demarco	11 Lark Street	6/5/2008	34
John	Demarco	11 Lark Street	6/4/2009	40
John	Demarco	11 Lark Street	11/2/2008	34
John	Demarco	11 Lark Street	3/18/2008	49

Record: I◄ ◄ 10 of 1000 ► ►I ►▦ No Filter Search

Discussion:
The initial request, however, was to present a list of unique customers who have orders. We do not need any repeated customer names in the result set. To achieve this, we need an inner join and a GROUP BY clause by last name, first name, and address fields. Notice how the number of customers returned is the same as that returned by the subquery we used in the beginning of this example.

Code:
SELECT FirstName, LastName, Address
FROM Customers
INNER JOIN Orders ON Customers.CustomerID = Orders.CustomerID
GROUP BY FirstName, LastName, Address

Result:

LastName ▾	FirstName ▾	Address ▾
Ackerman	Nicholas	5 Buckingham Dr
Ames	Pindar	23 Cornell Dr
Andersen	Thomas	52 Betwood Street
Anderson	Joseph	34 Cortland Ave

Record: ◀ ◀ 10 of 190 ▶ ▶▶ ▶* 🗙 No Filter Search

276. Left Joins

List all customers whether they have orders or not

Discussion:

There are cases in which we do not want to retrieve only the matching records from two related tables. For instance, we might want to list all customers from the customers table and fields from their associated orders where they exist. In this case, the output of our query will list all of the records from the customers table and will list the OrderDate and ShippingCost values in the orders table for customers who have orders. In addition, for customers without orders, it will return blank values for the OrderDate and ShippingCost fields. The figure below shows the query design for an inner join, which is the default join type when we create a query in Access 2007.

Double-click on the relationship line between customers and orders. The Joins dialog box comes up. Change the join type to number 2: "Include ALL records from Customers and only those records from Orders where the joined fields are equal".

The query design now changes to:

A left join will output all of customers from the customers table and any related fields from the orders table based on matches on the CustomerID field. If there are any customers without orders, they will still appear in the result set. If there are any orders

327

without associated customers, they will not appear in the result set. Notice the relationship arrow that now has a point toward the Orders table. This is the visual sign that there is a left join relationship between these two tables.

Code:

SELECT lastname, firstname, Address, OrderDate, ShippingCost
FROM Customers LEFT JOIN Orders ON Customers.CustomerID =
Orders.CustomerID;

Result:

Note that the database returned 1011 records. This is because there are 1000 records in which the CustomerID in the customers table has an associated CustomerID in the orders table. In addition, we have 11 customers without a CustomerID in the orders table, but they will appear in the result set because this is a left join. Notice the blank values for the OrderDate and ShippingCost for some of the customers without any orders.

277. Right Joins

List all orders including those without customers
Discussion:

In this scenario, we want to produce a list of all orders from the orders table whether or not they have any matching records in the customers table. If a record from the orders table has a matching record in the customers table, this is fine and should actually be the case for all orders. If our query returns any records in which the fields from the customers table are blank, these are orphaned records. This means that we have orders without customers, and the integrity of our database is compromised. Let's start with a normal query and see how we can change it to a right join query.

Double-click on the relationship line between customers and orders. The Joins dialog box comes up. Change the join type to number 3: "Include ALL records from Orders and only those records from Customers where the joined fields are equal".

A right join will output all of the orders from the orders table and any related customers from the customers table based on matches on the CustomerID field. If there are any orders without customers, they will still appear in the result set. If this is the case, these orders are considered orphaned records, and they need to be investigated very closely and eliminated from the database. In addition, we need to have a look at the database design to see how it is possible that these orders are there in the first place. This can happen only if referential integrity is off. If it is off, turn it on.

Then, we need to deal with the orphaned records. We cannot have orders without customers because first, it does not make sense and second, because our database integrity is compromised. Maybe these were orders belonging to existing customers and entered with the wrong CustomerID as the foreign key while referential integrity was not on. If this is the case, change the value of the CustomerID field in the orders table to associate them with existing customers in the customers table. If we cannot find any customers to associate the orphaned orders, we must delete them from the database. Notice the relationship arrow that now has a point toward the customers table. This is the visual sign that there is a relationship with a right join between these two tables.

Code:

SELECT lastname, firstname, Address, OrderDate, ShippingCost
FROM Customers
RIGHT JOIN Orders ON Customers.CustomerID = Orders.CustomerID;

Result:

Notice that the database returned 1000 records. This is because there are 1000 records in which the CustomerID in the orders table has an associated CustomerID in the customers table. As you know, there are 11 customers without a CustomerID in the orders table, but they will not appear in the result set because this is a right join listing ALL records in the orders table and only associated customers in the customers table. Notice that we do not have any blank values for the lastname, firstname, and address fields from the customers table, which means we have no orphaned records in the orders table.

lastname	firstname	Address	OrderDate	ShippingCost
Kashisnky	Alfred	8 Kelton CT	1/9/2008	43
Parson	Dominic	28 Elizabeth S	1/10/2008	39
Ellison	Colin	123 Front Ave	1/10/2008	49
Steiner	Stephanie	88 Howland R	1/10/2008	35

Record: 10 of 1000 — No Filter — Search

CHAPTER 30
WORKING WITH SUB-QUERIES

A subquery is a normal SQL statement or a normal query nested in another query. Subqueries are primarily used to achieve results in a single step instead of using multiple queries. Specifically, subqueries are used in the following scenarios:

1. To create dynamic search lists with IN or NOT IN
2. To perform existence tests with EXISTS or NOT EXISTS
3. To perform dynamic aggregations with aggregate functions
4. To create temporary tables that combine data from multiple tables using UNION
5. To update records in update statements
6. To delete records in delete statements
7. To find duplicate records
8. To find related records in another table
9. To return a single value
10. To create dynamic and customized data categories using the switch() function

Let us explore the scenarios above through practical examples.

278.   Use a subquery with the IN predicate to find non-discounted products
Find orders for which you extended no discounts for at least one of the products included (solution 1)
Discussion:
Our business goal in this example is to retrieve orders for which we provided no discount for at least one of the products contained in the order. For at least one of the products contained in these orders, the discount rate was 0. Keep in mind that there might be multiple products in each order. In addition, notice that the ProductsOrders table is the table in between that establishes the many-to-many relationship between the Orders and Products tables. Consequently, the logic should be to first look in the

ProductsOrders table for all of the products with zero discounts. Using the OrderID from this result (the subquery) you will be able to find the corresponding orders in the Orders table. From the result, we can see that out of the 1000 orders in the Orders table, we provided at least a non-discounted product for 136 orders.

Code:
SELECT *
FROM orders
WHERE orderid
IN (SELECT orderid FROM ProductsOrders WHERE (Discount) =0)

Main Query Result:

Subquery Result:

Notice that we have a discrepancy: The subquery returned a list of 140 orders, while the main query returned a list of only 136 orders. What happened? As you can see in the picture below, there are some orders like OrderID=390 which contain two products, and we provided no discounts for either of them Order 390 appears twice in the subquery but only once in the main query, which means that the final count of 136 is correct.

279. Use a subquery with EXISTS to find non-discounted products

Find orders for which we extended no discounts for at least one of the products included (solution 2)

Discussion:

A more effective and faster solution than using the IN predicate is to use EXISTS. By using EXISTS, we expect the subquery to return some values. In this example, we are again looking for non-discounted products in orders, and we will obtain the exact same result as in the previous example. O and P are simply abbreviated names for the Orders and ProductsOrders tables respectively.

Code:
```
SELECT *
FROM Orders O
WHERE EXISTS (SELECT OrderID FROM ProductsOrders P WHERE O.OrderID
= P.OrderID AND discount = 0);
```

Result:

280.   Use a subquery with the IN predicate to find customers with orders in a specific quarter

Find customers with orders in the fourth quarter of the year 2010 (solution 1)

Discussion:

In this example, we will use the IN predicate with two date functions to retrieve customers with orders in the fourth quarter of 2010. Notice that we are looking for customer names and not orders placed in that period.

Code:

SELECT *
FROM Customers
WHERE CustomerID IN
(Select CustomerID FROM Orders WHERE
((((DatePart("q",[OrderDate]))=4) AND ((Year([orderdate]))=2010)))

Result:

281.   Use a subquery with EXISTS to find customers with orders in a specific quarter

Find customers with orders in the fourth quarter of the year 2010 (solution 2)

Discussion:

We can obtain the same output with the previous example by using EXISTS.

Code:

SELECT *

FROM Customers C

WHERE EXISTS

(Select CustomerID FROM Orders O WHERE C.CustomerID = O.CustomerID

AND ((((DatePart("q",[OrderDate]))=4) AND ((Year([orderdate]))=2010)))

Result:

CustomerID	FirstName	LastName	Address
7	Robert	Demaggio	34 Princeton Dr
9	Paul	Demarist	89 Mercer Street
12	Jim	Devito	102 Lexington Ave
13	David	Vanderback	91 Fifth Ave

Record: ◄ ◄ 1 of 59 ► ►I ►☆ No Filter Search

282.   Use a subquery with EXISTS to relate two tables on fields other than the primary keys

Find customers who reside in the same city as that of sales representatives

Discussion:

Our supervisor asks for a list of customers who live in the same city as our sales representatives. So, if we have a sales representative in Orlando, Florida, our supervisor wants us to identify all of the customers living in that city. We need to create a relationship between the Customers and SalesReps tables based on the city field. We can accomplish this task using the following SQL statement. As you can see from the result set, we have 58 customers living in the same cities as our salespeople.

Code:

SELECT *

FROM customers

WHERE exists

(SELECT *

FROM salesreps

WHERE customers.city = salesreps.city)

Result:

283.   Use a subquery with the NOT IN predicate to find orphaned records

Find orders without customers

Discussion:

We can easily retrieve orphaned records using a subquery. In this example, we are looking for orders without customers. If we find any orders without customers, you need to delete them from the database and check the referential integrity setting for the one-to-many relationship between the tables Customers and Orders. In this example, we use the table tbls_orders where I put some orphaned records for demonstration purposes. As you can see from the result set, three orphaned records are found.

Code:

```
SELECT *
FROM tbls_orders
WHERE CustomerID
NOT IN (SELECT CustomerID FROM Customers)
```

Result:

284. Use a subquery with NOT EXISTS to find unrelated records

Find customers without any orders

Discussion:

This time, we will use NOT EXISTS to find customers who have not submitted any orders at all. Thus, we are trying to find customers without any related orders in the orders table. This is not a problem when it comes to database integrity. It is just a business fact. We might want to initiate a promotional campaign for these customers, for example.

Code:

SELECT *

FROM Customers C

WHERE NOT EXISTS (SELECT CustomerID FROM Orders O WHERE C.CustomerID = O.CustomerID)

Result:

CustomerID	FirstName	LastName	Address
19	Erin	Erin	28 Karrie Terrace
37	Allan	Cimo	24 Crestwood CT
40	Kelly	Costa	45 Sixth Ave
66	Arnold	Webster	53 Southern Blvd

Record: 10 of 11 | No Filter | Search

285. Use a subquery to find above average priced products (working on one table)

Find products with prices above the average product price

Discussion:

In this example, we are looking for products with above average prices. We want the database to calculate the average price per product, compare every product price to the average price, and display only those products which exceed the average price. It looks like a lot for a single SQL statement, but it is possible. The essence of this SQL statement is in the WHERE clause where we ask the ProductUnitPrice to be bigger than the average ProductUnitPrice using the inequality predicate ">" and the aggregate function avg().

Code:

SELECT productname, ProductUnitPrice

FROM Products

WHERE (ProductUnitPrice) > (SELECT avg(ProductUnitPrice) FROM Products)

ORDER BY ProductUnitPrice DESC

Result:

286. Use a subquery, EXISTS, GROUP BY, HAVING, and the sum() function to isolate bigger orders (working with two tables)

List order information with shipped invoices above $500

Discussion:

This time, we need to retrieve orders with a total of over $500. Our problem is that we need to list order information from the Orders table while making calculations on the ProductsOrders table where we keep product prices and quantities. We can achieve this task using a subquery with EXISTS and GROUP BY, which will run very fast as well.

The crucial part of this piece of code is in the GROUP BY clause. We need to group by OrderID in the subquery since in the ProductsOrders table, the same OrderID appears multiple times because there might be multiple products in the same order. (Check the GROUP BY chapter for details). However, we want our subquery to produce only one OrderID per order. In addition, we use the HAVING clause because we do not know beforehand what orders have a total of $500 or more. By using the HAVING clause, we are telling the database to first calculate the order totals through the sum() function, group the results by order, and then, apply the filter (Sum([unitprice]*[quantity]))>500).

Code:

```
SELECT *
FROM orders O
WHERE EXISTS
(SELECT orderid, Sum([unitprice]*[quantity])
FROM ProductsOrders P
WHERE O.OrderID = P.OrderID
GROUP BY orderid
HAVING ((((Sum([unitprice]*[quantity]))>500)))
```

Result:

OrderID	CustomerID	SalesRepID	ShipperID	OrderDate
308	196	3	3	10/15/20
354	3	4	1	4/23/20
404	101	4	2	11/18/20
609	2	6	2	5/4/20
944	106	10	1	9/13/20

Record: I◄ ◄ 1 of 5 ► ►I ►▪ No Filter Search

287.   Create temporary tables using a subquery and UNION

Retrieve person information from customers and suppliers and create a temp table with the combined results

Discussion:

Let's assume that a fellow employee asks us for a combined list of names and addresses of our customers and suppliers because she wants to send out a common greeting postcard to all of them. We can create a temporary table with the combination of names using the SELECT INTO and UNION statements in combination. Notice how double quotes (") are used in the SQL statement for suppliers since in that table, there are no first and last name fields.

Code:

SELECT lastname, firstname, address, city, state, zip INTO tempPeopleTable
FROM
(SELECT lastname, firstname, address, city, state, zip
FROM customers
UNION
SELECT ContactName," , address, city, state, zip
FROM suppliers)

Result:

288. Update records in one table using criteria from another using a subquery

Update product prices in the products table using criteria from the suppliers table

Discussion:

Management has decided to increase the prices of products from suppliers in Boston and Dallas. This is because transportation costs from those cities have increased considerably lately. The problem is that we need to update prices in the products table while using criteria from the suppliers table. This time, we also need to use filtering criteria within the subquery statement. The subquery in this example needs to retrieve the SupplierIDs of suppliers in Boston and Dallas. The resulting SupplierIDs will be used by the main query to update product prices in the products table. Notice that in the products table, every record contains a SupplierID value.

Code:

UPDATE tbls_Products_Upd

SET ProductUnitPrice = ProductUnitPrice * (1+0.20)

WHERE SupplierID IN

(SELECT SupplierID FROM Suppliers

WHERE city= "Boston" or city = "Dallas")

Result:

289. Delete records in one table using criteria in another table

Delete order information in the orders table using criteria from the customers table

Discussion:

This time, our task is to delete orders from customers in Los Angeles and Orlando. These orders will be processed by another distribution center, and we do not want them to clutter our database and affect our reports. In essence, the subquery will retrieve the CustomerIDs of these customers from the Customers table. Then, the main query will use these CustomerIDs to delete the orders that contain them in the tbls_Orders_DEEL table. Always remember to run a SELECT statement first before deleting records. (Check chapter 28 for a full overview of DELETE statements).

Code:

DELETE

FROM tbls_Orders_DEL

WHERE CustomerID IN

(SELECT CustomerID FROM Customers

WHERE city= "Los Angeles" AND lastname = "Orlando")

Result:

290. Find duplicate records using a subquery

Find all duplicate records in a table

Discussion:

Our goal in this example is to use a subquery to find all duplicate records in the tbls_Orders table. Keep in mind that these records have identical field values and identical primary keys values. So, they are exact duplicates. If you need to find duplicate records based on the values of one or multiple fields but with different primary key values, consult chapter 22 where I list various scenarios of duplicate records. As you can see from the result set in this example, there are 11 duplicate records in this table.

Code:
```
SELECT *
FROM tbls_Orders WHERE OrderID IN(
SELECT OrderID
FROM tbls_Orders
GROUP BY OrderID
HAVING count(*)>1)
ORDER BY OrderID
```

Result:

291. Use the max() function to return a single value in the subquery

Find the latest shipped order from the orders table

Discussion:

Let's assume that we need to present all of the details (field values) of the latest order we shipped. We can, of course, find the maximum (latest) shipped date in the orders table and use this date as a criterion to list the details of our latest order. This way, however, we need to create two queries. In addition, if we need to use it again, we need to remember the names of the two queries and their association. Instead, with a subquery, we can perform both steps in one SQL statement as follows:

Code:

SELECT *

FROM Orders

WHERE shippeddate = (SELECT max(ShippedDate) FROM Orders)

Result:

OrderID ▼	CustomerID ▼	SalesRepID ▼	ShipperID ▼	OrderDate ▼
4	165	2	1	12/14/2010
＊ (New)				

Record: ◄ ◄ 1 of 1 ► ►I ►☰ ☒ No Filter | Search | ◄ ▥ ►

292. Create a crosstab report with a subquery

Create a crosstab report that shows the number of products in every discount percentage category

Discussion:

In this example, we have a request from management to present a report that will list all orders, the number of products in each order, and the discount category each product belongs to. For each order, management wants to know how many products were given a 0 discount, how many a 15% discount, and how many a 20% discount. This is a crosstab query, but we can actually use subqueries to create this report. As you can see from the code below, we can use a subquery to create the discount category we want. This is flexibility that we do not have with crosstab queries. We can include any discount categories we want and leave out the ones that we do not want to appear.

Code:

```
SELECT OrderID,

(SELECT Count(*) FROM ProductsOrders P
WHERE O.OrderID=P.OrderID AND (discount = 0) ) AS '0%',

(SELECT Count(*) FROM ProductsOrders P
WHERE O.OrderID=P.OrderID AND (discount = 0.15) ) AS '15%',

(SELECT Count(*) FROM ProductsOrders P
WHERE O.OrderID=P.OrderID AND (discount = 0.20) ) AS '20%'

FROM Orders AS O
```

Result:

The above SQL example will work in any relational database, and it represents a way to create crosstab reports. However, in Access 2007, we have the option to create the exact same report by taking advantage of the TRANSFORM and PIVOT statements for crosstab queries to obtain the same results in a faster and easier way without the need to write multiple subqueries. In addition, if we had 15 different discount levels, we would have to write 15 subqueries. Instead, by using crosstab queries, we can always write the same code below. However, in case we need to present only a few specific discount categories, subqueries give us tremendous flexibility for it.

Code:
```
TRANSFORM Count(ProductsOrders.[Discount]) AS CountDiscount
SELECT OrderID
FROM ProductsOrders
GROUP BY OrderID
PIVOT Discount
```

Notice that 1000 orders returned using subqueries, while only 919 returned using TRANSFORM. This is because TRANSFORM left out orders that contained no products, while the subqueries code returned all orders—even those without any products displaying 0s for all three discount categories of "0", "15%", and "20%". This is not a problem of the crosstab or subqueries code. It is simply a business fact that there are some orders in the database that are not processed yet. This fact makes things a bit more complicated, but it happens. So, I want you to know how crosstab queries and subqueries fare under these circumstances.

Result:

APPENDIX I
THE SAMPLE DATABASE

For all of the examples in this book, you can download the sample database from http://www.databasechannel.com/sampledata/Access2007.

The Entity Relationship Diagram (ERD) of the database is shown below:

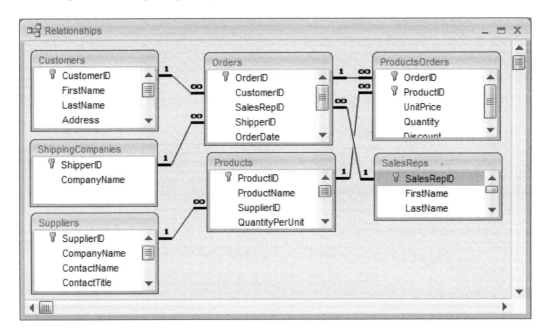

1. There is a one-to-many relationship between Customers and Orders.
2. There is a many-to-many relationship between Orders and Products with the table ProductsOrders functioning as the join table. The table ProductsOrders holds all of the details about each particular order and what products it contains. Its primary key is the combination of the primary keys of the Orders and Products tables.

3. As you can see from the ERD, there are also one-to-many relationships between the ShippingCompanies and Orders tables, Suppliers and Products, and SalesReps and Orders. The SalesReps table is our employees table, i.e. our salespeople.

The tables you see in the ERD diagram are the main tables in the database. However, I have created copies of the main tables so that you can work on examples without affecting the main tables. All of the secondary tables have the prefix "tbls", and you can work on them at will, deleting or updating data without affecting the main tables of the database. Just in case something goes wrong, however, you can download the database again as you please.

INDEX OF TERMS

Made in the USA
San Bernardino, CA
05 September 2013